PSYCHOLOGY PRACTITIONER GUIDEBOOKS

EDITORS

Arnold P. Goldstein, Syracuse University
Leonard Krasner, Stanford University & SUNY at Stony Brook
Sol L. Garfield, Washington University in St. Louis

ANXIETY DISORDERS

Pergamon Titles of Related Interest

Clark/Salkovskis COGNITIVE THERAPY FOR PANIC
AND HYPOCHONDRIASIS
Ellis/McInerney/DiGiuseppe/Yeager RATIONAL-EMOTIVE THERAPY
WITH ALCOHOLICS AND SUBSTANCE ABUSERS
Ellis/Sichel/Yeager/DiMattia/DiGiuseppe RATIONAL-EMOTIVE
COUPLES THERAPY
Last/Hersen HANDBOOK OF ANXIETY DISORDERS
Meichenbaum STRESS INOCULATION TRAINING
Poppen BEHAVIORAL RELAXATION TRAINING AND ASSESSMENT
Saigh POSTTRAUMATIC STRESS DISORDER: A Behavioral Approach
to Assessment and Treatment

ANXIETY DISORDERS
A Rational-Emotive Perspective

RICKS WARREN
Anxiety Disorders Clinic, Lake Oswego, OR;
Pacific Institute for Rational-Emotive Therapy, Lake Oswego, OR
and Pacific University, Forest Grove, OR

GEORGE D. ZGOURIDES
University of Portland, Portland, OR;
Anxiety Disorders Clinic, Lake Oswego, OR
and Tualatin Valley Mental Health Center, Portland, OR

PERGAMON PRESS
Member of Maxwell Macmillan Pergamon Publishing Corporation
New York • Oxford • Beijing • Frankfurt
São Paulo • Sydney • Tokyo • Toronto

Pergamon Press Offices:

U.S.A.	Pergamon Press, Inc., Maxwell House, Fairview Park, Elmsford, New York 10523, U.S.A.
U.K.	Pergamon Press plc, Headington Hill Hall, Oxford OX3 0BW, England
PEOPLE'S REPUBLIC OF CHINA	Pergamon Press, Xizhimenwai Dajie, Beijing Exhibition Centre, Beijing 100044, People's Republic of China
GERMANY	Pergamon Press GmbH, Hammerweg 6, D-6242 Kronberg, Germany
BRAZIL	Pergamon Editora Ltda, Rua Eça de Queiros, 346, CEP 04011, Paraiso, São Paulo, Brazil
AUSTRALIA	Pergamon Press Australia Pty Ltd., P.O. Box 544, Potts Point, NSW 2011, Australia
JAPAN	Pergamon Press, 8th Floor, Matsuoka Central Building, 1-7-1 Nishishinjuku, Shinjuku-ku, Tokyo 160, Japan
CANADA	Pergamon Press Canada Ltd., Suite 271, 253 College Street, Toronto, Ontario M5T 1R5, Canada

Copyright © 1991 Pergamon Press, Inc.

Library of Congress Cataloging in Publication Data

Warren, Ricks.
    Anxiety disorders : a rational-emotive perspective / by Ricks Warren, George D. Zgourides.
       p.   cm. -- (Psychology practitioner guidebooks)
    Includes bibliographical references and index.
    ISBN 0-08-040623-8 (H) : -- ISBN 0-08-040622-X (F)
    1. Anxiety. 2. Rational-emotive psychotherapy.   I. Zgourides, George D. II. Title. III. Series.
    RC531.W37 1991
    616.85'223--dc20
                                   90-49533
                                        CIP
Printing: 1 2 3 4 5 6 7 8 9 Year: 1 2 3 4 5 6 7 8 9 0

22542422

To Terri—empirical evidence that dreams can come true.
Ricks Warren

To my family.
George Zgourides

Contents

Foreword

When I began to develop rational-emotive therapy (RET) in 1953 and started practicing it early in 1955, I was largely working with clients who had moderate and severe anxiety disorders, particularly those who were anxious about failing at work and love. After practicing classical psychoanalysis and psychoanalytically oriented psychotherapy for a number of years before that time, and after discovering how ineffective these therapies were in relieving anxious and phobic states, I began to see clearly that it was not the activating events (As), including childhood traumas, of people's lives but largely their irrational beliefs (Bs) *about* these As that led to their emotional and behavioral consequences (Cs) of anxiety, panic, phobias, and obsessive-compulsiveness. I formulated this ABC theory of anxiety from observing scores of clients (especially those with sexual, relationship, and family anxiety), and from studying many philosophers who seemed to realize, far more than psychotherapists then did, the important cognitive roots of emotional disturbance (Ellis, 1972b, 1989, 1991).

Because I had also used behavioral methods (especially in vivo desensitization) to overcome my own public speaking and social anxiety in the 1930s, before I even thought of becoming a psychologist (Ellis, 1972b, 1991), I also realized, as I started to create RET, that although cognitive disputing (D) is of vital importance in helping people to overcome their irrational beliefs (Bs), strong behavioral methods of acting against one's anxieties and phobias are also required. Thus, in my first comprehensive book on RET, *Reason and Emotion in Psychotherapy* (Ellis, 1962), I noted, "rational-emotive therapy is one of the relatively few techniques which includes large amounts of action, work, and 'homework' assignments" (p. 334). "The theory states . . . that the *two* main counter-propagandizing forces that will help [clients] change their underlying beliefs and their disturbed behavior are thinking *and* acting: challenging and contradicting their internalized sentences, on the one hand, and forcing themselves to *do* the things of which they are irrationally afraid, on the other" (p. 335). "Rational-emotive therapy . . . emphasizes overt activity and homework assignments by the patient" (p. 336).

So, from the start, I formulated and utilized RET both cognitively and behaviorally and made it into the pioneering form of cognitive-behavioral therapy (CBT) that has been followed by almost all the other popular forms of CBT that exist today. Without my concern about combatting my own early anxiety and without my observation of the behavioral inhibitions of scores of my anxious and phobic clients, I would probably never have created RET. So I am grateful to my many anxious and panicked clients who led me to develop it.

In spite of my involvement with my own and my clients' anxiety that greatly influenced me to devise and to use RET in the 1950s, RET at first did not specifically emphasize the treatment of anxiety disorders because I soon saw, as I started to employ it with a great many clients, that it was equally applicable to just about all the common neurotic and borderline disorders—including severe depression, self-hatred, hostility, self-pity, low frustration tolerance, procrastination, addiction, and other cognitive-behavioral problems. So in my major writings on RET, I have mainly dealt with all these kinds of disorders (Ellis, 1957a, 1962, 1971a, 1973d, 1985b, 1988; Ellis & Dryden, 1987, 1990; Ellis & Grieger, 1977, 1986; Ellis & Harper, 1961, 1975), and I have only occasionally written specifically about the rational-emotive theory and practice of anxiety disorders (Ellis, 1967, 1970, 1971b, 1972b, 1973d, 1979b, 1979c, 1980a, 1982, in press).

Anxiety, however, is unquestionably one of the main and most frequent human disturbances, and it has many important manifestations. As *Anxiety Disorders: A Rational-Emotive Perspective* by Ricks Warren and George Zgourides shows, the anxiety disorders include panic, social phobia, simple phobia, obsessive-compulsive disorder, post-traumatic stress disorder (PTSD), and generalized anxiety disorder. Quite a batch of emotional-behavioral disturbances! Each one of these disorders has literally millions of sufferers in Western civilization; and if we include worldwide victims, we can probably find billions of people who, at one time or other, are afflicted with various forms of severe anxiety. Moreover, as the authors of this book remind us, the other major emotional disorders—especially, depression, self-hatred, and hostility—tend to include significant aspects of anxiety; and one of the most common of all human problems, low frustration tolerance, is synonymous with what I have called discomfort anxiety (Ellis, 1979a, 1980a).

I am therfore delighted that Ricks Warren and George Zgourides, two leading practitioners of RET, have produced this present detailed volume on the rational-emotive diagnosis and treatment of anxiety disorders. In doing so, they have systematically covered, in chapter after chapter, the general etiology of each major form of anxiety or phobia, given its Diagnostic and Statistical Manual of Mental Disorders, 3rd ed., Revised, (DSM-III-R, American Psychiatric Association, 1987) diagnostic criteria, reviewed the assessment instruments, discussed the non-RET treatments, given a RET model for each specific anxiety disorder, and presented a RET plan of treatment. This is indeed a comprehensive approach.

In covering the cognitive-behavioral and the RET literature on anxiety, and also by covering the kinds of RET interventions and cases they have worked on in their own extensive antianxiety practices, Warren and Zgourides have herewith presented a wealth of research and clinical material that includes and supplements the most important aspects of the RET approach to assessing and treating the main anxiety disorders. Their book is more thorough-going and more specific than any other existing RET approach to these disorders. It is exceptionally clear, scientific, and often profound. A careful reading of this well-organized book is likely to benefit virtually all clinicians who see anxious and phobic clients and who want to offer these clients maximum help.

Albert Ellis, Ph.D., President
Institute for Rational-Emotive Therapy

Chapter 1

A Brief Overview of Anxiety Disorders

Recent research has led to the following fascinating discoveries about anxiety:

- The prevalence of anxiety disorders in the general population is greater than that of any other mental disorder, including depression and substance abuse (Barlow, 1988);
- One study found that 40% of the patients in a cardiology practice were suffering from panic disorder (PD) (Beitman, DeRosear, Basha, Flaker, & Corcoran, 1987);
- About 35% of the general population has had one or more panic attacks in the last year (Norton, Dorward, & Cox, 1986);
- It is estimated that between 7 and 12 million individuals are agoraphobic, with 75% of these being women (Barlow, 1988);
- About 80% of panic patients describe a significant life stressor prior to the first panic attack (Uhde, Roy-Byrne, Vittone, Boulenger, & Post, 1985).
- Between 5% and 10% of the population have specific fears significant enough to be diagnosed as having phobias (Myers, et al., 1984); and
- It is estimated that 80 million antianxiety agent prescriptions are written annually, with about 10% to 15% of Americans taking such prescriptions (Taylor & Arnow, 1988).

Until fairly recently, anxiety disorders received relatively little attention in professional literature. In the last 20 years or so, however, there has been a significant increase in clinical interest in these disorders. For example, in 1989 an entire issue of *Clinical Psychology Review* was devoted to social phobia, a disorder that previously had been labeled as "relatively unstudied" (Heimberg, Dodge, & Becker, 1987). This increased interest is partially due to reconceptualization of anxiety disorders by the American Psychiatric Association, improvements in psychological therapies, large multisite surveys (e.g., Epidemiological Catchment Area study), and an increased understanding of the biological and neurochemical mechanisms involved in the genesis of panic and anxiety. For example, given these major changes during recent decades, Barlow (1988) reported that virtually all panic clients can live panic-free lives given current treatments. These are exciting times for clinicians and researchers who are involved in anxiety research and therapy.

In the *Diagnostic and Statistical Manual of Mental Disorders,* third edition, revised (DSM-III-R) of the American Psychiatric Association (1987), anxiety disorders are classified as mental disorders rather than as syndromes or mere clusters of symptoms. What is a mental disorder, and how does an anxiety disorder differ from an anxiety syndrome, a cluster of anxiety symptoms, or just normal anxiety or worry?

A mental disorder is defined in DSM-III-R as "a clinically significant behavioral or psychological syndrome or pattern that occurs in a person and that is associated with present distress (a painful symptom), or disability (impairment in one or more areas of functioning), or with a significantly increased risk of suffering death, pain, disability, or an important loss of freedom" (p. xxii). Two key elements to understanding the concept of disorder as presented in this definition concern the phrase *clinically significant* and the term *disability,* as the presence or absence of these factors permits differentiation between anxiety syndromes and disorders. Anxiety is best viewed as clinically significant when it causes disability by interfering enough in the individual's daily living activities to cause distress and/or dysfunction. People with full-blown anxiety disorders certainly experience significant disability or interference in everyday living as a result of their anxiety (for example, as is evidenced by an agoraphobic person who is literally trapped in his or her home).

In addition to degree of disability or interference experienced, the intensity and frequency of the anxiety symptoms must be considered in determining the presence of a disorder versus a syndrome, particularly because certain of the anxiety disorders likely exist along a continuum in terms of severity (e.g., generalized anxiety disorder [GAD]—PD without agoraphobia—PD with agoraphobia continuum). For example, occasional panic (i.e., high intensity–low frequency) may pose no real problem other than episodic discomfort that an individual accepts and endures when it arises. Likewise, frequent bouts of low-level worry (low intensity–high frequency) may not interfere enough with the person's life to be a major source of concern. Anxiety disorders,

Table 1.1. Anxiety Syndromes

1.	Fear
2.	Generalized or chronic anxiety
3.	Episodic, intense anxiety attacks
4.	Anticipatory anxiety
5.	Mild episodic anxiety
6.	Mild anxiety and mild depression
7.	Anxiety related to specific social, family, and work situations
8.	Anxiety following traumatic events

Note. Adapted from Taylor and Arnow (1988).

however, typically involve both high-intensity and high-frequency symptoms, which are more likely to cause emotional problems and disability and lead the person to seek professional assistance.

Most people can relate to having experienced some level of anxiety or worry at some point in their lives. It is when the anxiety becomes chronic, intense, and debilitating that it is best classified as a disorder. Otherwise, the client is said to suffer from an anxiety syndrome, state, or symptom constellation. For example, Taylor and Arnow (1988) listed anxiety syndromes that, depending on intensity and frequency, may or may not involve an actual disorder (see Table 1.1). Clinicians treating individuals suspected of having an anxiety disorder are advised first to rule out the aforementioned syndromes as part of the differential diagnostic process to determine the appropriate treatment.

Sometimes an individual experiences a cluster of symptoms rather than a syndrome or disorder. As mentioned earlier, some individuals experience panic attacks but do not qualify for diagnosis of PD, while others experience limited symptom attacks and qualify for a diagnosis of agoraphobia without a history of PD. Panic attacks involve four or more DSM-III-R panic attack symptoms, whereas limited symptom attacks involve fewer than four symptoms. Panic symptoms include shortness of breath, dizziness, shaking, choking, and fear of dying, to mention just a few (see chapter 3, Table 3.1, for a complete listing of DSM-III-R panic symptoms).

DSM III-R ANXIETY DISORDERS

The following are the DSM-III-R anxiety disorders, each of which will be reviewed in later chapters:

1. *Panic disorder with agoraphobia (300.21):* These individuals experience panic attacks that are often unpredictable (spontaneous) and usually frightening. These panic-disordered individuals may also show mild to severe avoidance of public and social situations where they believe

help may be difficult or impossible to locate (e.g., shopping malls, public transportation). They typically worry about having future panic attacks and are often reluctant to enter situations where they fear attacks may occur.

2. *Panic disorder without agoraphobia (300.01):* These panic-disordered individuals experience panic attacks, but they do not avoid public and social situations.

3. *Agoraphobia without history of panic disorder (300.22):* These individuals fear public and social situations but do not experience full symptom panic attacks. Instead, they may have intense anticipatory anxiety or limited symptom panic attacks.

4. *Social phobia (300.23):* People with social phobia have a persistent, strong desire to avoid situations involving social interactions (e.g., public speaking, writing, eating, or performing in the presence of others). Extreme fears of being exposed to scrutiny by others and of behaving in ways that will lead to humiliation, shame, or embarrassment are characteristic.

5. *Simple phobia (300.29):* The essential feature here is a persistent fear of and strong desire to avoid specific objects or situations. Examples include fear of animals, closed places, heights, and germs.

6. *Obsessive compulsive disorder (300.30):* These individuals experience anxiety-evoking recurrent thoughts, ideas, images, or impulses that are seen as senseless or repugnant (obsessions) and/or anxiety-reducing behaviors or thoughts performed in a ritualistic manner (compulsions). Examples of compulsions include repetitive handwashing or checking door locks.

7. *Posttraumatic stress disorder (PTSD) (309.89):* People with PTSD develop a complex of symptoms following a traumatic event that typically is either life threatening or seen as life threatening (e.g., natural disasters, accidents, assault). Symptoms usually include reexperiencing the traumatic event via dreams or intrusive thoughts, emotional numbness, social withdrawal, and loss of interest in previously enjoyed activities. Exaggerated startle responses, problems with memory and concentration, sleep disturbance, depression, and generalized anxiety are common. Activities or situations that remind one of the traumatic event often are anxiety provoking and avoided.

8. *Generalized anxiety disorder (GAD) (300.02):* These individuals typically experience chronic and intense worry, which may include a number of unpleasant symptoms such as trembling, shortness of breath, and palpitations.

In addition to the foregoing, the following DSM-III-R disorders include anxiety as a predominate feature: (a) anxiety disorder not otherwise specified (300.00); (b) adjustment disorder with anxious mood

(309.24); and (c) organic anxiety syndrome (294.80). Although a review of these disorders is beyond the scope of this book, mental health professionals diagnosing anxious individuals should be careful to rule out these and other psychiatric disorders (e.g., borderline personality disorder) in addition to evaluating for anxiety due to other factors, including street drug use, various medications, and certain physical disorders.

One of the purposes of the DSM-III-R is to simplify the differential diagnosis process by providing mental health professional with a set of distinct diagnostic criteria for each of the mental disorders. By determining the presence of the correct combination of criteria via careful interviewing and/or use of other assessment instruments, the clinician is able to determine whether the client suffers from a disorder, and if so, which one(s). If not all criteria are met, the client is considered to have a syndrome rather than a disorder. Finally, in addition to the diagnostic criteria, the DSM-III-R also contains a useful set of decision trees that make the diagnostic process more efficient and precise.

A PROPOSED TREATMENT PLAN
FOR ANXIETY DISORDERS

Many anxiety disorders have similar underlying treatment methods; thus we present the following generic treatment plan. In the following chapters, when the treatment of choice deviates from the plan, we describe the differences and explain the rationale for the preferred therapy.

1. Determine the presence of an anxiety disorder via DSM-III-R diagnostic criteria. Screen for secondary disorders, such as avoidant personality disorder, depression, or alcohol and substance abuse problems. Alcohol problems are frequently associated with the anxiety disorders, particularly panic disorder and social phobia. See Cox, Norton, Swinson, and Endler (1990) and Kushner, Sher, and Beitman (1990) for recent reviews of the relation between alcohol/substance abuse and the anxiety disorders.

2. Obtain a detailed social history (e.g., via Ellis and Dryden's [1987] biographical information form). Pay close attention to whether the client's family and relatives appear predisposed to develop anxiety disorders.

3. Utilize appropriate assessment instruments to determine the presence and severity of the disorder and to obtain baseline readings for use later in the therapeutic process and in follow-ups.

4. Consult with medical professionals to determine if physical conditions, medications, or lifestyle habits are prompting or exacerbating the client's condition. A thorough medical examination and lab work are necessary to rule out such organic and lifestyle factors.

5. Introduce the client to the basics of rational-emotive therapy (RET), as described in chapter 2, as well as to the three-component (i.e., biopsychosocial) model of anxiety disorders. Provide pertinent handouts.

6. Administer the personality data form, part 1 (see Appendix C). Discuss with the client the information gathered from this form and how it relates to his or her emotional dysfunctions. Discuss implications for the upcoming therapy.

7. Introduce the client to the RET self-help form (see Appendix A) and its use in identifying and disputing irrational beliefs.

8. Introduce the client to the appropriate therapeutic procedures (e.g., in vivo exposure).

9. Assist the client in identifying and challenging anticipated irrational beliefs and cognitive distortions prior to the preferred procedure.

10. Conduct a debriefing after the procedure to identify and challenge both old and new irrational beliefs.

11. Have the client practice therapeutic procedures between sessions and use the RET self-help form at home during the week to facilitate the process of identifying and disputing cognitive distortions.

12. Initiate any adjunctive therapies deemed to be appropriate (e.g., relaxation training, assertion skills training, rational humorous songs, shame-attacking exercises).

13. Repeat steps 8 through 12 for the remainder of the therapy.

14. Use these steps and RET principles in individual and/or group format(s), given the special needs and concerns of the client.

15. If a particular therapy program is warranted (e.g., Heimberg & Becker's [1984] social phobia treatment program), use RET techniques as an adjunct to other cognitive restructuring and behavioral exercises.

THEORETICAL MODELS

Taylor and Arnow (1988) stated that "anxiety is best viewed from the biopsychosocial perspective, which posits that various systems interact in complicated ways to determine the final presentation of anxiety for a particular individual" (p. 41). They described the subjective, cognitive, physiological, and behavioral dimensions of anxiety as the "various systems" that interact with one another. Moreover, their model incorporates psychodynamic, developmental, learning, psychophysiological, neurophysiological, and molecular theories of anxiety.

In this section, we briefly summarize a variety of theoretical models that address anxiety disorders from a biopsychosocial perspective. These models are further described in the ensuing chapters.

Lang's (1968, 1978) three-system model of fear and Foa and Kozak's (1985, 1986) adaptation of Lang's (1977, 1979) bioinformational conceptualization of fear to the theory and treatment of anxiety disorders provide useful models for understanding and treating such disorders. First, as Lang's three-system model suggests, fear consists of cognitive, physiological, and behavioral components. Thus, once fear is acquired via direct experience, vicarious experience, or direct instruction, it is manifested in the three components. Individuals differ as to which response system is dominant, and within individuals the three systems are not always highly correlated (Emmelkamp, 1982; Rachman, 1978). Thus, for example, some individuals report negative self-statements and endorse irrational beliefs but may show little physiological arousal or avoidance, while others may not report such maladaptive cognitions yet may engage in significant avoidance. Recent studies have explored the utility of tailoring cognitive-behavioral treatments to individual variations in response systems.

Building on Lang's analysis of fear structures, Foa and Kozak (1985, 1986) conceptualized anxiety disorders as specific impairments in affective memory networks. According to Foa and Kozak, fear is represented in memory as a network that includes three types of information: (a) information about feared stimuli; (b) information about verbal, physiological, and overt behavioral responses; and (c) interpretive information about the meaning of the stimulus and response elements. For example, the fear structure of simple phobics may contain information that stimuli (e.g., heights, snakes) are dangerous, while those of agoraphobics contain information that anxiety responses themselves (e.g., rapid heartbeat) are dangerous.

Foa and Kozak (1985) noted that "neurotic fear structures are distinguished by the presence of erroneous estimates of threat, high negative valence for the threatening event, and excessive response elements (e.g., physiological, avoidance)" (p. 466). Consistent with this hypothesis, Butler and Mathews (1983), in a questionnaire study, found that anxiety neurotics, compared to depressives and normals, are more likely to interpret ambiguous information as threatening, overestimate the probability of the occurrence of the aversive events, and rate the negative events as more costly. Warren, Zgourides, and Jones (1989) obtained similar results using a modified version of the Agoraphobic Cognitions Questionnaire (Chambless, Caputo, Bright, & Gallagher, 1984).

Foa and Kozak also indicated that the fear structure of anxiety-disordered individuals, compared to those of normals, are more resistant to modification. This may be due to failure to access the fear structure, either because of active avoidance or because the content of the fear structure is difficult to encounter in everyday life (e.g., thunderstorms). On the other hand, even with exposure, change may be impeded by various impairments in the mechanisms of change, such as excessive arousal impeding habituation, erroneous rules of inferences, and other information-processing impairments. Foa and Kozak (1985) discussed the specific characteristics of fear structures of the various anxiety disorders and exposure methods for modifying them. These will be discussed throughout the book in relevant chapters.

Foa and Kozak (1986) also proposed that regardless of the specific therapeutic intervention used, two conditions are required for the reduction of fear. First, information matching at least some components of the fear structure must be presented to the individual to access the fear structure from storage in long-term memory. Second, new information incompatible with the existing fear memory must be made available so that a new memory can be formed. This is usually accomplished by various forms of exposure resulting in emotional processing (Rachman, 1980).

Clark and Beck's (1988) model of anxiety is also similar to the foregoing models. Anxiety disorders are viewed as related to overestimates of danger that arise from four basic cognitive errors: (a) overestimation of the probability of the feared event, (b) overestimation of the severity of the feared event, (c) underestimation of coping resources to deal with the event, and (d) underestimation of rescue factors (i.e., assistance available from others). According to Clark and Beck (1988), humans are evolutionarily programmed to respond to perception of danger with a set of cognitive, physiological, and behavioral responses (e.g., the fight-or-flight response, which protects individuals from harm).

Barlow (1988) presented a model for the etiology of anxious apprehension that appears to provide a reasonable account of the development of each of the anxiety disorders and that is compatible with Lang's (1977, 1979), Foa and Kozak's (1985, 1986), and Clark and Beck's (1988) models. Barlow (1988) hypothesized an interaction between biological vulnerability; psychological vulnerability related to developmental experiences involving mastery, controllability, and predictability; stressful life events; the occurrence of true and/or false alarms (i.e., the fight-or-flight response, which is essentially a panic attack); and the development of anxious apprehension or worry over future alarms. We discuss Barlow's model in more detail, describe specific adaptations of this model to each of the anxiety disorders, and relate these to our RET model of anxiety.

Finally, Bandura's (1977, 1986) self-efficacy theory provides a useful model for explaining both the maintenance and modification of phobic behavior. "This theory states that psychological procedures, whatever their form, alter the level and strength of self-efficacy. It is hypothesized that expectations of personal efficacy determine whether coping behavior will be initiated, how much effort will be expended, and how long it will be sustained in the face of obstacles and aversive experience" (p. 191). Bandura (1988) has recently expanded on the role of self-efficacy in the regulation of anxiety arousal. In this discussion Bandura notes, "it is not the sheer frequency of frightful cognitions but rather the perceived self-inefficacy to control their escalation or perseveration that is a major source of anxiety arousal" (p. 89). Similarities between this position and Barlow's (1988) emphasis on perceived controllability as the central factor in anxiety disorders are evident.

Bandura suggested that one's self-efficacy expectations are altered by four main sources of information: (a) performance accomplishments, (b) vicarious experience, (c) verbal persuasion, and (d) physiological states. Bandura discriminated between efficacy and outcome expectations. To oversimplify, efficacy expectations are related to the question, "Can I do it?" (i.e., "Can I engage in exposure to my feared situation?"). Outcome expectations are related to the question, "Will it matter?" (i.e., "Will exposure lead to anxiety reduction?"). Bandura hypothesized, consistent with empirical evidence, that efficacy expectations are more powerful causative agents than outcome expectations, and that direct performance accomplishments most powerfully alter perceived coping self-efficacy. Loyd Williams (e.g., Williams, Dooseman, Kleifield, 1984; Williams, Turner, & Peer, 1985) is probably the most notable clinician researcher who has applied self-efficacy theory and related guided mastery treatment for phobias.

For each of the anxiety disorders, we also (a) review recent literature, including etiology, DSM-III-R diagnostic criteria, assessment instruments, and non-RET treatments; (b) review treatment approaches similar to RET; (c) review specific RET methods used to treat the disorder, if such information exists; (d) discuss the theoretical appropriateness of RET, including differences between RET and other cognitive methods; (e) present a RET treatment protocol; and (f) provide case example(s). Subsequent chapters also include therapist-client dialogues that demonstrate the kind of interactions most commonly used by RET therapists who treat anxiety-disordered clients. Finally, the appendices contain some useful RET forms.

Chapter 2
Basics of Rational-Emotive Therapy

In a recent survey of clinical and counseling psychologists, D. Smith (1982) concluded that the cognitive-behavioral orientations "represent one of the strongest, if not *the* strongest theoretical emphases today" (p. 808). This survey also found that cognitive-behavioral and/or rational therapy was the predominate orientation among the 10 most influential therapists. Albert Ellis, who was voted today's second most influential therapist, pioneered the advent of cognitive-behavioral therapy via RET some 30 years ago (Ellis, 1957b). In 1985 Ellis received the Distinguished Professional Contribution to Knowledge award from the American Psychological Association (APA).

The purpose of this chapter is to summarize the basic theory and practice of RET, particularly as it is most relevant to the understanding and treatment of anxiety disorders. The reader is encouraged to consult recent RET practitioners' texts for more detailed coverage of RET theory and how-to-do-it instructions (Ellis & Dryden, 1987; Greiger & Boyd, 1980; Walen, DiGiuseppe, & Wessler, 1980). The recent RET practitioner guidebook on treating alcohol and substance abuse may also be a useful reference (Ellis, McInerney, DiGiuseppe, & Yeager, 1988).

THE BASICS

In its simplest form, RET espouses the notion that emotional reactions are not directly caused by events but by one's beliefs about those events. Thus, at the core of RET theory is the famous Epictetian quote, "People are not disturbed by things but by their view of things." Figure 2.1 illustrates the ABC theory of RET. In the figure the dark arrow between B and C signifies the primary role of beliefs in creating emo-

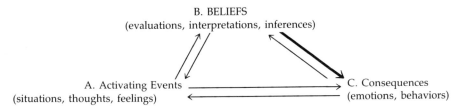

FIGURE 2.1. ABC theory of RET

tions. RET theory also acknowledges, however, that A, B, and C influence one another.

Consider the following example. For the person with a public speaking phobia, A refers to the situation of giving a speech, while C refers to both the anxiety expressed when thinking about or actually giving a speech and to possible behavioral avoidance of the fear-evoking activity. RET holds that it is not A that directly causes C, but rather the B (or Bs) that one has about A. Furthermore, A influences B in the sense that without a speech to give, the relevant beliefs would be less likely to occur. B influences A in that whether the phobic approaches A is influenced by his or her beliefs regarding both the desirability of giving a speech and his or her ability to do so. C influences B in that the phobic's emotional state affects the likelihood of the occurrence of different types of thoughts. For example, the more anxious the speaker is, the more likely he or she is to worry about that anxiety being seen by others and to predict a poorer performance. In a similar way, C influences A, because when the speaker is anxious he or she may also be more likely to avoid the A of giving a speech. Finally, A may directly influence C, as, for example, when the speaker is startled by an unexpected audience reaction and does not have time to process cognitively the sudden stimulus.

In summary, while RET acknowledges a reciprocally influencing relationship among situation, thought, feeling, and behavior, at the core of RET theory is the notion that beliefs play a primary role in creating and maintaining emotional disturbance.

ETIOLOGY OF IRRATIONAL BELIEFS

Similar to other cognitive therapies (e.g., Beck, Rush, Shaw, & Emery, 1979) that view irrational beliefs as learned through direct instruction, modeling, or other actual experiences, RET also hypothesizes that the tendency to think irrationally is a biological vulnerability of the human species. On the positive side, though, Ellis also views the ability to use reason and logic to challenge such irrational thinking and self-defeating behavior as a biological capacity. According to RET theory, parents and other cultural inputs influence us, but it is our predisposition to crooked thinking that permits us to accept irrational indoctrination (Ellis, 1976, 1979c).

Concerning anxiety disorders, Ellis's biological theory of irrational beliefs appears consistent with Eysenck's (1967) view that individual differences in neuroticism, including having a labile or overactive autonomic nervous system (ANS), probably render certain individuals more susceptible to developing an anxiety disorder.

RATIONAL AND IRRATIONAL BELIEFS

The Bs with which RET is most concerned are rational and irrational beliefs. Essentially, rational beliefs aid in obtaining one's goals and usually are sound in terms of logic and reason. Irrational beliefs, on the other hand, block one's goals and usually fail the test of reason. For example, the belief, "I must perform perfectly well when giving a speech," fails the test of logic as there is no guarantee that one will do so well, and there is no evidence that one really must perform well at an activity just because of one's desires. Further, such a belief usually leads to extreme anxiety that may block the goal of enjoying oneself while giving a good speech.

In other words, irrational beliefs tend to lead to debilitative rather than facilitative emotional and behavioral consequences. Examples of debilitative emotions include extreme anxiety, depression, anger, guilt, and shame. Debilitative or destructive behavioral consequences include withdrawal, avoidance, aggression, drug abuse, and other self-defeating behaviors. Examples of facilitative emotions include such positive emotions as curiosity, excitement, joy, happiness, but also negative or unpleasant ones such as disappointment, regret, irritation, and sorrow. Facilitative or constructive behaviors include approaching feared situations, tackling unpleasant but necessary chores, facing inevitable conflicts, and risking possible rejection. Thus, rather than encouraging people to become unemotional, the goal of RET is to assist people in becoming more positively emotional. In fact, RET helps clients look for those irrational beliefs that are suspected of keeping them unemotional (e.g., avoiding the experience of natural grief or sorrow).

What are the major irrational beliefs hypothesized by Ellis and RET theorists as being the most frequent contributors to debilitative emotions and behaviors? Over the 30 years of RET's existence, Ellis's views on this central issue of RET have steadily evolved. In the beginning, Ellis postulated 11 specific irrational beliefs thought to be most frequently associated with emotional maladjustment (Ellis, 1962). Although recently recognized problems with the measurement of irrational beliefs limit conclusions (e.g., T. Smith, 1982), the bulk of experimental evidence supports the role of these irrational beliefs in emotional problems. Ellis's (1962, pp. 60–88) original 11 irrational beliefs are as follows:

1. The idea that it is a dire necessity for an adult human being to be loved or approved by virtually every significant person in his community.
2. The idea that one should be thoroughly competent, adequate, and achieving in all possible respects if one is to consider oneself worthwhile.
3. The idea that certain people are bad, wicked, or villainous and that they should be severely blamed and punished for their villainy.
4. The idea that it is awful and catastrophic when things are not the way one would very much like them to be.
5. The idea that human unhappiness is externally caused and that people have little or no ability to control their sorrows and disturbance.
6. The idea that if something is or may be dangerous or fearsome one should be terribly concerned about it and should keep dwelling on the possibility of its occurring.
7. The idea that it is easier to avoid than to face certain life difficulties and self-responsibilities.
8. The idea that one should be dependent on others and needs someone stronger than oneself on whom to rely.
9. The idea that one's past history is an all-important determiner of one's present behavior and that because something once affected one's life, it should indefinitely have a similar effect.
10. The idea that one should become quite upset over other people's problems and disturbance.
11. The idea that there is invariably a right, precise, and perfect solution to human problems and that it is catastrophic if this perfect solution is not found.

The reader is encouraged to consult Ellis's text for one of Ellis's most lucid and cogent explanations for the irrationality of these beliefs.

More recently, Ellis (1979c, 1988) described the preceding irrational beliefs as derivatives of the following three basic "musturbatory ideologies":

1. I must perform well and/or win the approval of others, or else it's awful, and I am inadequate or worthless as a person.
2. You must treat me fairly and considerately and not unduly frustrate me, or it's awful, and you are a rotten person.
3. My life conditions must give me the things I want easily and with little frustration and must keep me from harm, or else life is unbearable, and I can't be happy at all.

Thus, Ellis and RET view the three musts as the primary contributors to other more specific irrational beliefs, such as the 11 listed earlier, as well as responsible for the following specific types of irrational thinking (Ellis & Dryden, 1987):

1. *Demanding:* The musts and shoulds that escalate preferences into demands. For example, "I must avoid errors" rather than "I would prefer to avoid errors."
2. *Catastrophizing:* Viewing negative events as more than extremely bad, having no right to occur, and "unstandable." For example, "It's awful to be rejected."
3. *Rating of self and others:* Overgeneralizing from traits or actions to one's entire self. For example, "I would be worthless if I lost my job," or "You're a bad person if you treat me badly."

The specific irrational beliefs, the three musts, and the three types of irrational thinking are referred to in RET as *evaluative beliefs* or thinking processes. They represent one's appraisal of the degree of badness or goodness of events or of one's interpretations of or inferences about events. RET also acknowledges the existence of many other kinds of cognitive distortions, such as those described by Beck (Beck, Rush, Shaw, & Emery, 1979) and Burns (1980), and hypothesizes that they stem from the primary musts and evaluative beliefs. Some of the most common distortions are as follows:

1. *Selective abstraction:* Focusing on a particular detail while ignoring other relevant aspects of a situation—for example, a speaker who focuses on the one person who leaves the room but ignores the attention given by most others in the audience.
2. *Arbitrary inference:* The process of drawing a conclusion without evidence. For example, a person having a panic attack infers that her rapid heartbeat means a likely heart attack, while disregarding results of medical tests that indicate the presence of a healthy heart.
3. *Personalization:* Relating external events to oneself in the absence of reasonable evidence. For example, the student who is sensitive to criticism interprets a grade from the teacher as being indicative of the teacher's opinion of him or her.
4. *Mind reading:* Assuming that one knows the motives, intents, or

other things going on in others' minds. For example, the social phobics "know" that others are judging them harshly when they appear nervous.

5. *Emotional reasoning:* Using one's emotional state as evidence for the existence of an objective condition. For example, the chronic worrier expects danger to be forthcoming because he or she feels extremely anxious.

6. *Overgeneralizing:* Using *always, never,* and fortune-telling, or "knowing" what to expect of the future. For example, the social phobic states, "I always behave nervously," or the obsessive compulsive "knows" that failure to perform rituals will lead to future disaster.

7. *Minimization and magnification:* Downplaying one's positive traits or accomplishments and exaggerating the negative aspects of one's performance or circumstances.

Ellis (Ellis & Dryden, 1987) delineated two basic forms of psychological disturbance that are consequences of holding the aforementioned musts: ego disturbance and discomfort disturbance. Ego disturbance refers to anxiety, depression, and other debilitative emotional and behavioral states that result from rating oneself as inadequate, inferior, or worthless if one does not perform certain tasks well or if one fails to obtain desired love or approval from others. Discomfort disturbance refers to anxiety, depression, or debilitative emotional and behavioral reactions that occur when one's demands for comfort or the absence of discomfort are not met.

Ego and discomfort disturbances often occur together. As Ellis (1982) explained,

> Whenever ego anxiety is profound, it leads to such heightened feelings of discomfort (such as panic, horror, or terror) that people conclude that these feelings absolutely *must* not, *should* not exist, that it is awful if they do, and that life is too much of a hassle for them to experience almost any enjoyment whatever under these conditions. They then are in the throes of discomfort anxiety. And whenever extreme discomfort anxiety or feelings of low frustration tolerance exist, most humans sooner or later tend to put themselves down for having and indulging in such feelings. They tell themselves conditions like, "What a baby I am! I should be able to face my panic and get over it and I obviously cannot. I'm just a rotter and a highly incompetent person!" (p. 35)

DISPUTING IRRATIONAL BELIEFS

RET argues that the way to change irrational beliefs once they are discovered is to dispute them. RET favors frequent, vigorous disputing and recommends a variety of methods, including cognitive, emotive, and behavioral disputes (Walen et al., 1980).

Cognitive disputes involve intellectually understanding why irrational beliefs are unreasonable and self-destructive, repeatedly questioning the validity of the beliefs, and practicing verbally, covertly, and in writing more rational alternative beliefs. Emotive disputes involve trying to generate force and vividness in disputing. Ellis has created rational humorous songs and other emotionally evocative techniques to achieve this end. Behavioral disputes involve acting against the irrational beliefs and in accordance with rational beliefs. Risk-taking and shame-attacking exercises are examples of behavioral and emotional disputational strategies. RET also makes an important distinction between empirical disputing and evaluative or philosophical disputing. RET favors the latter as the most important, as it directly attacks the major musts that are thought to be central to disturbance.

Returning to our speech phobic client, we can outline his situation in the ABC format.

A. *Activating event:*
   1. Anticipating giving a speech
B. *Beliefs:*
   1. I know I'll do badly. *(overgeneralizing)*
   2. If I did do badly, I couldn't stand it; it would be awful *(catastrophizing)*, and I'd be less of a person. *(self-rating)*
C. *Consequences (emotions and behaviors):*
   1. Extreme anxiety
   2. Avoiding preparation of the speech
D. *Disputes*
   1. How do I know that I'll do badly? Maybe I will, but hopefully I won't, particularly if I work very hard at challenging my irrational beliefs.
   2. If I did do badly, I could stand it even though I wouldn't like it. It would be unfortunate but not really catastrophic.
   3. How is my worth as a person determined by my speech-giving ability? It isn't! Speech–giving is only one performance and at worst it's a problem for me, but I'm not the same as my speech-giving ability!

The first dispute is empirical because one could gather evidence of how likely it is that one will speak badly. Disputes 2 and 3 are evaluative or philosophical because they challenge the client's basic assumptions or meanings.

Finally, appropriate behavioral disputes for the client might include in-session or homework assignment exposures to various types of performance situations, especially as an adjunct to the foregoing empirical and evaluative disputes.

VALUES IN RET

RET does not claim to be a value-free therapy (Ellis & Dryden, 1987). On the contrary, RET advocates several values that it considers to be conducive to psychological well-being. In 1985 Ellis received the Humanist of the Year award, and many of the values that he advocates for RET are consistent with ethical humanism, although they are also compatible with the core teachings of most major religions.

The philosophy of acceptance of self, others, and the conditions of the world is probably the most important value in RET. This acceptance does not imply passive resignation to detrimental personal characteristics or environmental conditions. It does, however, posit that such acceptance reduces debilitative emotional responses and sets the stage for reasoned problem solving so that conditions can be changed to increase the quality of life.

Central to the philosophy of acceptance is an understanding of the role of shoulds or musts in RET. To grasp why certain types of shoulds or musts are irrational, we must first discuss the uses of musts and shoulds that are not irrational. The shoulds of probability reflect one's estimates, based on personal experience or empirical statistics, of the likelihood of an event's occurrence. For example, if one thinks that an airplane should arrive safely without accident, one almost always would be correct in that prediction. Another use of should refers to the fact that it would be better if certain events occurred. For example, the thought, "I should (it would be better to) approach rather than avoid certain anxiety-provoking situations" is rational if evidence indicates that such an approach is a step toward accomplishing one's eventual goal of functioning with less fear.

The irrational use of shoulds is the demanding or "musturbatory" type. If the person in the previous example fails to face a specific uncomfortable situation and then thinks, "I should have faced it!" he or she may be saying, "Since it would have been better to have acted courageously, I should have faced it!" The likely meaning here would be, "I must do what is best," or "I have no right to have made the mistake of avoiding rather than confronting." These meanings of shoulds are absolutistic, allow no room for human fallibility, and go against accepting the reality that has already occurred. In other words, a person behaves in a certain way for specific (though not always obvious) reasons, which, as explained by Hauk (1973), include ignorance, stupidity, or disturbance. Ignorance refers to a lack of information or awareness that could facilitate certain choices. Stupidity refers to low intelligence that hampers a person in his or her ability to think clearly through available options. Disturbance refers to self-defeating emotions and behaviors that result from irrational beliefs. For example, a person with a fear of riding in elevators who, therefore, avoids them may not know the statistics on elevator safety or the therapeutic benefits of exposure versus avoidance in overcoming fear. It may be difficult for this person to understand the rationale behind how exposure therapies work, or the client may hold the belief that it is better to avoid discomfort rather than to tolerate it.

The value of tolerating frustration and discomfort is another core value advocated by RET and is most relevant to anxiety disorders (Ellis, 1979a, 1979b, 1979c, 1980a, 1982). In differentiating between low frustration tolerance (LFT) and discomfort anxiety (DA), Ellis has explained that LFT is the broader, more inclusive term referring to one's tendency to view any form of discomfort as almost intolerable and to be avoided whenever possible. Discomfort may include frustration, boredom, physical pain, or emotional pain, such as embarrassment, sadness, and anxiety. It is this latter type of discomfort that Ellis refers to as DA. Thus, we would view an individual's avoidance of confronting the situation he or she fears, whether it be heights, snakes, speeches, public restrooms, shopping malls, or the experience of anxiety itself (e.g., rapid heartbeat, shortness of breath, feelings of impending doom), as due to LFT in general terms and to DA in more specific terms.

The concept of DA is similar to that of anxiety sensitivity (AS), an individual difference variable that refers to the individual's belief that the experience of anxiety and fear may cause illness, embarrassment, or additional anxiety (Reiss, Peterson, Gursky, & McNally, 1986). These two concepts appear to differ significantly, however, in DA's primary focus on the discomfort of anxiety itself and the predicted discomfort that could result from the consequences of panic or anxiety (e.g., fainting, heart attacks), rather than the adverse consequences per se. While Reiss and his colleagues and other researchers have obtained empirical data supporting the role of AS as a risk factor for developing and maintaining anxiety-related problems, similar research validating Ellis's concept of LFT or DA as a central component of anxiety disorders has yet to be conducted. Nevertheless, on logical grounds and given the related research supporting AS and preliminary RET research, we view LFT and DA as central to the etiology and maintenance of anxiety-related problems. In a recent study, Warren, Zgourides, and Jones (1989) found support for the prediction that irrational belief is related to avoidance behavior. Future research is needed to determine if the irrational beliefs most predictive of avoidance are in fact indicative of a philosophy of LFT.

In terms of treatment, for example, the RET approach to LFT and DA involves teaching clients that it is in their long-term self-interest to experience short-term pain for long-term gain (i.e., to become long-range rather than short-range hedonists). Several therapeutic options are available for use in this process (e.g., bibliotherapy). Therapists should also have clients determine and compare the advantages and disadvantages of tolerating momentary discomfort for future gains. Increasing frustration tolerance involves learning to challenge such thoughts as, "I must not experience discomfort! It's terrible if I do! I can't stand it!" and to develop a more accepting attitude toward discomfort in general as part of life.

Another value central to RET and anxiety disorders is long-range versus short-range hedonism. RET advocates an approach to life that is risk-taking, enjoyment-maximizing, and meaning-fulfilling. It recommends, therefore, that individuals risk short-term pain for long-term gain. This concept is consistent with that of LFT and its rational alternative high-frustration tolerance (HFT) in that the willingness to tolerate short-term pain, whether it is anxiety, frustration, or arduous tasks, may result in a more general and long-term satisfaction with life. Thus, the student who diligently studies to achieve a career objective, the couple who face their problems rather than ignore them, or the phobic who confronts anxiety-provoking situations are cases of individuals who exhibit HFT and behave according to long-range rather than short-range hedonism.

Finally, Ellis distinguishes between "preferential" and "general" RET (Ellis, 1980b; Ellis & Dryden, 1987; Warren, McLellarn, & Ponzoha, 1988) and predicts that preferential RET, which takes a philosophical stand about absolutistic shoulds and musts causing emotional disturbance, will be more effective than general RET, which is a more general form of cognitive-behavioral therapy. This delineation of the two kinds of RET poses problems when evaluating existing RET outcome studies, although we hope that greater specification of treatment procedures used in studies will eventually correct this problem.

SELF-ACCEPTANCE

RET appears to be the only system of psychotherapy that clearly differentiates between the concepts of self-esteem and self-acceptance (Boyd & Grieger, 1982; Ellis 1977c) and strongly recommends the latter (Warren et al., 1988). For logical and practical reasons, Ellis advocates teaching clients self-acceptance rather than self-esteem. According to Ellis, self-esteem involves self-rating (e.g., "I'm a good person when I perform well, display positive characteristics, or win the approval of others. I'm less of a person when I perform poorly, display negative characteristics, or fail to win approval").

RET promotes self-acceptance rather than self-rating for several reasons. First, human beings are beings-in-process, with behaviors and traits that are constantly changing. Second, there is no accurate way to measure such behaviors and traits. For example, one person may value persistence while another does not. Third, it is impossible to keep track of all of a person's various personality characteristics and behavioral performances. Thus, if one rates oneself as weak or inferior because one suffers from an anxiety disorder, one is on dubious scientific grounds due to overgeneralizing from one aspect of self to the whole self, possibly ignoring other traits such as intelligence, perseverance, caring for others, and job competence.

On practical grounds, self-rating appears to lead eventually to debilitative emotions and interference with obtaining chosen goals. Thus, even if one rates oneself as a superior person because of a promotion at work or competence as a parent, one will usually remain more vulnerable to anxiety or depression, particularly if one begins to do poorly at work or at parenting. In other words, "What goes up usually comes down." If one can gain worth from success, one can lose it by failure. As Wessler and Wessler (1980) noted, with one's self-worth constantly on the line, life becomes a test rather than an adventure. Further, by focusing on proving oneself, one can become sidetracked from truly enjoying life. See Kuiper and Olinger (1986) for a relevant discussion of "Dysfunctional Attitudes and a Self-Worth Contingency Model of Depression" (p. 115).

Self-acceptance is particularly important to counteract what Ellis refers to as "problems about problems" (e.g., Ellis, 1980b; Ellis & Dryden, 1987; Yankura & Dryden, 1990). For example, simple phobics, who have the problem of avoiding heights or enduring such situations with dread, often develop a secondary problem of depression and low self-esteem as they denigrate themselves for "having such a stupid phobia." The RET therapist persistently works to help such clients unconditionally accept themselves in spite of their phobic handicaps. Thus, energy consumed by self-berating can be spent more productively on tolerating the short-term discomfort of overcoming a phobia. Otherwise, the client, as Ellis puts it, "will have two problems for the price of one." Other writers have recently described similar phenomena. For example, Barlow (1988) and Taylor and Rachman (1990) discussed fear of sadness and other aversive affective states, and Teasdale (1985) discussed depression about depression.

Throughout the book we present RET theories to explain various aspects of the etiology and maintenance of the anxiety disorders and propose related therapeutic interventions. Evidence supporting the validity of our theoretical concepts and the effectiveness of the suggested therapy techniques varies from one anxiety disorder to another, and many of our hypotheses await further empirical testing. We also encourage interested readers to consult *Inside RET: A Critical Appraisal of the Theory and Therapy of Albert Ellis* (Bernard & DiGiuseppe, 1989) for up-to-date critiques of theoretical, philosophical, research, and clinical aspects of RET.

In the following chapters we apply the philosophy and practice of RET, with a primary focus on preferential RET methods, to understanding and treatment of each of the DSM-III-R anxiety disorders. When RET has been empirically tested as a treatment for a specific anxiety disorder, we summarize the findings. When RET has not been utilized or when a related cognitive-behavioral intervention appears to be the treatment of choice, we describe the tested intervention and discuss how RET might be used either solely or in conjunction with this alternative approach. We assume that practitioners who use this book as an aid to treating anxious clients will already have experience in cognitive-behavioral therapy. For practitioners or students not trained in these methods, we hope that our text will contribute to the development of relevant knowledge and therapeutic skills.

Chapter 3

Panic Disorder

Of all the anxiety disorders, during the 1980s PD has probably received the most widespread research and clinical attention (Barlow, 1988). This phenomenon appears to be related most directly to the creation of a separate PD diagnostic entity in the DSM-III (1980) as well as to Klein's (1964) hypothesis that panic and anticipatory anxiety are two qualitatively distinct and biologically different forms of anxiety. More recently, panic has received additional attention with the reconceptualization of agoraphobia (i.e., a pattern of avoidance behavior primarily resulting from the person's fear of having panic attacks in public settings) as a subcategory of PD.

PD is characterized by the occurrence of unexpected panic attacks, which are discrete periods of intense apprehension, terror, or feelings of impending doom. These attacks are distinguished from high levels of general anxiety by their sudden and unexpected onset and tendency to surge to a peak, usually within 10 minutes. During a panic attack that meets DSM-III-R criteria, at least 4 of 13 specific autonomic and cognitive systems are present, which may include palpitations or accelerated heart rate (tachycardia); smothering sensations or shortness of breath (dyspnea); unsteady feelings, dizziness, or faintness; and fear of dying, losing control, or going crazy. People with PD typically either experience such attacks or fear their recurrence. Those who also exhibit significant avoidance behavior may meet DSM-III-R diagnostic criteria for PD with agoraphobia.

In terms of the onset of PD, Epidemiologic Catchment Area (ECA) findings have indicated that for individuals currently meeting the appropriate diagnostic criteria, as well as individuals with severe and recurrent or simple panic attacks not fully meeting criteria, the modal age of onset for the first panic attack is from 15 to 19 years. In contrast, the onset of PD tends to peak between the ages of 25 and 44, which suggests a prolonged incubation period between the first panic attack and eventual development of the disorder (Von Korff & Eaton, 1989).

Stressful life events have been consistently associated with time periods preceding the onset of agoraphobics' panic attacks (Pollard, Pollard, & Corn, 1989), PD (De Loof, Zandbergen, Lousberg, Pols, & Griez, 1989), and agoraphobia (Last, Barlow, & O'Brien, 1984). It is likely, however, that this phenomenon is not specific to PD but is also pertinent to the onset of other anxiety and psychiatric disorders (De Loof et al., 1989). Consistent with this position are the results of a recent study by Rapee, Litwin, and Barlow (1990), who found that PD patients did not report significantly more major life events preceding the onset of their disorder than did patients with other anxiety disorders and normal controls. In addition, while no difference was found between PD patients and those with other anxiety disorders, both groups rated the importance of the life events as significantly more negative than did the normal controls.

Besides the subjective distress and at times terror of unpredictable panic attacks, people who experience attacks or have PD may also experience a variety of serious related problems. For example, people without PD but who have frequent panic attacks usually suffer from significant psychological distress (e.g., phobias, avoidance behavior, major depression; Katon, Vitaliano, Russo, Jones, & Anderson, 1987). Those with PD, however, are at exceptional risk. For example, PD patients are the most frequent users of mental health and medical services (Boyd, 1986) and psychotropic medications (Weissman & Merikangas, 1986). Furthermore, people receiving diagnoses other than PD, but who have panic attacks, are more likely to seek treatment than people with another disorder without panic attacks (Boyd, 1986). There is additional evidence that people with PD suffer severe impairments in the quality of life (Markowitz, Weissman, Quellette, Lish, & Klerman, 1989) and are at high risk for attempting suicide (Weissman, Klerman, Markowitz, & Quellette, 1989). More specifically, the diagnosis of PD is associated with health problems similar to or greater than those associated with major depression. These problems include, among others, substance abuse, impaired social and marital functioning, and financial dependency (Markowitz et al., 1989). As for suicide attempts, Weissman et al. (1989) reported that people with recurrent panic attacks are 18 times more likely than people without a psychiatric disorder to attempt suicide. The authors also reported that 20% of people with PD (compared to 15% for major depression) and 12% of people with occasional panic attacks had attempted suicide.

According to Telch, Lucas, and Nelson (1989), when agoraphobia is classified as a subtype of PD, the lifetime prevalence for the disorder ranges from 5.4% (ECA; Karno et al., 1987) to 8.1% (Munich Follow-up Study [MFS]; Wittchin, 1986). There is also accumulating evidence that the phenomenon of panic is not limited to those with PD. In fact, it is known now that panic frequently occurs as a part of all of the other anxiety disorders, other emotional disorders, and in the general population. The prevalence of normals who report panic attacks ranges from about 9.3% for those who have had at least one DSM-III–defined attack to 34.4% for those who have had at least one attack during the previous year (Norton, Harrison, Hauch, & Rhodes, 1985). In addition, in a specific study of unexpected, DSM-III-R attacks, Telch, Lucas, and Nelson (1989) found that approximately 12% of a large sample of surveyed students reported one or more attacks during their lifetimes.

ETIOLOGY OF PD AND AGORAPHOBIA

The most prominent etiological models of PD are the biological and cognitive-behavioral models, which have been reviewed extensively in the professional literature (e.g., Margraf & Ehlers, 1989a; Margraf, Ehlers, & Roth, 1986; Rachman & Maser, 1988). Our purpose here is to summarize briefly the major components and current status of these models as a background for presenting our RET model.

The biological or medical-illness (MI) model (Margraf & Ehlers, 1989a) was originally developed by Klein (e.g., 1964, 1980), who proposed that panic attacks occur spontaneously as a result of an innate alarm mechanism that is triggered by separation anxiety. Furthermore, anticipatory or general anxiety, as well as avoidance behavior, were viewed as a result of unpredictable or spontaneous panic. Similarly, Sheehan (e.g., Carr & Sheehan, 1984) proposed that panic attacks were part of an "endogenous" type of anxiety that is a "metabolic disease" (pp. 99–111). In general, both Klein's and Sheehan's theories are representative of today's MI model of PD and agoraphobia.

The MI model has had great heuristic value, spawning voluminous research that has advanced to a significant degree the field's understanding of panic and generated numerous psychopharmacological treatments. On the other hand, as an explanatory model, most predictions have not been substantiated, nor have most significant research findings been corroborated. For example, studies examining drug specificity have indicated that two separate drug classifications—tricyclic antidepressants and benzodiazepines—both are effective for two separate types of anxiety: anticipatory anxiety and panic attacks. Also contradicting a strict biological model of PD, newly developed psychological treatments have shown great promise for PD sufferers. In addition, studies examining separation anxiety, experimental panic induction (e.g., via lactate infusions), spontaneity of panic attacks, and specific genetic vulnerability for PD have failed to confirm MI model predictions and actually are more consistent with cognitive-behavioral or psychophysiological model predictions. These types of studies again confirm Taylor and Arnow's (1988) assertion that anxiety disorders, including PD, are best viewed from a biopsychosocial perspective that incorporates biological, psychological, and social components.

Biological model adherents have also proposed the existence of specific neuroanatomical substrates for panic attacks, and the locus coeruleus (LC) has been hypothesized most often as the specific area of impairment (e.g., Redmond & Huang, 1979). According to Margraf and Ehlers (1989a), the LC hypothesis in its original global form has not yet been substantiated by empirical research.

Gorman, Liebowitz, Fyer, and Stein (1989) proposed a "neuroanatomical hypothesis for PD" (p. 148). These investigators hypothesized that the three distinct aspects of PD—the acute panic attack, anticipatory anxiety, and phobic avoidance—"arise from excitation in three distinct neuroanatomical locations, respectively: the brain stem, limbic lobe, and prefrontal cortex. Reciprocal innervation among nuclei in these three centers explains the genesis of the disease and its clinical fluctuations over time" (p. 149).

Gorman et al. (1989) explained the role of specific medications in addressing the separate components of PD and corresponding neuroanatomical locations. Cognitive and behavioral aspects of PD are also addressed, and a number of experimental tests for the neuroanatomical hypothesis are delineated. Gorman et al. (1989) creatively integrated neuroanatomical, cognitive, and behavioral concepts and provided a well-conceived view of possible biological substrates of PD and agoraphobia. Nonetheless, whether such biological mechanisms are unique to panic versus anxiety and hyperarousal in general, and whether such mechanisms are agents versus results of chronic anxiety, remains to be confirmed.

Finally, concerning biological causes, clinicians should be aware of some of the most common organic conditions associated with panic and anxiety, as it is not uncommon for physical conditions to coexist and exacerbate psychological symptoms (Barlow, 1988). For example, mitral valve prolapse, audiovestibular dysfunctions, hypoglycemia, and hyperthyroidism are disorders that at times are associated with panic and anxiety. Toxic and withdrawal effects of various drugs, such as caffeine, alcohol, cocaine, opiates, and certain over-the-counter medications (e.g., theophylline for asthmatic conditions), can also produce somatic sensations that may either mimic anxiety symptoms or serve as panic triggers. For a more comprehensive review of medical conditions that may be associated with anxiety symptoms, see Barlow (1988), Goldberg (1988), and Warren and Winkler (1990).

Concerning cognitive-behavioral theories of PD, a variety of models have been proposed (e.g., Barlow, 1986; Margraf & Ehlers, 1989b), with the similarities between these models far exceeding the differences.

Barlow (1988) described a comprehensive cognitive-behavioral-physiological model of the etiology of PD. Due to nonspecific biological vulnerability, which "may involve an overactive hypothalamic-pituitary-adrenocortical system and/or labile neurotransmitter system" (Barlow, 1988, p. 269), stress that typically is the result of negative life events leads to an alarm reaction. The alarm reaction is an innate response to perceived threat or danger and basically is the emotion of fear with its associated action tendencies of fight or flight. Because the alarm is elicited by accumulated stress and not by objective danger, the reaction is considered a false alarm.

As true alarms are associated with true danger, it is likely that humans are prepared to learn associations between alarm reactions and contiguous stimuli. For example, sudden attack by a large dog will naturally elicit the fight or flight response, which in turn protects the potential victim from a possibly life-threatening situation. In the future, the individual may demonstrate learned avoidance of situations reminiscent of the dog's attack or those likely to involve other dogs.

False alarms consist of a complex configuration of physiological arousal, cognitive perceptions of loss of control, impending doom, and strong escapist urges. These component sensations become associated with the entire alarm reaction and/or situational cues. This process results in interoceptive conditioning and learned alarms. Due to biological and/or psychological vulnerabilities (the latter often being related to developmental learning processes involving perceptions of mastery or control), individuals develop anxious apprehension or worry about the occurrence of future alarms. This worry involves attention narrowing and self-focused attention, with the likely result of increased awareness of somatic cues, which then presents the individual with an increased frequency of alarm (i.e., panic attack) triggers. Depending on cultural factors, learned coping styles, situational factors, social support systems, and perceived safety signals, varying degrees of avoidance may develop. Such avoidance may involve activities that produce feared somatic cues (e.g., exercise that produces tachycardia), places (e.g., shopping malls), forms of transportation (e.g., public buses), and a variety of situations in which the individual feels trapped or that may have been the scene of previous panic attacks (e.g., dental chairs, airplanes).

In summary, Barlow's (1988) theory of panic etiology integrates biological, cognitive, and behavioral factors with concepts from interoceptive conditioning and emotion theory.

The other well-known cognitive-behavioral theory of PD and agoraphobia is Clark's (e.g., 1986, 1988) and Beck's (e.g., 1988) cognitive approach to PD, which in many respects is similar to Barlow's (1988) model. However, differences do exist: Both Clark and Beck respectively focus (a) less on emotion theory concepts and developmental and learning experiences related to mastery and control, and (b) more on the cognitive components of the immediate panic cycle. In addition, while Barlow (1988) posited stress-induced false alarms or panic attacks, Clark and Beck proposed that panic attacks do not occur unless stress-related and/or non-stress-related factors (e.g., sexual arousal) body sensations are misinterpreted as dangerous. Furthermore, Clark (1988) postulated that "panic patients have a tendency to misinterpret bodily sensations even when they are not anxious. This relatively enduring cognitive *trait* would then be amplified when an individual enters an anxious *state*" (p. 77). Clark also proposed that this trait either may predate the first panic attack or follow it as a consequence. For example, introverts typically are more fearful of hyperventilation sensations than extroverts.

Clark's (1986) cognitive model of panic attacks can be summarized briefly as follows (see Figure 3.1). When internal (e.g., dyspnea) or external (e.g., supermarket) stimuli are perceived by the individual as threatening or dangerous, apprehension or fear occurs, which leads to a variety of body sensations that are also interpreted as catastrophic (e.g., indicative of a heart attack, loss of control). Further apprehension concerning the perceived physical and/or psychological danger creates a vicious cycle that is difficult to break.

The cognitive model does not require that catastrophic misinterpretation of body sensations or mental events always occur on a conscious level, a notion that is consistent with experimental findings that threat cues can be detected and discriminated without awareness (Mathews & MacLeod, 1986). Moreover, the cognitive model includes a role for biological factors in the genesis of panic attacks. For example, people who suffer from a deficiency of central adrenergic $alpha_{2-auto}$ receptors are more likely to experience sudden, variable, or intense surges in noradrenaline and sympathetic nervous system activation in response to perceived threat (Clark, 1988).

The cognitive model is consistent with numerous other experimental findings. For example, danger-related ideation is often associated with panic attacks (e.g., Hibbert, 1984); body sensations usually precede catastrophic ideation (Hibbert, 1984; Ley, 1985); and cognitive factors sig-

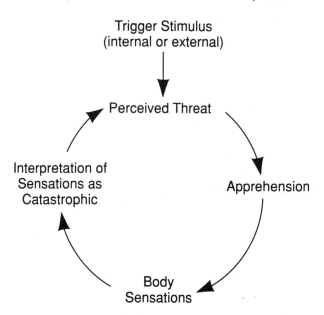

FIGURE 3.1. A cognitive model of panic attacks. From *Behaviour Research and Therapy, 24,* p. 463. D. M. Clark, A Cognitive Approach to Panic, 1986; Copyright 1986 by Pergamon Journals Ltd., reprinted by Permission.

nificantly influence whether individuals panic in response to hyperventilation (Margraf, Ehlers, & Roth, 1989; Salkovskis & Clark, 1990), lactate infusion (van der Molen, van den Hout, Vroemen, Lousberg, & Griez, 1986), and CO_2 inhalation (Rapee, Mattuk, & Murrell, 1986; Sanderson, Rapee, & Barlow, 1989).

Similar to Clark and Barlow, Beck (1988) proposed that:

> certain individuals are predisposed both neurophysiologically and cognitively to experience panic attacks under specifiable circumstances. The neurophysiological and cognitive aspects may represent different sides of the same coin. The predisposition may take the form of a chronically increased physiological arousal (in some of the patients), an increased tendency to exaggerate or misconstrue the meaning of certain symptoms, and most likely an inability to appraise these misinterpretations realistically. (pp. 92–93)

Margraf and Ehlers (1989b) presented a psychophysiological model of panic attacks almost identical to the cognitive model, but also delineating factors that reduce the likelihood of full development of a panic attack. Such variables include situational factors that connote safety versus danger, habituation and fatigue, and perceived availability of coping strategies.

Table 3.1 lists the DSM-III-R diagnostic criteria for PD. Table 3.2 lists the DSM-III-R diagnostic criteria for PD with agoraphobia (300.21).

Table 3.1. DSM-III-R Diagnostic Criteria for Panic Disorder

A. At some time during the disturbance, one or more panic attacks (discrete periods of intense fear or discomfort) have occurred that were (1) unexpected, i.e., did not occur immediately before or on exposure to a situation that almost always caused anxiety, and (2) not triggered by situations in which the person was the focus of others' attention.

B. Either four attacks, as defined in criterion A, have occurred within a four-week period, or one or more attacks have been followed by a period of at least a month of persistent fear of having another attack.

C. At least four of the following symptoms developed during at least one of the attacks:
    (1) shortness of breath (dyspnea) or smothering sensations
    (2) dizziness, unsteady feelings, or faintness
    (3) palpitations or accelerated heart rate (tachycardia)
    (4) trembling or shaking
    (5) sweating
    (6) choking
    (7) nausea or abdominal distress
    (8) depersonalization or derealization
    (9) numbness or tingling sensations (paresthesias)
    (10) flushes (hot flashes) or chills
    (11) chest pain or discomfort
    (12) fear of dying
    (13) fear of going crazy or doing something uncontrolled

Note: Attacks involving four or more symptoms are panic attacks; attacks involving fewer than four symptoms are limited symptom attacks (see Agoraphobia without History of Panic Disorder, p. 241).

D. During at least some of the attacks, at least four of the C symptoms developed suddenly and increased in intensity within ten minutes of the beginning of the first C symptom noticed in the attack.

E. It cannot be established that an organic factor initiated and maintained the disturbance, e.g., Amphetamine or Caffeine Intoxication, hyperthyroidism.

Note: Mitral valve prolapse may be an associated condition, but does not preclude a diagnosis of Panic Disorder.

Note. Reprinted with permission from the *Diagnostic and Statistical Manual of Mental Disorders, Third Edition, Revised.* Copyright 1987 American Psychiatric Association.

REVIEW OF ASSESSMENT INSTRUMENTS

A variety of methods are available for the assessment of PD and agoraphobia. These include structured and unstructured clinical interviews, self-report measures, physiological measures, and self-monitoring devices.

The Anxiety Disorders Interview Schedule-Revised (ADIS-R) (Di Nardo et al., 1985) provides a comprehensive DSM-III-R–compatible assessment of PD and agoraphobia, as well as the other anxiety

Table 3.2. DSM-III-R Diagnostic Criteria for Panic Disorder with Agoraphobia

---

A. Meets the criteria for Panic Disorder.

B. Agoraphobia: Fear of being in places or situations from which escape might be difficult (or embarrassing) or in which help might not be available in the event of a panic attack. (Include cases in which persistent avoidance behavior originated during an active phase of Panic Disorder, even if the person does not attribute the avoidance behavior to fear of having a panic attack.) As a result of this fear, the person either restricts travel or needs a companion when away from home, or else endures agoraphobic situations despite intense anxiety. Common agoraphobic situations include being outside the home alone, being in a crowd or standing in a line, being on a bridge, and traveling in a bus, train, or car.

Note. Reprinted with permission from the *Diagnostic and Statistical Manual of Mental Disorders, Third Edition, Revised.* Copyright 1987 American Psychiatric Association.

disorders. Unstructured clinical interviews include a history of the development of panic attacks and a behavioral analysis of antecedents and consequences of panic and avoidance behavior. Self-report measures useful for assessing PD include the Trait version of the State-Trait Anxiety Inventory (STAI-T; Spielberger, Gorsuch, & Lushene, 1970), and the Eysenck Personality Questionnaire—Neuroticism scale (EPQ-N; Eysenck & Eysenck, 1975). The Beck Depression Inventory (BDI; Beck, Ward, Mendelsohn, Mock, & Erbaugh, 1961) can be used to assess associated depression. Other self-report measures that have been devised to assess specific panic-related phenomena include the Body Sensations Questionnaire (BSQ; Chambless et al., 1984), which directly measures fear of body sensations associated with panic and general anxiety; and the Anxiety Sensitivity Index (ASI; Reiss et al., 1986), which, like the BSQ, assesses discomfort with body sensations but also assesses distress over being anxious. The ASI discriminates between agoraphobics and patients with other anxiety disorders and between patients with other anxiety disorders and college students.

The Panic Appraisal Inventory (PAI; Telch, 1987) consists of three separate scales that assess the cognitive appraisal of panic anticipation, consequences (physical, social, loss of control), and coping ability. Telch, Brouillard, Telch, Agras, and Taylor (1989) found that each of the subscales discriminates between patients with PD uncomplicated and PD with agoraphobia. Anticipated panic was found to be the best predictor of avoidance behavior. Another measure of cognitions associated with panic and agoraphobia is the Agoraphobic Cognitions Questionnaire (ACQ; Chambless et al., 1984). The ACQ, like the PAI, measures the frequency of catastrophic thoughts concerning possible negative consequences of experiencing anxiety. Warren, Zgourides, and Jones (1989) developed an expanded ACQ that includes ratings of perceived probability and cost (i.e., the degree of badness) of the untoward events (e.g., having a heart attack). Frequency × probability × cost scores, as well as probability scores alone, were significant predictors of avoidance in a composite sample of anxiety disordered, mixed diagnosis clients, and normals.

Measures to assess agoraphobic avoidance include the Fear Questionnaire (FQ; Marks & Mathews, 1979), the Mobility Inventory for Agoraphobia (MI; Chambless, Caputo, Jasin, Gracely, & Williams, 1985), and standardized and individualized behavioral avoidance tests (Barlow, 1988). The FQ yields avoidance scores associated with agoraphobia, blood-injury phobia, and social phobia, as well as anxiety-depression ratings. The instrument also has a global measure of the degree of disturbance of phobic systems. Because the FQ is widely used at anxiety disorders treatment centers around the world, the clinician can easily compare clients' scores with normative standards. As Barlow (1988) noted, there exists data that suggest that a cutoff score of 30 on the agoraphobic subscale identifies severe agoraphobic avoidance, while a score below 10 identifies a clinically successful treatment outcome (Mavissakalian, 1986a, 1986b). The MI measures avoidance of a variety of places or situations when the individual is either alone or accompanied. The instrument also contains a measure of panic frequency for the preceding week.

Behavioral avoidance tests can be standardized, such as the behavioral walk, which involves having clients walk as far as they can along a segmented predetermined course. Unstandardized behavioral tests can be developed from clients' fear and avoidance hierarchies.

As inexpensive portable heart rate monitors (Leelarthaepin, Gray, & Chesworth, 1980) become increasingly available, physiological assessment may become a more viable part of mental health treatment. Although physiological assessment typically suffers from problems of reliability, discriminant validity, and lack of sensitivity in measuring treatment effects, some pretreatment physiological measures may predict the client's response to treatment. Specifically, clients who at pretest show the highest heart rates during behavioral avoidance tests may be more likely to respond to treatment than those who have lower heart rates (Barlow, 1988).

In conclusion, self-monitoring devices are probably more valid than retrospective reports (Barlow, Hayes, & Nelson, 1984). As Rapee, Craske, and Barlow (1990) noted, recent PD treatment outcome studies have utilized ongoing self-monitoring of panic attacks as the major dependent variable (e.g., Barlow, Craske, Cerny, & Klosko, 1989). Self-monitoring forms also are useful for measuring general anxiety, depression, positive affect, and fear of having a panic attack (Barlow, 1988).

REVIEW OF NON-RET
TREATMENTS

Research on drug treatments for PD with and without agoraphobia has increased dramatically in recent years (Barlow, 1988). The most widely studied and accepted medications for the treatment of PD include the tricyclic and monoamine oxidase inhibitor (MAOI) antidepressants (e.g., Lydiard & Ballenger, 1988; Sheehan & Raj, 1988) and the benzodiazepine antianxiety agents (e.g., Pollack & Rosenbaum, 1988; Woods & Charney, 1988). Given the dietary restrictions necessary to avoid potentially dangerous reactions when taking MAOIs, tricyclics and benzodiazepines usually are the preferred drug therapies for PD and agoraphobia.

Imipramine (Tofranil) is generally accepted by physicians and nonmedical therapists as the most effective tricyclic panic blocker, although the empirical status regarding the drug's effectiveness with PD is far from conclusive. While imipramine appears to confer an advantage on exposure-based treatments for PD and agoraphobia, in the absence of exposure instructions, significant reductions in panic attacks may not occur (Telch, Agras, Taylor, Roth, & Gallen, 1985). Furthermore, general resistance to taking medication, inability to tolerate side effects, and relapse on discontinuation of medication are well-known problems associated with antidepressant treatment of PD.

Alprazolam (Xanax) is probably the most widely accepted benzodiazepine treatment for PD and agoraphobia. Results from a recent large-scale, multicenter study indicated that about 55% to 60% of patients taking alprazolam were panic free following drug treatment (Ballenger et al., 1988). Similar results have been reported in other studies (e.g., Klosko, Barlow, Tassinari, & Cerny, 1990). Unfortunately, there are also serious problems associated with alprazolam treatment, including risks of physical dependency, rebound panic, and a relapse rate that approaches 90% once complete withdrawal is achieved. In addition, benzodiazepines may impede the process of habituation when the client is exposed therapeutically to feared situations. Imipramine, on the other hand, tends to facilitate exposure via desensitization of the noradrenergic neurotransmitter system, a biological "toughening up" process that has been demonstrated in animal laboratories (Barlow, 1988).

For a more extensive review of drug treatments for PD and agoraphobia, the reader is referred to Barlow (1988), Marks (1987), and Taylor and Arnow (1988).

Exposure-based treatments for agoraphobia have been conducted since the 1960s and are considered to be the treatment of choice for this disorder. Psychological treatments for panic attacks with or without be-havioral avoidance were not developed or formally introduced until the 1980s. In the following paragraphs, we summarize the outcome of re-search on exposure-based treatments for agoraphobia and the newly developed cognitive-behavioral treatments for PD.

Summarizing the results of 24 controlled outcome studies of expo-sure treatments for agoraphobia, Jansson and Öst (1982) concluded that 70% of patients showed substantial improvement, with therapeutic gains maintaining at follow-up of 4 or more years, on the average. Barlow (1988) concluded that the treatment of choice for agoraphobia (i.e., ex-cluding direct treatments for panic) is a gradual, self-paced exposure to the avoided situations. In this procedure, therapists are weaned slowly from involvement by the end of treatment. Inclusion in the treatment process of communication training (Arnow, Taylor, Agras, & Telch, 1985) and the patient's spouse (Cerny, Barlow, Craske, & Himada, 1987) appear to enhance therapeutic outcome. Preliminary evidence also sug-gests that panic management training likely improves outcome of ex-posure treatments for agoraphobic avoidance (Bonn, Readhead, & Tim-mons, 1984; Chambless, Goldstein, Gallagher, & Bright, 1986).

With respect to direct psychological treatments for panic attacks and PD, notable excitement and optimism characterizes the current state of affairs, as discussed by Barlow (1988):

> During the past several years, we may have discovered something un-precedented in the annals of psychotherapy research. Preliminary evi-dence from a number of centers around the world suggests that we can eliminate panic . . . with specifically targeted psychological treatments, panic is eliminated in close to 100% of all cases, and these results are maintained at follow-ups of over one year. If these results are confirmed by additional research and replication, it will be one of the most impor-tant and exciting developments in the history of psychotherapy. (p. 447)

The preliminary evidence to which Barlow refers in the preceding paragraph includes both controlled and uncontrolled studies. In un-controlled research, Clark, Salkovskis, and Chalkley (1985) and Salkov-skis, Jones, and Clark (1986) found voluntary hyperventilation, breath-ing retraining, and reattribution of panic symptoms to hyperventilation to be effective for virtual elimination of panic attacks, with improve-ments maintained at 2-year follow-up. In another uncontrolled study, PD clients who received cognitive therapy experienced complete ces-sation of panic attacks after 12 weeks of treatment, with improvements in panic and associated symptoms maintained at 1-year follow-up (So-kol, Beck, Greenberg, Wright, & Berchick, 1989). Michelson et al. (1990) reported the effectiveness of a cognitive-behavioral treatment that included cognitive therapy, breathing exercises, applied relaxation, and interoceptive exposure with 10 DSM-III-R diagnosed PD patients. After 13 2.5-hour group sessions over a 12-week period, all patients were free of spontaneous panic attacks. Further, significant improvement was observed on most measures, and all subjects met criteria for high end-state functioning. Gitlin et al. (1985) found a similar cognitive-behavioral package effective in eliminating panic attacks in 10 of 11 PD patients.

Several recent controlled studies demonstrating similar success have been reported. Unpublished results from a controlled study that compared cognitive therapy with supportive counseling found that patients experienced complete elimination of panic attacks with cognitive therapy, and superior effects compared to the supportive therapy (Beck, 1988). Öst (1988) found applied relaxation to be superior to progressive relaxation in the treatment of PD. Each of eight patients treated with applied relaxation were panic free at posttreatment and at 19-month follow-up. Cognitive-behavioral treatment, which included cognitive restructuring, relaxation training, and exposure to interoceptive cues, successfully eliminated panic in 87% of PD patients (Barlow et al., 1989). For a more extensive review of psychological treatments for panic attacks and PD, see Rapee (1987).

Klosko et al. (1990) recently completed the first controlled study comparing cognitive-behavioral and psychopharmacological therapies in the treatment of PD. Cognitive-behavior therapy and alprazolam were compared in a double-blind medication placebo study. The panic-control treatment (PCT) proved to be at least as effective as, and on some measures more effective than, alprazolam. The percentage of clients who completed treatment and who were panic free is as follows: alprazolam, 50%; medication placebo, 36%; PCT, 87%; and waiting-list control, 33%. Similarly, Clark (1989a), in comparing cognitive therapy and imipramine in the treatment of PD, found cognitive therapy to be superior, with approximately 90% of patients remaining panic free at posttreatment.

Finally, and in addition to these first two psychological versus drug treatment studies, a comparative review of studies that evaluated the effectiveness of tricyclics, MAOIs, benzodiazepines, and behavior therapy in the treatment of panic was recently published. On the basis of this review, Clum (1989) concluded that, although it is premature to draw final conclusions, behavior therapy appears to be the treatment of choice for panic. Behavior therapy was rated as superior to other therapies on the basis of fewer treatment dropouts, fewer relapses, and greater reductions in the number and frequency of patients' panic attacks.

A RET MODEL FOR PD AND
AGORAPHOBIA

In research with agoraphobics, McNally and Foa (1987) found a pattern similar to Butler and Mathews (1983; see chap. 1): compared to normals, agoraphobics rated events related to physiological arousal as more threatening, probable, and costly. Given these findings, we conclude that anxiety disordered clients are generally characterized by their propensity to catastrophize concerning danger-related events. PD and agoraphobic clients typically evidence a more specific tendency to catastrophize about physiological arousal and other somatic sensations.

As we have discussed previously, RET distinguishes between inferential and evaluative beliefs and thinking styles, as described by Ellis (1980b):

> RET hypothesizes that most antiempirical statements by which people disturb themselves stem from overt or implicit *musts:* from absolutistic premises that humans *bring* to many situations and that then almost compel them to misperceive these events. Thus if you begin with the irrational premise, "I *must* not die dramatically in an airplane accident," you will easily tend to make several antiempirical conclusions, such as 1) "There is a *good chance* that the plane I fly in will get into an accident, and 2) If I do get in an air crash, it will be awful." (p. 329)

Thus, RET hypothesizes that the agoraphobic's tendency to catastrophize in response to body sensations is related to underlying musts. Of the three musts proposed by Ellis and described in chapter 2 of this book, we view the second must (i.e., "I must not experience discomfort") as the most likely to be implicated in the occurrence of the individual's first panic attack. Under the broad category of the second must falls the demand that one must not experience danger to one's physical or psychological well-being.

The manner in which PD sufferers develop irrational musts is described later in this chapter. We speculate that due to biological vulnerability, certain individuals develop irrational beliefs and thinking styles more easily in response to life experiences that involve issues of mastery and control and the threat of potential or actual danger to one's physical or psychological integrity. Thus, these individuals are more vulnerable to having a panic attack in response to stress-related arousal or other sudden, unexplained body sensations. Moreover, stress-related arousal may itself be related to biological vulnerability (e.g., having an overly labile autonomic nervous system), whereas the occurrence of the initial panic attack may be related to more immediate experiences (e.g., one's parent having had a heart attack).

We further speculate that individuals who develop PD subsequent to previous panic attacks engage in what Barlow (1988) referred to as "anxious apprehension" (p. 234). In terms of RET theory, anxious apprehension is best translated as becoming hypervigilant and worrying about the signs of future attacks. We further view the concept of worry as a form of catastrophization (i.e., increasing in one's mind the likelihood and awfulness of a panic attack).

This awfulness is probably related to irrational beliefs concerning the consequences of having panic attacks, most typically involving fear of physical danger (e.g., having a heart attack) and social and psychological danger. This latter category of danger may be divided further into fear of losing one's mind, embarrassment, criticism from self or others, and the pure discomfort of panic. In addition, we hypothesize that variations on the theme of the three basic musts also are implicated here. Individuals who believe that they must perform well and/or win the approval of others, or else things are awful, they cannot stand it, and their self-worth will be diminished, are at risk of developing anxious apprehension with respect to future attacks, and therefore at greater risk of developing PD.

AVOIDANCE

Research studies have begun to examine why some individuals with PD do not develop significant avoidance while others do. Before presenting a RET perspective on this question, we review recent empirical findings.

Surprisingly, neither duration of the history of panic attacks nor frequency and severity of panic appear to determine the degree of avoidance (Craske & Barlow, 1988). To date, the variable that best predicts avoidance is the anticipation of panic (Telch, Brouillard et al., 1989).

Anticipation of panic, perceived consequences of panic, and perceived self-efficacy in coping with panic have been found to discriminate between patients with PD and those with PD with agoraphobia (Telch, Brouillard et al., 1989). Catastrophic cognitions (Fleming & Faulk 1989) and fear of body sensations (Chambless & Gracely, 1989) also discriminate between PD and agoraphobic clients. Other variables associated with avoidance include low masculinity sex role scores (Chambless & Mason, 1986), social-evaluative anxiety (Pollard & Cox, 1986), unexpected panics (Rachman & Lopatka, 1986), and cognitive bias (i.e., the frequency × probability × cost of catastrophic cognitions and the occurrence of events they represent), and irrational beliefs (Warren, Zgourides, & Jones, 1989). Finally, Rapee and Murrell (1988) found scales measuring social phobia, introversion, and unassertiveness related to avoidance. In addition, clients with greater avoidance, when compared to clients with less avoidance, were more likely to perceive influences and triggers for panic attacks rather than view panic as independent of external factors.

Craske and Barlow (1988) stated that the origin of avoidance may be related to anticipatory anxiety about the occurrence of panic and strength of the action tendency to avoid versus approach, which appears to be related to a history of mastery and control experiences, learned styles of responding to stress, social demands (e.g., cultural factors such as male versus female socialization; Chambless & Mason, 1986), and potential for secondary gain. Once developed, avoidance may be maintained by unexpected panics, overestimations of panic occurrence, fear reduction from escape or avoidance, social demand, secondary gain, and safety signals (Craske & Barlow, 1988). Empirical evaluation of these proposed factors will be an important area for future research.

From a RET perspective, individuals who hold dogmatic musts related to performance, approval, and discomfort would be predicted to overestimate the probability of the occurrence of panic and panic consequences, as RET proposes this relationship between underlying irrational musts and tendencies to catastrophize. The hypothesis that underlying musts are related causally to inaccurate negative inferences related to perceived probabilities of panic, panic consequences, and avoidance has not been tested, although one study found irrational beliefs to be predictive of avoidance (Warren, Zgourides, & Jones, 1989).

Of the three must-related beliefs, we hypothesize that the belief that one must not experience discomfort is associated particularly with avoidance. We also predict that PD individuals with equal expectations for the occurrence of panic and feared physical, social, and loss of control consequences of panic vary in the degree of approach versus avoidance, depending on the level of discomfort tolerance. Our reasoning is similar to Craske and Barlow's (1988) discussion of courageous behavior:

> Courageous behavior is related closely to high fear tolerance. The assessment of differential courage requires assessment of approach to situations or activities of which two groups are equally fearful or equally expectant of the occurrence of panic. If panickers without extensive avoidance were more courageous, they would be equally fearful of the situation that agoraphobics typically avoid, but approach regardless. (p. 677)

TREATMENT OF PD: A RET PERSPECTIVE

Emmelkamp and his colleagues conducted the only controlled studies of RET with DSM-III diagnosed agoraphobics. Research has yet to evaluate RET for DSM-III-R diagnosed PD with or without agoraphobia. Emmelkamp, Kuipers, and Eggeraat (1978) found prolonged exposure in vivo to be clearly superior to cognitive restructuring, which consisted of RET and self-instructional training (SIT). A subsequent study (Emmelkamp & Mersch, 1982) compared cognitive restructuring, which again consisted of RET and SIT (but compared to Emmelkamp et al., 1978, emphasized RET and insight into irrational beliefs) with prolonged exposure in vivo and a combined treatment, which consisted of prolonged exposure in vivo and SIT. Although at posttreatment the combined treatment and exposure were superior to cognitive restructuring, at 1-month follow-up there were no significant differences between groups, except on assertiveness, where cognitive restructuring was superior. Emmelkamp and Mersch (1982) noted that from treatment to follow-up the exposure groups slightly relapsed while the cognitive restructuring group improved. SIT did not enhance the effectiveness of exposure in vivo.

As a true test of RET, a major deficiency was present in both studies—the behavioral (i.e., exposure) component of RET was omitted. Emmelkamp et al. ((1978) acknowledged this shortcoming. According to Ellis (1962),

> the effect of cognitive restructuring might be increased if this procedure was combined with real-life exposure in phobic situations. In the clinical use of Rational-Emotive Therapy, for example, use is often made of *in vivo* homework assignments. (p. 40)

In response to Emmelkamp et al. (1978), Ellis (1979b) emphasized this point.

> Pure cognitive restructuring works relatively poorly for almost any kind of phobia. . . . For unless phobic individuals *act* against their irrational beliefs that they *must* not approach fearsome objects or situations and that it is *horrible* if they do, can they ever really be said to have overcome such beliefs? (p. 162)

Ellis (1979b) also suggested that treatment for agoraphobia might be enhanced if both ego and discomfort anxiety were addressed (see chapter 2). Emphasizing the role of discomfort anxiety, Ellis stated,

> But "fear of fear" or "anxiety about anxiety" is a shorthand phrase for "fear of the *discomfort* of fear" or "anxiety about the *discomfort* of anxiety" . . . if it is true that agoraphobics (and many other serious phobics) are high physiological reactors—and my own clinical observation of them for many years leads me to strongly espouse this hypothesis—then we can predict that they would tend to feel more discomfort, and presumably more discomfort anxiety, than certain other kinds of phobics. (p. 163)

The third study (Emmelkamp, Brilman, Kuiper, & Mersch, 1986) directly compared RET, SIT, and in vivo exposure. Results indicated that in vivo exposure was definitely more effective than RET and SIT. In an effort to enhance RET, based on Ellis's (1979b) recommendations, Emmelkamp et al. (1986) emphasized rationally disputing beliefs related to ego and discomfort anxiety. In addition, exposure procedures were implemented. Nevertheless, RET subjects fared poorly. When RET and SIT subjects subsequently received in vivo exposure, significant improvements were noted. Emmelkamp et al. (1986) concluded that exposure in vivo was superior to cognitive treatments and "that there was no evidence that priming agoraphobic patients with cognitive therapy enhanced the overall effects of exposure treatment" (p. 51).

While this third study contained important improvements over the first two, factors that may have compromised the effectiveness of RET still remained. While the exposure was included, it was conducted following six sessions of purely cognitive RET and a 1-month waiting period. We hypothesize that RET would be more effective if cognitive restructuring and exposure were systematically integrated throughout treatment, as Heimberg, Dodge, and Becker (1987) recommended for enhancing the cognitive-behavioral treatment of social phobia. Similarly, Marshall (1985) also noted the importance of optimal timing and integration of cognitive and behavioral procedures. Finally, Michelson (1987), in discussing the results of Emmelkamp et al. (1986), raised concerns about the fidelity of the cognitive treatments (RET and SIT), given that they were administered by advanced clinical psychology students who served as therapists: "Hence it would be necessary to replicate the findings in an independent center where cognitive therapists whose treatment integrity and fidelity were closely monitored and objectively addressed" (p. 260).

The approach to treatment of PD with or without agoraphobia that we outline next attempts to remediate previous deficiencies in the RET treatment of agoraphobia and to improve on traditional RET by incorporating recently validated, direct physiological treatment of panic (e.g., Clark, 1989a; Klosko et al., 1990).

To understand and treat PD and other anxiety disorders, it is valuable for the clinician to conceptualize panic along the following dimensions (Barlow, 1988):

1. *Uncued, unexpected panic* involves the classic spontaneous panic attack, perceived as arising out of the blue.
2. *Cued, expected panic* occurs, for example, when a simple phobic claustrophobic expects to panic when entering an elevator.
3. *Uncued, expected panic* involves thoughts and feelings of imminent panic; for example, "When I got up this morning, I knew I'd have a panic attack."
4. *Cued, unexpected panic* occurs, for example, when a social phobic

does not expect to panic but does so on speaking at a business meeting.

Within a sample of PD patients (Street, Craske, & Barlow, 1989), the relative frequencies of each of the four types of panic were as follows: uncued, unexpected = 12.5%; cued expected = 68.1%; uncued, expected = 1.4%; and cued, unexpected = 18.1%.

As Barlow (1988) explained, cues may be cognitive (i.e., thoughts or images) or physical sensations of which the panicker may or may not be aware. Thus, "the term cued is phenomenological in that it refers only to patients' perceptions of the presence of a discriminated cue and not to the actual presence of a cue" (p. 588).

Night panic is another phenomenon with theoretical and treatment implications. According to Barlow (1990), about 40% of PD patients report night panic, which (a) typically wakes the individual rather than occurring after awakening; (b) is not typically associated with rapid eye movement (REM) sleep, dreams, or nightmares; and (c) typically occurs 2 or 3 hours after the individual falls asleep, especially when entering delta or slow-wave sleep. Nocturnal panics can be viewed as pure examples of spontaneous panic devoid of cognitive components (Roy-Byrne, Mellman, & Uhde, 1988), but according to Barlow's (1988) and Clark and Salkovskis's (in press) cognitive-behavioral models of panic PD patients, as well as a substantial portion of the general population (Craske & Krueger, 1990), may stay attuned to personally significant stimuli (e.g., feared body sensations; changes in breathing) even while asleep. Such cues may be detected and interpreted as dangerous without conscious awareness (Mathews & MacLeod, 1986) and thus trigger fear or panic. When one awakes in such a state, additional danger-based interpretations are likely to follow, which further intensifies the panic.

As discussed earlier, recent research has indicated that panic attacks occur frequently in all anxiety-disordered, other psychiatric-disordered, and normal individuals. Hence, newly developed psychological treatments that appear remarkably effective in decreasing and eliminating panic attacks may also prove to be valuable interventions for clients with anxiety disorders other than PD and agoraphobia. The treatment model described throughout the remainder of this chapter is applicable not only to PD patients but also to a certain portion of patients with other anxiety disorders for whom panic attacks are a feature (e.g., when phobic situations are confronted).

Barlow concluded that the cognitive-behavioral treatments of panic have virtually eliminated panic attacks in 80% to 100% of PD patients (Rapee & Barlow, 1989), which we believe is a remarkable finding. Klosko et al., 1990, however, noted that for PD patients who with treatment cease to have panic attacks, significant general anxiety often remains. Hence, we predict that the RET approach to PD and agoraphobia consists of the procedures that will strengthen existing treatments for panic-related anxiety disorders, including general anxiety and emotional disturbances about having a panic-related disorder.

Barlow and Craske (1989) published a step-by-step PD client manual, and Craske and Barlow (1990) published a corresponding treatment guide. In addition, Clark and Salkovskis (in press) provided an in-depth guide for cognitive therapy for panic. Given the availability of these texts, we summarize the basic cognitive intervention that has been tested empirically and discuss areas in which RET appears to be an appropriate adjunctive therapy.

As Craske and Barlow (1990) summarized, current, effective treatments for PD include, at least to some degree, (a) education about the nature of panic attacks, (b) breathing retraining or relaxation training, (c) cognitive therapy to deal with erroneous beliefs about panic and its consequences, (d) exposure to interoceptive somatic cues, and (e) exposure to avoided situations, if agoraphobic avoidance is present. Each of these procedures is described next, in addition to some useful assessment and self-monitoring procedures (e.g., from Barlow, 1988; Barlow & Craske, 1989).

Initial Session

During the first session, we gather information about the client's history of panic attacks and avoidance patterns to establish an appropriate DSM-III-R diagnosis (see chapter 1 for a discussion of our general treatment plan and approach). Emphasis is on the client's description in minute detail of the circumstances surrounding both the first panic attack and the most severe attack. The purpose of this questioning is to discover the client's particular pattern of body sensations and associated catastrophic interpretations that culminate in panic.

Education about Panic Attacks

By the end of the initial session, we use the client's psychosocial data to explain the cognitive-behavioral model of panic as it relates specifically to him or her (i.e., using Clark's 1986 cognitive diagram). We then give the client a handout, "The Causes of Anxiety and Panic Attacks" by Rapee, Craske, and Barlow (1988), the contents of which are contained in Barlow and Craske's (1989) client manual, *Mastery of Your Panic and Anxiety*. This handout presents, from a cognitive-behavioral

PANIC ATTACK RECORD

NAME: _____

DATE: _____   TIME: _____   DURATION: _____ (mins.)

WITH: SPOUSE _____   FRIEND _____   STRANGER _____   ALONE _____

STRESSFUL SITUATION: YES / NO   EXPECTED: YES / NO

MAXIMUM ANXIETY (CIRCLE)
0 ------------- 1 ------------- 2 ------------- 3 ------------- 4 ------------- 5 ------------- 6 ------------- 7 ------------- 8
   NONE   MODERATE   EXTREME

SENSATIONS (CHECK)

POUNDING HEART	_____	SWEATING	_____	HOT/COLD FLASH	_____
TIGHT/PAINFUL CHEST	_____	CHOKING	_____	FEAR OF DYING	_____
BREATHLESS	_____	NAUSEA	_____	FEAR OF GOING CRAZY	_____
DIZZY	_____	UNREALITY	_____	FEAR OF LOSING CONTROL	_____
TREMBLING	_____	NUMB/TINGLE	_____		

FIGURE 3.2. Self-monitoring form for panic attacks. From *Journal of Anxiety Disorders, 4,* p. 175. R. M. Rapee, M. G. Craske, and D. H. Barlow, Subject-Described Features of Panic Attacks Using Self-monitoring, 1990; Copyright 1990 by Pergamon Journals, Ltd., reprinted by permission.

perspective, a detailed explanation of panic and the physiological symptoms that make up the fight or flight response. The client is asked to read this material two or three times before the next session so that he or she will have an accurate understanding of panic.

We also give the client a packet of questionnaires and self-monitoring forms, including the FQ, STAI-T, EPQ-N, MI, BSQ, BDI, our expanded version of the ACQ, and the Belief Scale, a single construct measure of irrational beliefs (Malouff & Schutte, 1986; Warren, Zgourides, & Jones, 1989). This packet is also readministered at posttreatment. Our primary self-monitoring form is the Panic Attack Record (see Figure 3.2) of the Phobia and Anxiety Disorders Clinic of the State University of New York at Albany (Barlow, 1988; Barlow & Craske, 1989). The Weekly Record involves end-of-day ratings from 0 to 8 of average anxiety, maximum anxiety, average depression, average pleasantness, medications taken, and fear of panic attacks. We use this instrument for the first 2 weeks and the final week of treatment to serve as pre- and posttest measures. The client is then given several Panic Attack Records and asked to complete one as soon as possible after each panic attack that occurs during the entire course of treatment. In addition to checking all sensations that occurred, the client underlines the first symptom noticed. This information is used to help identify the sequence and pattern of body sensations that trigger the client's panic.

In addition, on the reverse side of the Panic Attack Record, the client may be asked to record the main thoughts that occurred both preceding and following the panic attacks. This information is useful for increasing awareness of how thoughts contribute to panic and for eventual cognitive restructuring.

During the second session, the client's completed questionnaires are reviewed. Information from the Panic Attack Record, as well as discussion of the client's understanding of the panic and reaction to the cognitive-behavioral handout, are used to illustrate further the cognitive-behavioral model of panic.

Breathing and Relaxation Training

Because 60% to 70% of individuals who panic experience hyperventilation symptoms during attacks (Craske & Barlow, 1990), we also include as part of the education portion of treatment a discussion of the nature of hyperventilation, which involves an increased rate and/or depth of respiration that prompts an imbalance of O_2 and CO_2 with subsequent physiological sensations virtually identical to those comprising a DSM-III-R panic attack. These symptoms, although harmless to physically healthy persons, can be misinterpreted and lead to a panic attack. (See Barlow and Craske, 1989, for a more detailed explanation of hyperventilation and its treatment.)

We conduct a session of progressive muscle relaxation (Bernstein & Borkovec, 1973), audiotape the exercise, and instruct clients to practice it at least once each day. After 2 weeks, a "letting go" recording is made on the reverse side of the first tape. This exercise eliminates the muscle-tensing component and includes attention to slow diaphragm breathing and cue-controlled procedures in which the client pairs the words *relax* or *calm* with a series of exhalations at the end of the tape. Separate daily practice of diaphragm breathing is also assigned and later integrated into the cue-controlled relaxation procedures. Thus, the client develops a portable relaxation skill that can be used to reduce general anxiety and arousal, thereby decreasing those body sensations that have become panic triggers. Moreover, the client is taught to use relaxation and slow breathing to disrupt the panic attack cycle, as diaphragm breathing can modify chronic hyperventilation by correcting the acute overbreathing that occurs during panic attacks. Finally, development of breathing and relaxation skills plays a vital role in restoring the client's sense of control and mastery over his or her fear reactions.

It should be noted, however, that clients may experience relaxation-induced anxiety (Heide & Borkovec, 1983) and may actually panic in response to various somatic sensations associated with relaxation (Barlow, 1988). Therapists may choose to discuss the types of sensations they may experience during relaxation, as a way to reduce the likelihood of panic reactions, or they may not do so and instead use this reaction to vividly demonstrate the role of catastrophic-misinterpretation of body sensations in producing panic. In any case, for those clients who do experience relaxation-induced anxiety, continued relaxation practice with appropriate educational inputs will typically take care of this problem. Essentially, practicing relaxation exercises may be another interoceptive exposure exercise for some panic patients.

Cognitive Restructuring

Education about the nature of panic and the reattribution of panic symptoms to a normal, survival-oriented fight or flight response is an important aspect of cognitive restructuring. Some patients have reported that the most helpful component of a cognitive-behavioral treatment for panic has been the corrective information that reduced catastrophic beliefs about panic attacks (Gitlin et al., 1985, as reported in Rapee & Barlow, 1989).

The most beneficial and intensive cognitive restructuring interventions teach the client to revise probability overestimates for the occurrence of panic-related consequences (e.g., fainting, losing control) and to decatastrophize the perceived aversiveness of these feared events. Cognitive-behavioral interventions aimed at both of these targets are implemented at various times during therapy (e.g., when conducting exposure to feared body sensations). Examples of interventions for revising probability estimates and decatastrophizing appear at the conclusion of this chapter.

Overestimating Probabilities

PD clients often overestimate the probability both of having a panic attack in specific situations and experiencing dangerous consequences as a result of panic. Moreover, many of these overestimations are based on emotional reasoning. For example, "Because I feel faint, I'm going to faint" or "Because I feel like I'm going to lose control and run out of the room, it's very likely that I'll do that." We have found it useful to help clients learn to make more accurate predictions by teaching them about the hazards of emotional reasoning.

Therapist: What leads you to think that you actually will pass out if you panic?

Client: I don't know. It just feels like I will when I get lightheaded.

Therapist: So, in a sense you are using your feelings that you are going to pass out as evidence that you will.

Client: Right.

Therapist: How would you evaluate how good that evidence is?

Client: Not too good, I guess.

Therapist: Why?

Client: Well, I've had the feeling that I would pass out thousands of times, but I've never actually passed out.

Therapist: Right. So, rather than feeling like you're going to faint being evidence of the likelihood of fainting, what is it really more likely to be evidence of?

Client: Do you mean hyperventilation and fight or flight stuff?

Therapist: Yes. Why don't you tell me how hyperventilation, for example, might make you feel lightheaded?

Probability overestimations also can be maintained by the presence of various forms of avoidance behaviors, both subtle and obvious. For example, Clark (1989b) described a client who continued to fear falling when she panicked, although this actually never had happened. In this case, when the woman was afraid she would hold onto something (e.g., a shopping cart), a subtle form of avoidance. Such clients are taught to view fear of falling, for example, as an interpretation of wobbly or weak legs, resulting from fight or flight processes, and to refrain from the avoidance behavior of holding onto a shopping cart. Then, a valid behavioral experiment to test the prediction that wobbly legs will lead to falling down can be conducted. For example, the client can deliberately refrain from holding on to shopping carts or leaning against a wall to prevent falling when she is anxious and her legs feel weak and wobbly. The client could also be asked during the therapy session, after suitable bodily sensations are induced, to hop up and down on one foot. Clark and Salkovskis (1990) report this procedure as quite useful when appropriate, and they, incidently, model this procedure to workshop participants in a superb fashion!

Distraction can also serve as a form of subtle avoidance. As many phobia treatment programs teach distraction as an active coping skill (e.g., focusing on various details of the environment instead of one's anxiety), when distraction is therapeutic and when it is antitherapeutic becomes an important point for therapists to be clear on (Craske, Street, & Barlow, 1989); Clark and Salkovskis (1990) offer what appears to us to be a potential resolution to this issue. Distraction can be profitably used to decrease the nuisance value of anxiety symptoms (e.g. relax tense muscles, help focus and concentrate more clearly). However, when one believes that without the use of distraction (e.g. focusing on one's breathing, thinking pleasant thoughts, deliberately avoiding fearful thoughts) some disaster, such as fainting, collapsing, losing control, or going crazy, will occur, then the distraction is avoidance that prevents disconfirmation of catastrophic predictions.

In terms of clients' tendencies to overestimate the probability of having a panic attack, rather than specific consequences of an attack, the foregoing procedures are also useful. In addition, the therapist assists the client's review of the frequency of panic attacks in various situations, as well as any variables that may discriminate between previous situations where panic has occurred and anticipated ones. Such interventions serve to challenge overgeneralizations. For example, "Because I panicked before at the corner store, I'll always panic there." Discussion might reveal that the previous panic at the corner store occurred after the client was exhausted from her daily routine and before she had learned breathing and cognitive coping skills. She might also recall situations wherein she did not panic at the store.

It is important for the therapist not to convey to the client the message that there exists a 100% guarantee or certainty that panic will never occur again in specific situations. Although research has indicated that lower probability estimates of the likelihood of having a panic attack are associated with less avoidance behavior (Telch, Brouillard, et al., 1989), research has also indicated that unexpected panics may increase future avoidance (Rachman & Lopatka, 1986). Thus, RET therapists teach clients to play the odds more accurately but not to believe unrealistically that they never will panic. The goal of therapy is to help the client reach a healthy balance between being prepared to deal with potential panics and hypervigilantly assuming that a panic definitely will occur.

When clients overestimate the probability of experiencing physical disaster (e.g., a heart attack) during a panic attack, developing a list of evidence for and against such a possibility may be a useful intervention. Here, the results of recent medical examinations and accurate information as to why the physical sensations are unlikely to indicate a heart attack are important. Thus, for example, if hyperventilation or discussion of anxiety-provoking topics results in chest pain or numbness in the client's arm, and if subsequent application of relaxation procedures reduces or eliminates the symptoms, the client should be asked, "If you actually were having a heart attack, would such symptoms come and go in this manner?"

When using medical examination results as evidence of the absence of a medical condition, the exact nature of the examination and the client's understanding of the results are vital. For example, a recent client rated the likelihood of having heart disease and a subsequent heart attack at 80 on a scale of 1 to 100, despite a relatively recent cardiology exam that yielded negative results. Further discussion indicated that the client had not asked questions important to her understanding of her symptoms. We compiled a detailed list of such questions and arranged for a consultation with a cardiology nurse practitioner who was known to have an understanding of anxiety. After talking with the nurse, the client rated the likelihood of having heart disease at 20. This rating remained stable throughout therapy, and her fear of having a heart attack eventually subsided.

Interoceptive Exposure

As discussed earlier, we ascertain the client's feared body sensations from information gathered via clinical interview, Panic Attack Records, the BSQ, and discussion. Even more useful, however, are the body sensation provocation exercises designed by Barlow and colleagues for the assessment of fear of specific body sensations. The therapist models and the client performs each of the exercises listed in Figure 3.3. Following each exercise, the client reports the sensations experienced and rates from 0 to 8 the intensity of the sensations, the intensity of anxiety experienced, and the similarity of the sensations to those experienced during actual panic attacks. (See Barlow and Craske, 1989, and Rapee and Barlow, 1989, for details on administering these exercises.)

After the relevant information is gathered and ratings are completed, we have sufficient information to build a hierarchy of feared body sensations. Following Barlow and Craske's (1989) model, items included in the hierarchy are the ones rated as being at least 3 on the 0 to 8 scale of similarity to a natural panic attack and at least 3 on the intensity scale. These items are then ranked from least to most anxiety provoking. In conducting these exercises, we usually model each exercise and often perform it with the client. The client is instructed to continue practicing the exercises at home between sessions. Table 3.3 shows the instruction sheet clients are given to facilitate practice at home. Figure 3.4 contains the exposure record sheet on which clients monitor their exposure exercises.

Exposure to Avoided Activities and Situations

Once the client has completed the interoceptive exposure hierarchy, he or she is instructed to practice confronting items on a hierarchy of avoided activities, which are the ones the client perceives as likely to

INTEROCEPTIVE EXPOSURE RECORD

Client Name: _____

0 = None
8 = Extreme

Excercise	Sensations	Intensity of sensation 0 -8	Intensity of anxiety 0 - 8	Similarity to natural panic 0 - 8
Shake head from side to side, 30 seconds.				
Place head between legs for 30 seconds and lift head.				
Run on spot, 1 minute.				
Hold breath, 30 seconds.				
Spin in chair, 1 minute.				
Complete body muscle tension, 1 minute.				
Hyperventilate, 1 minute.				
Breathe through straw, 2 minutes.				
Stare at bright light, 1 minute, and then read.				
Hot stuffy room, 5 minutes.				

FIGURE 3.3. Interoceptive Exposure Record. From *Mastery of your Anxiety and Panic* by D. H. Barlow and M. G. Craske, 1989, Albany, New York. Copyright 1989 by Graywind Publications. Reprinted by permission.

Table 3.3. Instructions for Exposure Exercises

1. Start with the least (0 to 8) anxiety-provoking exercise and work your way to the top.
2. Continue the exercise for 30 seconds after you first notice your sensations (only 10 seconds for breath holding and shaking head from side to side).
3. After the 30 seconds are up, stop the exercise and rate the intensity of your anxiety and fear from 0 to 8, using the Exercise Exposure Record.
4. Apply breathing, relaxation, and rational thinking skills to manage the anxiety. For example, you might think, "I can tolerate these feelings; they are not dangerous."
5. Repeat the same exercise until your anxiety rating is down to a 2 or less (your rating should be the maximum level of anxiety you experience during the exercise or immediately afterwards) before you start using your coping skills.
6. Wait until the physical sensations have disappeared and you no longer feel anxious before repeating the same exercise again.
7. If your anxiety and fear does not decrease to a 2 after five practice trials, stop this exercise for today and do the same thing tomorrow.
8. When anxiety and fear is down to a 2 or less, start with the next exercise on your hierarchy. If your anxiety and fear rating of your first exercise has already gone down to a 2, and you haven't practiced it for a full week, continue to practice that previous exercise as well as practicing the next exercise. Continue practicing both exercises until the end of the week, even if your anxiety and fear ratings both go down to a 2 or less. Do not practice more than two exercises per day or per week.
9. Continue these procedures until you have gone through your entire hierarchy, reducing your anxiety and fear ratings to 2.
10. Remember to avoid distracting yourself during the 30 seconds when you are focusing on the sensation. Allow the sensations to be as intense as they are. Use imagery if needed to help stimulate the sensations, and remember to separate the unpleasantness from the actual anxiety and fear.

Note: Adapted from Barlow & Craske, 1989.

produce the feared body sensations. Activities include walking or running, engaging in sexual intercourse, watching an exciting and/or horror movie, taking a steamy shower, wearing turtleneck sweaters, drinking coffee, or driving on curved roads.

The final and primary component of treatment for agoraphobics involves having the client practice confronting items on a hierarchy of avoided situations, which may include shopping malls, elevators, theaters, and driving a car. During the exposure, the client is instructed to deliberately induce the feared body sensations (i.e., often via hyperventilation) to densensitize to them. The client takes control by assuming an active rather then avoidant approach to the feared situations, and he or she uses breathing and relaxation skills to cope with panic and anxiety sensations that are likely to arise during the exposure exercises.

Preferential RET Interventions

Though the aforementioned cognitive-behavioral procedures are consistent with what Ellis termed "general RET," those described next are representative of what Ellis termed "preferential RET" (Ellis, 1980b).

Day	Exercise	Trial	Anxiety and fear (0–8)

FIGURE 3.4. Exercise Exposure Record. From *Mastery of your Anxiety and Panic* by D. H. Barlow and M. G. Craske, 1989, Albany, New York. Copyright 1989 by Graywind Publications. Reprinted by permission.

Decatastrophizing. RET distinguishes between inferential and evaluative beliefs. Inferential beliefs include those discussed earlier as probability overestimates concerning the likelihood of experiencing certain negative consequences of panic attacks. Typical feared consequences include many of those that appear on the ACQ and that can be divided into two categories: physical danger (e.g., vomiting, fainting, choking, having a heart attack, having a stroke) and social and psychological danger (e.g., losing control, going crazy, acting foolish, screaming).

As indicated earlier, Ellis posited that such feared events are seen as highly probable because the client demands that they must not occur and are rated as terrible if they do. Consistent with Barlow and Craske's (1989) panic therapy, treatment focuses both on revising probability overestimates and changing catastrophic thinking. Consider the following discussion of catastrophization:

> Unnecessary anxiety and fear often arise from viewing an event as "dangerous," "insufferable," or "catastrophic," when in actuality it is not. . . . Ask yourself what is the worst possible thing that could happen . . . and what if people did think poorly of you, does that mean you will never enjoy life again? In other words, in actuality, you can stand or tolerate or bear any misfortune that happens to you. It is only the statement that creates the anxiety—the statement that you cannot stand it. In its most extreme form, decatastrophizing goes so far as pointing out that anybody can stand anything until they die and then there is no reason to stand it anymore. Decatastrophizing can be summed up in one phrase— so what? (Barlow & Craske, 1989, pp. 8–2, 8–3)

Barlow and Craske (1989) continued,

> If the worst that is considered likely to happen is death or loss of a significant other . . . then decatastrophizing may not be as effective because in your own mind, it is not appropriate to say that it is not so bad to die or not so bad to lose someone very close to you. Fears of death or loss are generally more appropriate to the analysis of overestimation— that is, how likely is it that you will die the next time you panic? (p. 8–3)

Barlow has indicated elsewhere (1990), however, that at times he uses decatastrophizing with fears of death related to panic, depending on the particular client's receptivity to this approach.

Nevertheless, the RET approach includes decatastrophizing for the typical physical danger concerns of panickers (e.g., death, having a stroke); but rather than saying "that it is not so bad to die or not so bad to lose someone very close to you" (Barlow & Craske, 1989, p, 8–3), we distinguish between something being bad or extremely bad and something being terrible and catastrophic. Thus, it seems rational to view having a heart attack or dying as extremely bad, assuming that one's goal is to be alive and healthy. But when one views such events as awful and catastrophic, one often means that this event is so bad that it has no right to exist in one's life: "It must not occur; I must have a guarantee that it won't." The dispute for this belief involves working with the client to accept on philosophical grounds that both bad and good are parts of life (or death). Ellis's (1972a) *How to Master Your Fear of Flying* and Burns's (1989) *The Feeling Good Handbook* contain relevant material on coming to terms with the fear of death.

For other feared panic-related disasters that do not culminate in death (e.g., losing control, losing one's job), we help the client to distinguish between seeing the event as existing at some point on a continuum of badness, from "slightly bad" to "extremely or 100% bad, awful, and catastrophic." Defining the term *awful* as "I can't stand or tolerate badness; it must not happen to me, and I wouldn't be at all happy if this happened to me" forces one to see that there is no law of the universe that requires that tragic events only happen to others. A more rational response is, "I probably could stand or endure it, though I would find it extremely uncomfortable, unfortunate, and inconvenient. I probably could eventually achieve some degree of happiness, if not as high a degree, in my life by continuing to work at being involved in activities or relationships that are meaningful to me."

Besides using their reasoning abilities to decatastrophize, clients can be assisted in thinking of other times in their lives when they or others whom they know have coped with tragic circumstances. Hence, in addition to helping clients make more accurate estimates of the probability of feared panic consequences, we also work with them to decatastrophize, but not minimize, even the worst-case scenarios.

Should the client not be receptive to the foregoing approach, we tend to focus on probabilities. We predict, however, that clients who are willing to decatastrophize their worst fears through becoming more accepting of themselves, others, and life circumstances, will evidence significant improvements with respect not only to panic attacks but also to general anxiety and the length of time that treatment gains are maintained. A comparison of the effects of changing evaluations (i.e., catastrophization) versus inferences (i.e., probability thinking) with different types of fears (e.g., death versus fainting) would be an interesting area for future research.

Increasing Discomfort Tolerance. Some clients fear the discomfort of panic more than or rather than other actual events (e.g., having a heart attack). Here, decatastrophizing discomfort is indicated. As agoraphobics may catastrophize about the discomfort that they would experience if they were to panic in an avoided situation, we assist clients in developing a list of advantages and disadvantages to avoiding versus confronting feared situations. Low discomfort tolerance may also be addressed when clients try to avoid uncomfortable exposure, other in-session procedures, and homework assignments.

Increasing Self-Acceptance. A major goal of RET with PD clients is to help them better accept themselves and their disorder and symptoms, as these clients often consider themselves as weak or inferior when compared to others who do not have similar problems. For example, a recent male weightlifter who valued his masculinity reported considering suicide if he had to continue "to live like this." Discussion revealed that this client felt as if he were "not a man" if he had panic attacks and fears of being alone. Therapy addressed two basic concepts: what is required to be "a real man" and the rating of one's self-worth as a function of certain traits or performances.

In addition to the value of self-acceptance as a worthwhile, yet fallible, human being with an anxiety disorder, issues of self-acceptance in dealing with impaired performance because of the disorder are also important. As anticipatory anxiety may lead to difficulties in concentration or memory, in performing independent activities (e.g., driving, shopping), in marital and social relationships, and in reduced efficiency at work, clients are likely to look down on themselves for these secondary problems. This self-berating may lead to depression, which in turn prompts the client to avoid following through on PD treatment or engaging in approach rather than avoidance behaviors.

Another important area of self-acceptance to address in therapy is potential disapproval from others, as spouses and other members of the client's social network may not understand the client's fears or may criticize him or her for having an anxiety-related problem. The client may also anticipate disapproval should the panic consequences (e.g., fainting in public) actually occur. Therapy then focuses both on realistically assessing the likelihood of being rejected or criticized and also helping the client to challenge the perceived need for approval (i.e., especially when it it unlikely to be forthcoming) and its connection with self-worth.

Therapist: What would be the worst thing about having a panic attack at the mall?
Client: I might pass out.
Therapist: And if you actually did pass out, what would be the worst thing about that?
Client: Everybody would stare at me.
Therapist: What would bother you most about that?
Client: I'd feel so embarrassed!
Therapist: Would you feel embarrassed if you absolutely did not care what these people were thinking?
Client: If I really didn't care at all, I guess not. But I do care what they think.
Therapist: It sounds like we're talking about your caring that they might think something negative. I mean, if you thought they would admire you, would you feel embarrassed?
Client: I don't think they would admire me! They would think I'm weird.

Therapist: If they thought you are weird, how would you feel about yourself? Perhaps ashamed or like less of a person?

Client: Yes, I would feel like a failure if I passed out and people were judging me.

Therapist: Okay, I think it's becoming clearer why it's so scary for you to go to the mall. If you predict that you're likely to pass out and that this would lead to disapproval and feelings of being a less worthwhile person and a failure, no wonder you avoid going to the mall. It's like you're in danger not only of panicking but also of losing your self-worth.

At this point, the client's irrational beliefs related to performance and disapproval have been identified, so the stage is now set for challenging these beliefs.

Therapist: Can you see how these beliefs are blocking your goals of being able to get out of life what you want?

Client: Right.

Therapist: Let's examine the validity of your beliefs, using your own reasoning abilities to see if the beliefs really make sense. Now for the first belief, "If I pass out and people disapprove of me, I'm a failure." Is this really true?

Client: Well, I guess it doesn't make me a total failure. We've talked about this before, that my worth as a person can't be measured by my performances. For example, I'm a good mother, teacher, etc.

Therapist: Right! It would be a massive overgeneralization to rate your entire worth as a human being by whether or not you passed out.

Client: I wish I could think that way.

Therapist: You can with practice. And not just by repeating words, but by continuing to use your own reasoning abilities to understand the concept of self-acceptance versus self-rating.

Client: That makes sense. I'll keep working on it.

Therapist: Good. Now for the disapproval part. Let's assume that you become more accepting of your own fallibility, including the possibility of passing out. Could you still accept yourself if you thought others at the mall were thinking negatively of you?

Client: I really would prefer that they approve, but I guess I can stand it if they don't.

Therapist: Now you're making progress. Now, explain again to me why their disapproval would not decrease your self-worth.

Client: Because there's no way to prove it. I would still be the same person I was before they judged me. And, as much as we all want approval, we usually don't get it from everyone. My worth doesn't go up and down like a yo-yo depending on what thoughts go through someone else's head.

Therapist: Great! Now if you truly believed that, do you think that you would worry as much about having a panic attack and passing out at the mall?

Client: I guess not.

Here, the therapist does not expect the client to endorse the rational beliefs all at once. However, repeated similar discussions throughout therapy, reading of relevant materials, and use of many other RET techniques can help the client to make appropriate cognitive changes.

CASE EXAMPLE: FEAR OF SUFFOCATION

Mary, a 52-year-old married woman, was self-referred to the Anxiety Disorders Clinic for problems with panic attacks and fears of suffocating. In particular, she experienced difficulty attending regular meetings at work in which she felt claustrophobic and prone to suffocation. Mary also reported mild claustrophobia, sleep problems, inability to enjoy previously enjoyed activities, general emotional numbness, depression, and stress.

Interestingly, Mary was diagnosed with both PTSD and PD. The trauma that appeared to initiate both disturbances was a previous allergic reaction to iodine during a medical exam 1 year prior. During the reaction, the client felt hot, swollen, confused, and as if she were going to suffocate and die. After the reaction, she felt as if the medical professionals were judging her in a negative way. She later had flashbacks of the event, nightmares, and racing thoughts as she attempted to fall asleep at night.

Assessment inventories revealed moderate scores on depression and high scores on trait anxiety, catastrophic cognitions (i.e, fear of having a heart attack, choking, suffocating, and losing control), and fear of body sensations (i.e., heavy feelings in her chest, shortness of breath, swollen throat, and flushed face). On the Belief scale, Mary strongly endorsed those items having to do with the need for others' approval and achievement to see herself as worthwhile.

Treatment for Mary's PD and PTSD involved many of the techniques described earlier in this chapter, including relaxation and slow diaphragm breathing training, education about panic attacks (e.g., use of readings and handouts describing both conditions), imaginal exposure to the original traumatic event, and in vivo exposure to (a) feared body sensations (interoceptive exposure, hyperventilation), (b) related activities avoided for fear of creating unpleasant body sensations (e.g., taking hot showers, drinking wine), and (c) other places and situations (e.g., movie theaters, elevators).

In addition, therapy included RET to deal with problems related to self-berating, fear of disapproval, and fear of death. Areas in which Mary was self-berating included being depressed, less emotionally in control, emotionally numb, and having difficulty concentrating, forgetting, and making decisions. Mary also avoided telling family and friends about her condition for fear they would believe her to be weird or unstable. She was highly sensitive to others' opinions and greatly feared rejection and disapproval. In addition, Mary viewed death as a horrible occurrence that should be feared. In particular, she feared being buried alive in a casket and being trapped without air in the claustrophobic environment.

Among other things, it was explained to Mary that her extreme fear of death increased her risk of interpreting various body sensations (e.g., difficulty breathing) as likely to produce death and of worrying about these sensations to the point of perpetuating her anxiety. She was asked to read the portions of Ellis's (1972a) *How to Master Your Fear of Flying* that deal with overcoming fear of death. Like many, Mary viewed herself as reacting to death with conscious concerns (i.e., missing loved ones, being trapped in a casket). Eventually, Mary was able to endorse the rational position that once dead, she probably would not feel sad, miss people, or fear suffocating in a casket. Mary also came to see her eventual demise as being unfortunate and sad for others, but also a normal end to a full life.

At the conclusion of 6 months of treatment, Mary reported continued improvement in all areas, especially the elimination of her panic attacks. Her sleep was no longer disturbed with nightmares and flashbacks. She was able to confront previously avoided situations, using her relaxation and cognitive skills to cope with any unexpected problems. She also reported a decrease in unrealistic expectations for herself and others.

Chapter 4
Social Phobia

Social phobia is best distinguished from other anxiety disorders by the social phobic's excessive fear of negative evaluation (Turner & Beidel, 1989). The social phobic experiences an overwhelming sense of performance anxiety in the presence of others when confronted with activities that might prompt disapproval or rejection or lead to humiliation and embarrassment in response to others' scrutiny and criticism. This performance discomfort, in turn, leads to presituational catastrophization, increased ANS arousal, and subsequent avoidance of those situations that might expose the social phobic to scrutiny. Although many individuals experience some degree of apprehension in everyday social situations, the experience of increased anxiety for nonphobics is usually not a serious concern or problem. For the social phobic, however, such anxiety can be excessive and debilitating, as in the case of a musician who must rely on public performances for financial security but whose performance technique is compromised by sweating and trembling as a result of increased physiological arousal. Furthermore, Liebowitz, Gorman, Fyer, and Klein (1985) found that social phobics suffer impairment in a variety of areas, including work, educational achievement, lack of career advancement, and severely restricted social functioning.

First identified by Marks and Gelder (1966), social phobia is defined in DSM-III-R as "a persistent fear of one or more situations (the social

Note: Portions of this chapter have been reprinted by permission of the Oregon Psychological Association (Zgourides, G. D., 1990, Social phobia: A brief overview of the disorder. Oregon Psychology: The Journal of the Oregon Psychological Association, 36, 14–15) and Human Sciences Press (Zgourides, G., Warren, R., & Englert, M., 1989, Adaptation of group therapy procedures in the treatment of social phobia: A case study. Phobia Practice and Research Journal, 2, 87–101).

phobic situations) in which the person is exposed to possible scrutiny by others and fears that he or she may do something or act in a way that will be humiliating or embarrassing" (p. 241). The most common situations in which the disorder is manifested include fear of performing or speaking in public, fear of conversing or interacting with a member of the opposite sex or with an authority figure, fear of eating in the presence of others, fear of writing in the presence of others (i.e., scriptophobia), and fear of urinating in public restrooms (i.e., paruresis; American Psychiatric Association, 1987; Heimberg, Dodge, & Becker, 1987; Thyer, 1987). Social phobics' somatic symptoms (e.g., trembling, sweating, shortness of breath, faintness), which occur in response to increased sympathetic ANS activity, are often identical to those symptoms reported by other anxiety sufferers (e.g., individuals with PD); nonetheless, there may also occur other somatic symptoms (e.g., spasm of the urethral sphincters in the paruretic; Zgourides, 1988) not generally characteristic of other anxiety disorders. Such atypical symptomatology is thought, at least in some cases, to result from the invasion of an individual's personal space (Middlemist, Knowles, & Matter, 1976) or violation of his or her "comfort threshold" (Zgourides, 1987) and necessitates implementation of a treatment program tailored to his or her specific needs.

Although many social phobics experience circumscribed fear in the form of situationally specific phobias (e.g., fear of using public toilets), recent research (e.g., Amies, Gelder, & Shaw, 1983) has suggested that some social phobics instead experience a general fear of social encounters. Accordingly, social phobia, which often first appears during adolescence or young adulthood, presumably a time when individuals are especially sensitive to criticism and prone to experiencing anxiety in response to developmental issues and stresses (Von Korff, Eaton, & Keyl, 1985), appears to involve a range of cognitive and behavioral responses in terms of severity and pervasiveness, from the experience of only minor difficulty in certain settings to complete debilitation in virtually all social situations.

Although the reported prevalence rates for this disorder range from 0.9% to 15.2% (Barlow, 1985; Curran, Miller, Zwick, Monti, & Stout, 1980; Myers et al., 1984), Robins et al. (1984) reported that approximately 2% of the general population is afflicted with a form of social phobia. Liebowitz et al. (1985) and Taylor and Arnow (1988) indicated that social phobia is the third most commonly treated anxiety disorder in their respective practices. Finally, although social phobia was previously considered to be one of the least studied of the anxiety disorders (Liebowitz et al., 1985), this trend appears to have changed (Heimberg, 1989).

ETIOLOGY OF SOCIAL PHOBIA

The most recent conceptualization of social phobia as reported in the professional literature refers to cognitive, physiological, and behavioral dimensions of the disorder (Heimberg, Dodge, & Becker, 1987; Heimberg, Dodge, Hope, Kennedy, & Zollo, 1987). Concerning the physiological component, a more than usual amount of sympathetic ANS activity appears to be characteristic of social phobics, this activity being due either to the phobic's increased physiological reactivity (Beidel, Turner, & Dancu, 1985) or overattention to bodily changes (Nichols, 1974). Interestingly, although many of the somatic symptoms reported by social phobics are similar to those reported by other anxiety sufferers, some findings (Amies et al., 1983; Taylor & Arnow, 1988) have suggested that social phobics tend to report those symptoms that are more visible to others, such as blushing and twitching. Interestingly, however, some evidence suggests that the degree to which socially anxious subjects report such symptoms exceeds the extent to which they are actually noticed by peers (Barlow, 1988). For a comparative list of these commonly reported symptoms of social phobics and agoraphobics, see Amies et al. (1983).

Bruch (1989) reviewed literature that emphasizes the notion that certain types of shyness have a genetic component. In other words, socially shy individuals may have a general genetic predisposition toward a low sympathetic threshold, which under certain environmental circumstances prompts development of a social anxiety disorder via the biopsychosocial mechanisms described in this chapter. In addition, Barlow (1988) reviewed evidence suggesting that elements of social phobia may be related to human beings being prepared, in a sociobiological sense, to fear certain social stimuli (e.g., angry, critical, or rejecting faces; Ohman, 1986; Ohman, Erixon, & Lofburg, 1975). Ohman (1986) demonstrated the ease with which fear can be conditioned to angry faces and the resistance of such conditioned fear responses to extinction. The importance of eye contact for the conditioning to take place was also demonstrated and appears to reflect the clinical discomfort often reported by clients when they perceive themselves to be the center of attention (Barlow, 1988). Other developmental antecedents of social phobia described by Bruch (1989) include adolescent self-consciousness, peer neglect, childhood illness, and being the firstborn child.

In terms of the cognitive component of the disorder, social phobia typically develops as a result of fear of negative evaluation and the generalization of this anxiety to one or more social situations. In other words, the perceived threat of social examination involves either shame and embarrassment (Buss, 1980; Trower & Turland, 1984) that is associated with one's perception of how others, particularly strangers, are thinking (Beck & Emery, 1985) or failure to meet excessively high, self-imposed performance standards (Alden & Cappe, 1981). This threat is in contrast to agoraphobics, who tend to fear losing control (e.g., having a heart attack) as a result of misinterpretation of uncomfortable physiological symptoms (Beck & Emery, 1985). As characterologically shy individuals associate their anxiety, whether prompted by internal cues (e.g., rapid heartbeat) or external ones (e.g., others' negative evaluations), with specific social encounters (e.g., a date), causal misattribution leads to irrational expectations of negative criticism and potential humiliation. Social phobics become convinced that others are examining their behavior and, because they hold irrational self-expectations of perfection, self-worth issues emerge. Believing that a person must perform perfectly to receive others' acceptance and approval and that making a mistake would be terrible, social phobics interpret their imperfect qualities and behaviors as being worthy of others' rejection. The harder they try to overcome their social handicap, the more sympathetic arousal and performance anxiety they experience in the feared situation, leading then to avoidance of anxiety-arousing settings to avoid feelings of low self-esteem and others' rejection. This sense of low self-esteem is likely to increase the tendency to prompt withdrawal from anxiety-arousing situations, as phobics are unable to estimate adequately their ability to cope effectively with such situations (i.e., they have low self-efficacy; Bandura, 1977; Taylor & Arnow, 1988). Other cognitive factors associated with social phobia include overestimation of the probability of the occurrence of unpleasant social events (e.g., criticism), negative self-statements (Cacioppo, Glass, & Merluzzi, 1979; Hartman, 1984; Heimberg, Acerra, & Holstein, 1985), excessive cognitive and behavioral responses to perceived negative criticism or feedback (O'Banion & Arkowitz, 1979; Smith & Sarason, 1975), perfectionistic social standards (Alden & Cappe, 1981), doubts regarding one's ability to make a favorable social impression (Shlenker & Leary, 1982), excessive self-focus or self-consciousness (Trower & Turland, 1984), and exaggerated fears of others' responses to one's display of anxiety (Taylor & Arnow, 1988).

Avoidance of fear-evoking situations is the most common behavioral response of social phobics, although some phobics are willing to tolerate feared situations with great anxiety (Heimberg, Dodge, & Becker, 1987). Actual avoidance, however, may lead to depression and additional anxiety, generating low self-efficacy, performance anxiety, further avoidance, and cognitive dissonance. In some cases, as the avoidance-anxiety-avoidance cycle continues, the circumscribed fear and subsequent performance anxiety and avoidance of specific situations may become a generalized fear and generate avoidance of many or all public interactions. Given the hypothesis that certain of the anxiety disorders exist along a continuum of severity, it is possible for such avoidant behavior to generalize beyond the realm of the circumscribed fear to include additional situations, possibly leading to a more pervasive fear and avoidance of many or all public settings.

Though a number of studies have failed to detect social skills deficits in socially anxious patients (Lucock & Salkovskis, 1988), some social phobics may have poor social skills (Heimberg, Dodge, & Becker 1987). Interestingly, timing and placement of responses appears to better differentiate the socially skilled and unskilled than does simple frequency of responses (Fischetti, Curran, & Wessberg, 1977).

In summary, social phobics' excessively high personal standards and hypercognitive self-monitoring of performance prompt sympathetic ANS arousal, overattention to physiological sensations, subsequent anxiety, preoccupation with performance, and avoidance to reduce anxiety and feelings of low self-esteem. As the entire process reinforces the hypercognitive activity and acts to maintain this cognitive-physiological-behavioral cycle, the person's self-confidence needed to interrupt the cycle deteriorates. In other words, the social phobic becomes the victim of a vicious cycle existing along cognitive, physiological, and behavioral dimensions. Along similar lines, Hope, Gansler, and Heimberg's (1989) model incorporates social psychology literature on attentional focus and casual attribution into clinical psychology literature on social phobia: "Excessive self-focused attention is increased by physiological arousal, interferes with task performance under some conditions, increases the probability of internal attributions, and intensifies emotional reactions" (p. 49). In addition, Hope et al. (1989) also stated that a type of causal attribution—self-serving bias (i.e., the tendency to attribute success to self and failure to outside influences)—may be reserved for social anxious individuals.

Finally, as discussed in relation to simple phobia (chapter 5), Barlow (1988) posited a role for panic attacks in the etiology, maintenance, and treatment of social phobia. Salkovskis et al. (1986) provided initial evidence for the utility of directly treating panic of social phobics.

DSM-III-R DIAGNOSTIC CRITERIA
FOR SOCIAL PHOBIA

The DSM-III-R diagnostic criteria for social phobia (300.23) are listed in Table 4.1.

An accurate diagnosis, particularly in terms of identification of concurrent disorders, is important to the eventual development of an ef-

Table 4.1. DSM-III-R Diagnostic Criteria for Social Phobia

A. A persistent fear of one or more situations (the social phobic situations) in which
the person is exposed to possible scrutiny by others and feels that he or she may
do something or act in a way that will be humiliating or embarrassing. Examples
include: being unable to continue talking while speaking in public, choking on food
when eating in front of others, being unable to urinate in a public lavatory, hand-
trembling when writing in the presence of others, and saying foolish things or not
being able to answer questions in social situations.
B. If an Axis III or another Axis I disorder is present, the fear in A is unrelated to it,
e.g., the fear is not of having a panic attack (Panic Disorder), stuttering (Stuttering),
trembling (Parkinson's disease), or exhibiting abnormal eating behavior (Anorexia
Nervosa or Bulimia Nervosa).
C. During some phase of the disturbance, exposure to the specific phobic stimulus (or
stimuli) almost invariably provokes an immediate anxiety response.
D. The phobic situation(s) is avoided, or is endured with intense anxiety.
E. The avoidant behavior interferes with occupational functioning or with unusual so-
cial activities or relationships with others, or there is marked distress about having
the fear.
F. The person recognizes that his or her fear is excessive or unreasonable.
G. If the person is under 18, the disturbance does not meet the criteria for Avoidant
Disorder of Childhood or Adolescence (p. 243).

Note. Reprinted with permission from the *Diagnostic and Statistical Manual of Mental Disorders, Third
Edition, Revised.* Copyright 1987 American Psychiatric Association.

fective treatment intervention and program. Human service professionals, on diagnosing social phobia, should also screen for the possibility
of simultaneously occurring depression (e.g., Dysthymia 300.40), as
symptoms of depression have often been shown to accompany social
phobia (Heimberg, Dodge, & Becker, 1987). Moreover, an accurate diagnosis may necessitate drawing a distinction between social phobia
and avoidant personality disorder (301.82), which is an Axis II classification involving generalized social isolation and avoidance. Although
there appears to be some deal of overlap when comparing social phobia and avoidant personality disorder, Heimberg, Dodge, and Becker
(1987) proposed a means of differentiation between the disorders: The
person with avoidant personality disorder typically has little or no desire to confront anxiety-provoking situations but instead adopts an avoidant lifestyle, while the person with social phobia typically desires or
attempts to confront anxiety-provoking situations, even if with great
anxiety. Initial evidence suggests that patients with avoidant personality disorder, compared to those with social phobia, are more sensitive
interpersonally, report greater social avoidance and distress, exhibit
significantly poorer social skills, and appear to possess more overall
general psychopathology (Barlow, 1988; Turner, Beidel, Dancu, & Keys,
1986).

Another recent distinction noted in DSM-III-R is circumscribed (e.g.,
public speaking phobia) versus generalized social phobia (e.g., fear of

most or all social interactions; Heimberg, Hope, Dodge, & Becker, 1990). Heimberg et al. (1990), in an initial study, found that while generalized social phobics were similar to public speaking phobics on the key dimensions of fear of evaluation and scrutiny by others, they reported more avoidance and distress, as well as negative self-statements during social interactions. On the other hand, public speaking phobics experienced greater cardiovascular arousal during a behavioral challenge simulating a situation similar to those for which they requested treatment. Interestingly, public speaking phobics underestimated the quality of their performance and overestimated the visibility of their anxiety symptoms (i.e., compared to observer ratings), while generalized social phobics actually exhibited more detectable anxiety and less able performances. Treatment implications are discussed later in this chapter.

Future studies are required to determine whether similar distinctions also exist between generalized and circumscribed social phobics other than public speaking phobics. It would also be of interest to compare generalized social phobics with avoidance personality disorder patients. We hypothesize that the overall psychopathology will vary on a continuum from circumscribed social phobia to avoidant personality disorder. Consistent with this hypothesis, a recent study found that generalized social phobics with an additional diagnosis of avoidant personality disorder were more timid in approaching new or ambiguous situations, more fearful of embarrassment due to others noticing somatic signs of anxiety, and were characterized by more overall risk aversion (Holt, Heimberg, & Hope, 1990).

Finally, one important possible complication of social phobia is the tendency of some phobic individuals to self-medicate, particularly with alcohol or other depressants (e.g., Schneier, Martin, Liebowitz, Gorman, & Fyer, 1989). A thorough evaluation of social phobics' substance use habits, therefore, is recommended to rule out this problem area, as anxiety treatment will be difficult or impossible if the client is committed to "downers" as the principal means of avoiding anxiety.

REVIEW OF ASSESSMENT INSTRUMENTS

The ADIS-R (Di Nardo et al, 1985) provides a useful structured interview for diagnosing social phobia. In addition, a variety of self-report measures are available for assessing social phobia and related fears. These include the Willoughby Personality Inventory (Willoughby, 1932), which effectively differentiates social phobics from other anxiety disorder patients and controls (Turner, Meles, & DiTomasso, 1983); the interpersonal sensitivity subscale of the Hopkins Symptoms Check List

(Derogatis, Lipman, & Cove, 1973); Social Phobia Subscale of the FQ (Marks & Mathews, 1979); the Social Interaction Self-Statement Test (Glass, Merluzzi, Biever, & Larsen, 1982); and the Social Fear Scale (Raulin & Wee, 1984). Three useful measures of shyness include the Stanford Shyness Inventory (Zimbardo, 1977), the Shyness Scale (Cheek & Buss, 1981), and the Social Reticence Scale (Jones & Russell, 1982).

Watson and Friend's (1969) Social Avoidance and Distress Scale (SAD), which is a 28-item true-false scale that measures social anxiety and avoidance, and Fear of Negative Evaluation Scale (FNE), a 30-item true-false scale that measures fear of others' possible negative appraisals and subsequent avoidance, have not been shown to discriminate between groups of anxiety sufferers (e.g., agoraphobics versus social phobics; Heimberg, Hope, Rapee, & Bruch, 1988; Turner, McCann, & Beidel, 1987). These two instruments, however, can be useful for initial anxiety screenings. In addition, pretreatment SAD (Holt, Heimberg, & Hope, 1990) and FNE (Mattick & Peters, 1988; Mattick, Peters, & Clarke, 1989) scores have been found to predict improvement from treatment.

Therapists assessing for social phobia may wish to screen for cognitive distortions via the Social Interaction Self-Statement Test (SISST; Glass, et al., 1982); the Belief Scale (Malouff & Schutte, 1986), a validated 20-item Likert Scale measure of irrational beliefs (Berotti, Heimberg, Holt, & Liebowitz, 1990; Malouff, Valdenegro, & Schutte, 1987; Warren & Zgourides, 1989; Zgourides & Warren, 1988); and a more comprehensive measure of irrational beliefs, the General Attitude and Belief Scale (Bernard, 1990; DiGiuseppe, Leaf, Exener, and Robins, 1988).

Turner, Beidel, Dancu, and Stanley (1989) developed and provided initial reliability (Turner et al., 1989) and validity data (Beidel, Borden, Turner, & Jacob, 1989; Beidel, Turner, Stanley, & Dancu, 1989) for a new instrument, the Social Phobia and Anxiety Inventory (SPAI). The SPAI is a 32-item Likert scale that measures the physiological, cognitive, and behavioral components of social phobia for a variety of fear-evoking situations and discriminates between social phobics, normal controls, and patients with other anxiety disorders.

Mattick and Clarke (1988) have developed two companion scales to assess social anxiety and social phobia. The Social Interaction Anxiety Scale (SIAS) assesses interpersonal anxiety, and the Social Phobia Scale (SPS) assesses anxiety about being observed by others. The SIAS and SPS differentiate social phobics from agoraphobics, simple phobics, and non-anxious groups. Normative data is available (Mattick & Clarke, 1988), and the scales are sensitive to treatment effects (Mattick & Peters, 1988; Mattick, Peters, & Clarke, 1989). Mueller, Heimberg, Holt, Hope, & Liebowitz (1990) have provided further validation for these measures.

In addition to self-report measures, behavioral approach tests, self-monitoring diaries (e.g. Mattick & Peters, 1988), "contrived behavioral assessments" (Barlow, 1988, p. 550; Farrell, Curran, Zwick, & Monti, 1983), physiological measures, (e.g. heart rate), and subjective anxiety ratings (e.g., 0-100 subjective units of distress scale [SUDS]) in antici- pation of and during simulated performances (Heimberg, Dodge et al, 1990) may be useful in a comprehensive assessment of social phobia.

REVIEW OF NON-RET TREATMENTS

Cognitive-behavioral clinicians have used a variety of therapeutic techniques to treat socially anxious individuals, including in vivo sys- tematic desensitization (Anderson, 1977), relaxation training (Öst, Jer- remalm, & Johansson, 1981), social skills training (Stravynski, Marks, & Yule, 1982), and exposure (Butler, Cullington, Munby, Amies, & Gelder, 1984; Glasgow, 1975; Lamontagne & Marks, 1973; Thyer, 1987).

Although exposure appears to be a central component of social pho- bia treatment, Butler (1985) described several problems that may arise during treatment. For example, certain social activities (e.g., signing a check) are not easily repeatable for providing extended exposure prac- tice. To correct for this, clients should be instructed to engage in more frequent, although brief exposures. Butler (1985) also noted that some socially phobic individuals who encounter anxiety-evoking situations on a frequent basis cope with their anxiety by distracting themselves from the task at hand. Exposure involving internal avoiding is not al- ways beneficial, as the irrational cognitions (e.g., "I must appear per- fect to others") common to these individuals may remain if not dealt with specifically. With respect to such cognitive distractions, Butler (1985) concluded that "attending to internal cues may maintain symptom monitoring while preventing full exposure" (p. 653). The solution to this problem, therefore, is to have the socially phobic client more fully engage in difficult exposures by (a) training the client in the use of appropriate listening, speaking, and social skills; (b) instructing the client to be more active in the exposure process; and (c) encouraging the client to provoke anxiety symptoms.

Given the theory that social phobia may be distinct biologically from the other anxiety disorders (Levin, Schneier, & Liebowitz, 1989), phar- macological treatment of the disorder has focused primarily on two ma- jor classes of drugs—beta blockers (Falloon, Lloyd, & Harpin, 1981; Gold, 1989; Liebowitz et al., 1987) and MAOIs (Gold, 1989; Leibowitz, Fyer, Gorman, Campeas, Lerin, 1986), although results appear to be inconclusive and sometimes contradictory (Falloon et al., 1981; Taylor & Arnow, 1988). For example, Gorman, Liebowitz, Fyer, Campeas, and

Klein (1985) found atenolol, a cardioselective beta blocker, to be effective with social phobics. Levin et al. (1989) reported that their controlled studies confirm the usefulness of phenelzine but not beta blockers. Concerning the efficacy of benzodiazepines, current thinking suggests that this class of medications may provide temporary relief from anxiety but in the long run interferes with the exposure process (Barlow, 1988). Although a pilot study (Reich & Yates, 1988) demonstrated the effectiveness of alprazolam in lessening dysfunctional symptoms for 14 social phobics during drug therapy, but not after discontinuation of the drug therapy, Shea, Uhde, Cimbolc, Vittone, and Arnkoff (1988) in a controlled study found a superiority of phenelzine over alprazolam. Furthermore, anxious clients taking benzodiazepines are at risk of abusing the medication and developing severe side effects (e.g., rebound anxiety). Finally, Levin et al. (1989) reported preliminary evidence for the usefulness of some other drugs in treating social phobia, particularly dopaminergic agonists and antagonists.

COGNITIVE THERAPY AND
SOCIAL PHOBIA

Clinical research attests to the effectiveness of multidimensional group therapy procedures in the treatment of social phobia (Heimberg, Becker, Goldfinger, & Vermilyea, 1985; Heimberg, Dodge, & Becker, 1987; Heimberg, Dodge, Hope et al., 1987; Heimberg, Dodge et al., 1990). Group therapy may be especially valuable for social phobics in that they (a) learn from others who share similar fears, (b) learn through helping others overcome their fears, (c) make a public commitment regarding their intent to change, (d) find encouragement through others' successes, (e) face fears first in a safe situation before attempting to confront situations external to the group, and (f) find the courage necessary to confront the actual fear-provoking situation (Sank & Shaffer, 1984). Whether the application of such group principles to individuals is an effective alternative to group therapy remains to be tested. Although there is still a paucity of data with respect to individual therapies and systematic, multilevel group programs, preliminary results indicate support for the use of cognitive restructuring and performance-based exposure techniques within a group format (Heimberg, Dodge, & Becker, 1987; Heimberg, Dodge, et al. 1990). Nevertheless, and regardless of the format used, effective psychological treatment of social phobia must include interventions that address the three components of the disorder—physiological, behavioral, and cognitive (Heimberg, Dodge, & Becker, 1987; and should include both in vivo exposure and cognitive restructuring strategies (Butler et al., 1984).

Heimberg and Becker (1984) devised a group therapy program and manual for treating social phobia, which was prepared under support of the National Institute of Mental Health (NIMH). The program consists of 12 weekly therapy sessions that include imaginal exposure; in vivo exposure; cognitive therapy; homework assignments; weekly assessments of clients' psychological functioning via two instruments, the BDI and the State-Trait Anxiety Inventory, forms Y-1 State and X-2 Trait (STAI:Y-1, STAI:X-2); use of a pretreatment assessment device, the Reactions to Treatment Questionnaire (RTQ; Heimberg & Becker, 1984); and use of Beck's Daily Record of Dysfunctional Thoughts (BDRDT) to facilitate practice exposures and cognitive restructuring exercises during the week and also to provide information for discussion during therapy sessions.

Each of the Heimberg and Becker (1984) sessions is devoted to specific tasks as outlined in their manual. The initial session is comprised of the following activities: assessments (BDI, STAI:Y-1, and STAI:X-2 to obtain baseline data concerning state and trait levels of anxiety experienced), therapist and client introductions, sharing of the client's fears and goals, explanations of the multicomponent nature of social phobia, assessment and anticipation of treatment outcomes, discussion of treatment components, discussion of the role of negative automatic thoughts in social phobia, sample role-plays, and discussion of the weekly homework assignment. Session 2 consists of assessments (BDI, STAI:Y-1), a review of completed homework (including a discussion of monitoring and recording automatic thoughts, BDRDT), further explanation of cognitive restructuring, exercises in disputing irrational thoughts, initial performance-based exposures, additional cognitive restructuring, and homework assignments. Sessions 3 through 11 involve the following: assessments (BDI, STAI:Y-1), discussion and review of previous homework assignments, continued exposures and cognitive restructuring, and projected homework assignments. Session 12 includes a discussion of therapeutic attainments, goals for the future, and termination.

Other cognitive therapies used to treat social phobia include systematic rational restructuring, which is a variant of RET (Kanter & Goldfried, 1979); the use of cognitive therapy and behavioral rehearsal in a group of anxious musicians (Kendrick, Craig, Lawson, & Davidson, 1982); the successful combination of cognitive and performance procedures (Butler et al., 1984; Stravynski, 1983); a combination of in vivo exposure and cognitive restructuring (Chhabra & Fielding, 1985); and attentional training (i.e., substitution of task-oriented positive cognitions for nontask-oriented negative ones via viewing of videotapes of performances) in a group of anxious musicians (Barlow, 1988).

A RET MODEL FOR SOCIAL
PHOBIA

In accordance with Barlow (1988) and Ellis (e.g., 1976), we hypothesize that certain individuals are predisposed by both biological and psychological vulnerabilities to develop social anxiety and avoidance (Bruch, 1989; Kagan, Reznick, & Snidman, 1988). Such individuals are more likely than others to develop fears in response to prepared social stimuli (e.g., anger, criticism, rejection, scrutiny). That social phobia typically begins during adolescence may be related to the developmental struggle involving emancipation from parents that results in greater reliance on peer relationships (Warren, Good, & Velten, 1984). With such increased importance on the acceptance of peers, social-evaluative concerns are heightened. Such concerns may also be related to parental fears of negative evaluation (Bruch, Heimberg, Berger, & Collins, 1987). Initial panic attack in response to extreme social rejection or criticism, as well as failure to acquire adequate social skills (which may elicit further social disapproval), may also contribute to the development of social phobia.

Due to psychological and biological vulnerabilities, individuals more easily develop irrational beliefs through the aforementioned learning experiences. For social phobics, two of Ellis's major must-related beliefs are central to the development and maintenance of social phobia. Thus, individuals who believe (a) "I must perform well and win the approval of others," and (b) "I must not experience discomfort" are likely to develop strong fears of negative evaluation and avoidance of situations in which such evaluation is predicted to occur. Avoidance is significantly related to low discomfort tolerance, associated with pain of embarrassment, humiliation, and/or shame that stems from irrational beliefs related to perceived negative evaluations of others, as well as one's self-criticisms. Hence, the social phobic suffers significantly from both ego and discomfort disturbances (Ellis & Dryden, 1987).

Consistent with Ellis (1980b), and as discussed in chapter 3, we view the social phobic's overestimations (i.e., compared to normals) of the likelihood of negative social events as byproducts of the aforementioned major irrational beliefs. Thus, similar to Butler and Mathews's (1983) findings for anxiety neurotics, social phobics are predicted to interpret ambiguous social events as personally critical, to overpredict the likelihood of the occurrence of negative social events, and to view such events as more costly. Similarly, from a fear structure perspective (Foa & Kozak, 1985), social phobics' "social fears are characterized by unusually high negative valence for social scrutiny and criticisms as well as overestimation of their likelihood. . . . In addition, these patients think that responses that exemplify anxiety are subject to social approbrium" (p. 477). Again, our RET model hypothesizes that these cognitive biases stem from basic demands for performing well, winning approval, and avoiding discomfort.

TREATMENT OF SOCIAL PHOBIA:
A RET PERSPECTIVE

Several reports concerning the use of RET or similar methods in treating socially anxious and/or phobic individuals exist in the professional literature. In treating 45 socially anxious individuals, Schelver and Gutsch (1983) found that "self-administered cognitive therapy (RET)" significantly decreased fear of negative evaluation, social anxiety, and trait anxiety. Although Stravynski, Marks, and Yule (1982) compared social skills training with and without cognitive modification (based on RET) in treating 22 social phobic patients but failed to demonstrate the superiority of cognitive combined with social skills interventions, Stravynski (1983) successfully used a combination of rational cognitive modification, social skills training, and in vivo exposure to treat an individual case of psychogenic vomiting. Biran, Augusto, and Wilson (1981) found in vivo exposure superior to RET in the treatment of three scriptophobics. Neither intervention was particularly successful in reducing self-reports of fear. The authors noted, however, that both subjects who received RET perceived it as an important part of the treatment and indicated that it relieved much of the shame they felt about having a phobia.

Heimberg, Dodge et al. (1990) commented on the Stravynski et al. (1982) and Biran et al. (1981) studies by stating that the effectiveness of the cognitive techniques in both studies may have been compromised due to the methods in which they were administered. For example, Stravynski et al. (1982) did not integrate the cognitive restructuring into the behavioral exposure, which may account for the negative outcome.

In contrast, Mattick and Peters (1988), in treating 51 social phobics, found a combination of cognitive restructuring ("systematic rational restructuring" with RET elements) and guided exposure to be more effective than guided exposure alone, supporting the addition of a cognitive component to exposure procedures. Furthermore, Mattick, Peters, and Clarke (1989) found rational restructuring (with elements of RET) to enhance the effectiveness of exposure in treating 43 social phobics. Alden (1989) compared group cognitive and relaxation procedures with either exposure, exposure plus interpersonal skills training, exposure plus interpersonal skills training with an intimacy focus, and a waiting-list control group in a 10-week treatment of avoidant personality disorder. The three treatment groups were comparable in producing gains superior to the control group. While skill training procedures did not significantly enhance the effects of graduated exposure procedures, inclusion of an intimacy focus appeared to enhance skill training, although the dropout rate was higher in this condition. Alden (1989) suspected that longer periods of treatment might increase treatment benefits.

Emmelkamp and his colleagues have conducted programmatic research on RET and other cognitive-behavioral treatments of social phobia. In an analogue study with socially anxious recruits (Emmelkamp, Mersch, & Vissia, 1985), and in another study with DSM-III diagnosed social phobics (Emmelkamp, Mersch, Vissia, & van der Helm, 1985), RET, self-instructional training, and in vivo exposure were equally effective. In a third study (Mersch, Emmelkamp, Bogels, & van der Sleen, 1989), RET and social skills training were also equally effective. Interestingly, in each of these three studies, only the cognitive component of RET was used, and therapy was short term (six to eight sessions). With a complete RET package, including cognitive restructuring and in vivo exposure, and along with a greater number of therapy sessions, RET is expected to produce additional benefits.

Finally, recent attempts have been made to match social phobics' individual response patterns to corresponding treatments. Öst et al. (1981) found, as predicted, that behavioral reactors did better with social skills training while physiological reactors did better with applied relaxation. In a subsequent study, Jerremalm, Johansson, and Öst (1986a) did not find differential effects when cognitive therapy was conducted with cognitive reactors and applied relaxation was implemented with physiological reactors. Similarly, Mersch et al. (1989) found both RET and social skills training equally effective with cognitive and behavioral reactors. The outcome of these studies, similar to those with simple phobics (see chapter 5), are inconclusive as to whether there is an advantage to matching mode of treatment to the social phobic's primary area of impairment. At this point, we agree with Barlow's (1988) conclusion for treatment of simple phobics: "For the time being, it makes eminently good clinical sense to assess and tailor exposure-based treatments, based on particular patterns of responding that are notably problematic for the individual patient" (p. 488). From our RET perspective, we recommend always including cognitive and behavioral (exposure) procedures, relaxation when physiological arousal is prominent, and social skills training when actual skills deficits are present. For generalized social phobics and avoidant personality disorder patients, interpersonal skills training, including the development of intimacy skills, may be appropriate (Alden, 1989).

Our RET approach to treating social phobia logically follows from the foregoing theoretical model. The central treatment goals include helping the socially phobic client to change his or her demands for perfect performances and approval from others to more adaptive desires to do well and secure others' approval. This, of course, involves assisting clients in gaining a greater degree of self-acceptance. In addition, therapeutic goals include increasing the client's discomfort tolerance so that he or she may better engage in the exposure aspects of therapy and better obtain long-term social or professional goals by learning to accept short-term discomfort. Mattick and Peters (1988) and Mattick, Peters, and Clarke (1989) provided empirical support for the greater effectiveness of exposure when combined with cognitive restructuring. These studies also provided empirical support for targeting irrational beliefs regarding perfectionistic self-expectations and demands for approval and reduction of related fear of negative evaluation. In fact, change in fear of negative evaluation was the best predictor of long-term improvement. As fear of negative evaluation decreases, so would the social phobic's various inferential cognitive errors related to others' potential evaluations.

In terms of our approach to treating social phobia, we include both exposure and cognitive restructuring, as well as skills training when indicated. For guidelines for implementing the exposure aspects of treatment, see chapter 5 and Butler's (1985) important recommendations for ways to address various difficulties that may occur in the exposure treatment of social phobics. It is also advisable that cognitive restructuring be integrated with exposure exercises both within and outside sessions, as Heimberg, Dodge et al. (1990) have emphasized.

In the remainder of this chapter, we present further illustrations of our RET approach to treating social phoba.

Dealing with Inferential Errors

Social phobics who hypersensitively perceive criticism when it is really not intended (arbitrary inference), take it as a personal failing when someone is upset with them (personalization), assume that others are observing and judging their anxiety response (mind reading), "know" others are being critical because "it feels like it" (emotional reasoning), and conclude that they will always be socially phobic (overgeneralization, fortune telling) are, of course, making numerous inferential errors. In RET, we help social phobics to become aware of such inferences, understand why these inferences are cognitive errors, and learn how to correct them by both rational disputes and behavioral exercises.

Overestimating the probability of negative social events is also an inferential error characteristic of social phobics (Lucock & Salkovskis, 1988). Treatment targets relevant cognitive distortions for change but emphasizes the importance of first addressing evaluative errors, from which the inferential errors actually flow.

The following is a sample discussion of probability estimates in which the therapist suggests a behavioral experiment.

Therapist: How certain are you that your employees are scrutinizing your public speaking during staff meetings?

Client: I'm sure they are.

Therapist: How sure? 25%, 50%, 100% maybe?

Client: Probably 100%, because I get twisted up when I talk in front of a group.

Therapist: Realistically, and given our earlier talks about probability versus possibility thinking, do you believe that your probability estimate is reasonable?

Client: Well, I suppose not. But I still get really uptight at those staff meetings.

Therapist: I understand that you get uptight, but I'm also glad that you are able to accept that your previous estimate of 100% was really unreasonable. What, in your opinion, is a more reasonable estimate?

Client: Maybe 25%.

Therapist: That sounds better, although I would be willing to bet that in actuality there is an even lower probability that others are scrutinizing your talking.

Client: Maybe so, but I'll need to think about that one some more.

Therapist: Sure. Also, perhaps we can devise an actual way to test the accuracy of your probability estimate.

Behavioral experiments can be effective methods for revising probability estimates. Such experiments can be creatively devised to fit clients' idiosyncratic fears. For example, in treating a client who feared fainting in front of others and the resulting embarrassment and humiliation, we conducted a behavioral experiment at a local shopping mall. The client predicted that should he faint, observing onlookers would see him as weak, weird, and inferior. To test these predictions, we devised (with the client's help) a simple questionnaire and interviewed a small sample of mall shoppers. Of the six interviewees, 100% stated that their first reaction to seeing someone faint would be to feel concern that there was a medical emergency and to decide how they might be helpful. None of the respondents indicated that they would see the fainter as weak, weird, or inferior for fainting. This behavioral experiment appeared to alter in a more powerful way the client's predictions of fainting-related disapproval than had previous discussions during sessions.

Dealing with Evaluative Errors: Discomfort Anxiety, Catastrophizing, and Self-Rating

Discomfort Anxiety. Ellis's concept of discomfort anxiety is relevant to the client's tendency to avoid social situations and/or exposure when anxious. Thus, at another level, RET may be a valuable therapeutic tool in terms of helping social phobics overcome the tendency to avoid both anxiety-provoking social situations and recommended therapeutic exposures. RET can be used to assist clients in refuting numerous irrational beliefs associated with potentially unpleasant social activities and therapeutic tasks. For a detailed description of discomfort anxiety, see chapter 2.

The social phobic is encouraged to accept philosophically that both good and bad social events are inherent in life and that there are no guarantees that bad events will not occur. Thus, clients are encouraged to desire that unpleasant social encounters not occur rather than demand that they must not occur. Rather than viewing so many negative social events as being terrible, clients are assisted in thinking of bad events as existing on a continuum of badness, with few events being classified as over 100% bad, which is one definition of awful or catastrophic.

Another component of the meaning of awful for many social phobics is that the event has no right to occur, they cannot be reasonably happy in spite of its occurrence, and one's self-worth is lowered because of its occurrence. The therapist seeks to assist the client in changing evaluations of disapproval, criticism, and rejection from awful, horrible, or catastrophic to anywhere from mildly to extremely unfortunate and inconvenient. This is accomplished via both cognitive and behavioral methods.

Dealing with Panic. As indicated earlier, panic attacks may play a role in the etiology and/or maintenance of some social phobias (Barlow, 1988). As the occurrence of panic attacks may actually compromise important performances (e.g., giving a public speech), panic management procedures, as described in chapter 3, may be an important component of treatment.

Dealing with Anger and Disapproval. As suggested earlier, humans may be prepared sociobiologically to fear angry, critical, and/or rejecting faces (Ohman, 1986). Perhaps this vulnerability, along with social learning experiences and the development of irrational beliefs, accounts for the extreme sensitivity of social phobics to the anger and/or disapproval of others. In our clinical experience, such individuals appear conflict phobic and may have difficulty with others' expressions of anger, especially when it is directed toward them by significant others.

"On the Receiving End of Anger" (see Appendix D), often used as a client handout, contains examples of how the RET therapist might approach problems of anger tolerance. The handout, the principles of which are considered applicable to dealing with anger from other sources, particularly where an ongoing relationship is involved (e.g., with a relative), incorporates relevant communication principles (Warren & Warren, 1985) and provides guidelines for the use of rational-emotive imagery (REI). REI was found in one study with general clinic outpatients to enhance the effectiveness of RET (Lipsky, Kassinove, & Miller, 1980).

Dealing with Social Skills Deficits. When assessment suggests that a social skills deficit may contribute to social anxiety and avoidance, direct skills training is indicated.

In the following example, portions of an actual case transcript illustrate the use of rational-role reversal (RRR; Kassinove & DiGiuseppe, 1975) with a 10-year-old boy ("Sam") with social anxiety, avoidance, and problems making friends. RRR was also found in the Lipsky et al. (1980) study to enhance the effectiveness of RET.

As the transcript illustrates, RRR involves the therapist and client switching roles, with the "client" guiding the "therapist" in clarifying concepts and reinforcing rational thinking.

Client (playing therapist):   How was your day, Sam?

Therapist (playing client):   Pretty good. I was at school today and tried some things you encouraged me to do, like play sports more and not worry about being criticized, making mistakes and stuff. So far it's going pretty well, but I think it would be helpful if we went over again what I'm supposed to think to myself when I'm making mistakes and being criticized. Is it OK if we go over that? When I think I might get criticized, I start feeling really depressed and kind of scared, like I don't want to chance it. And as you were telling me before, it's not me making a mistake or getting criticized that makes me upset, it's my own thoughts. Can you help me remember what those thoughts are that I had better try to avoid?

Client: One is, just think, well, everyone makes mistakes.

Therapist: Like you're trying to think, "So what if I make a mistake, everybody makes mistakes." Do you mean like it doesn't matter at all or that it's just not such a big deal?

Client: Not such a big deal. It's like playing baseball, and you forget to bring a bat.

Therapist: So, it's too bad but not terrible?

Client: Yes, if no one brings a bat, then you have to run back home and get it.

Therapist: So, instead of thinking it's terrible, I should think, "Well, it's not that bad, no big deal, everyone is going to make mistakes sometime." What if I find myself thinking, "I'm such a dummy for making that mistake! I shouldn't have made it?"

Client: You're not a dummy. Just think of the subjects that you're good at. Like eating lunch, I'll bet you're good at that.

Therapist: Yes, I'm good at that. I'm also pretty good at math, too. So, are you saying that it's not true that I'm a dummy?

Client: That's right.

Therapist: Why isn't it true?

Client: Because if you're a dummy, you don't know anything. All you do . . .

Therapist: Is sit around looking dumb all the time? I don't do that.

Client: You know how to talk. That means you're not a dummy. You know how to walk and run. You probably know how to skip.

Therapist: It's just not true if I think I'm a dummy. All I can say is, I made a mistake. Too bad! You know, if I find myself thinking that I never do anything right, that's the same sort of mistake.

Client: Yes.

Therapist: Because I do do some things right. So, if I think in the ways that you're teaching me to think, does that mean that if I make mistakes and get criticized that I'll feel great?

Client: No, you'll just feel good.

Therapist: So, I'll feel disappointed but not crushed. Does this stuff really work?

Client: Yes.

Therapist: Well, I'll take your word for it. It seems to be helping, but I want to keep remembering it so I won't forget. I want to drill this stuff into my head. What else can I do to make more friends?

Client: Say their name when you say, "Hi." Most of the time you don't think about saying their name because you're just passing by them or something. But you should try to fit their name in.

Therapist: I see. What is something else I can practice to help me have some friends?

Client: Talk more. Don't talk when others are talking. Don't interrupt.

Therapist: I think I'm doing better at that.

Client: Good! What else can you do to make friends?

Therapist: I can initiate activities myself. I can say, "Let's play." What if I go up to someone on the playground and say, "Hey, Jack, let's play" and he says, "No, I don't want to play with you"? Then what if I feel depressed and rejected?

Client: Find someone else to play with. Who cares? Think in your mind that they fall into a mud puddle that's seven feet deep. Make a joke about it in your head.

Therapist: What if I find myself thinking, "If this kid doesn't want to play with me, that must mean that I'm no good"?

Client: Go a different way.

Therapist: Try, try, again?

Client: Right, that's just his opinion.

Therapist: So, if he says to me, "I don't want to play with you, you're just a jerk," is that just his opinion?

Client: Yes. Other people might think, "Hey, you're wonderful."

In the preceding excerpt, the therapist is trying to review concrete social skills and several kinds of thinking that appear to be important in improving the client's social relationships (e.g., self-acceptance, de-catastrophizing rejection and disapproval). For a comprehensive RET approach to social difficulties, see Dryden (1982).

Ellis has produced several audiotapes that address some of the social phobic's central concerns. These include (a) Ellis's (1973b) *How to Stubbornly Refuse to Be Ashamed of Anything,* (b) Ellis's (1977b) *Conquering the Dire Need for Love,* (c) Ellis's (1984) *Unconditionally Accepting Yourself and Others,* (d) Ellis's (1977a) *Conquering Low Frustration Tolerance,* and (e) Ellis's (1973d) *Twenty-five Ways to Stop Downing Yourself.*

Ellis's well-known shame-attacking exercises are particularly appropriate for the social phobic's fear of negative evaluation and overestimates of the probabilities of various negative social events. Classic examples include having clients wear outlandish clothing or singing songs in public—the list of possibilities is seemingly endless. Clients can use such in vivo exercises to challenge their need for approval, particularly from total strangers, and to practice self-acceptance in the face of possible disapproval.

Risk-taking exercises, which can include assertiveness and approaching rather than avoiding conflict, can serve a similar function. For example, in the aforementioned behavioral experiment with the client who was fearful of fainting and subsequent disapproval, during the interviews with mall shoppers the client had several real-life opportunities to experience his fear of fainting while asking questions and standing alongside the therapist. After the individual interviews, debriefing revealed that the client had the thought, "Wouldn't it be terrible if I fainted right during the the interview on fainting? Wouldn't I really then make a fool of myself?" In preparation for the next interview, the client practiced questioning and answering his original irrational thoughts (e.g., "Why would it be terrible if I fainted during the interview? How would I really become a fool? I don't need their approval. I don't even know them! My worth as a person isn't connected to what they think of me.").

A variety of bibliotherapy sources are also recommended to the social phobic. These include Ellis's (1985a) "Intellectual Facism," Ellis's (1977c) "Psychotherapy and the Value of a Human Being," and Burns's (1980) *Feeling Good*. Readings that deal with overcoming dire needs for approval are included in Burns's (1980) *Feeling Good*, Ellis and Harper's (1975) *A New Guide to Rational Living*, and Ellis and Becker's (1982) *A Guide to Personal Happiness*. Ellis and Knaus's (1977) *Overcoming Procrastination* includes excellent client readings on increasing frustration tolerance.

In the remainder of this chapter, we present some samples of social phobics' ABCs and a case example of treatment of public speaking phobia.

SAMPLE ABCS

We consider the ABCs for an individual who is fearful and unable to urinate in a public restroom (i.e., the client has psychogenic urinary retention or paruresis).

A. *Activating event:*
   1. The need to urinate while away from home.
B. *Beliefs:*
   1. I must be able to urinate quickly and easily, as others are listening and waiting for me to start and finish. If I can't, they'll disapprove and think less of me, and that would be awful. Also, it means I'm inadequate and worthless.
   2. You must stay out of the restroom so that I can void, otherwise you'll frustrate me, and that would be awful.
   3. My life conditions must permit me to urinate easily whenever and wherever I wish, otherwise life is unbearable and I can't be happy at all.

The paruretic also may express one or more of the following types of irrational thinking:

1. *Demanding:* I must urinate quickly and easily, and with full force! People are waiting and will think that there's something wrong with me if I can't go. Yes, I must be accepted by everyone in the restroom.
2. *Catastrophizing:* It's terrible if I can't void when I want. This problem is "unstandable," and I'll never be able to use a public rest-

room. It would be horrible if people thought less of me because it takes me so long to get the "plumbing" working.

3. *Rating of self and others:* If I can't urinate in a public restroom, or if others think less of me because I'm taking so long at the urinal, it's horrible and this means that I'm a horrible person. Good people can void whenever and wherever they want.

C. *Consequences:*
    1. Extreme anxiety, avoidance of public restrooms.
    2. Restriction of fluid intake, refusal to accept extended social invitations.

We now consider the three types of irrational beliefs and self-statements typical of the person with a fear of writing in the presence of others (i.e., the client has scriptophobia).

1. *Demanding:* I must be able to write perfectly when others are watching. I have to be accepted, and people won't accept me if I look nervous and can't write. Any decent person should be able to write in public.
2. *Catastrophizing:* It would be awful if I had to stop writing my check at the checkout line in the store. All of those people in line would have to wait for me to finish the transaction. What if I couldn't? People would think I'm really weird, and that would be awful.
3. *Rating of self and others:* Any good person should be able to write a check in the store, so I must be a terrible person. If others think I'm bad, I must be bad.

The importance of having the client identify such irrational beliefs for the purpose of effective treatment planning becomes evident. Although the content of the two preceding examples is consistent, there are important differences, too. For example, the paruretic may be fearful of having others *hear* him urinate, while the scriptophobic is fearful of having others *watch* her tremble. Performance-based exposures must address these individual variables, as situationally specific exposure is likely to be a more efficient means of helping the client. Thus, the paruretic will want to seek out and practice challenging his irrational beliefs in various lavatories, while the scriptophobic will want to do the same in grocery stores. Of course, both will want to perform behaviorally active disputes (e.g., writing rational responses).

We now look at some disputes for our two clients' respective irrational beliefs.

D. *Disputes and effective new philosophy (for the paruretic):*
    1. Where is the law that says I must urinate quickly and easily or with full force? Who really cares? Actually, there is a low probability that people are listening for me to start and finish. Even

if they are, my self-worth is not dependent on their opinion of me. It doesn't matter if people think that there's something wrong with me, even if I can't go. I don't need anyone's approval!

2. It is inconvenient if I can't void when I want, but it is not terrible. I can stand this problem, as I have done so many times in the past. I have no reason to believe that I'll never be able to use a public restroom, nor do I have any reason to believe that people will think less of me because it takes me so long to get started. Even if people think I'm a weirdo, I still accept myself the way I am.

3. I'm not my actions! It's a free country, and I can take as long as I want at the urinal. If I perform poorly at something, that doesn't make me a bad person. I'm just a fallible human being who makes mistakes! Furthermore, being able to void in a public restroom doesn't make someone a good person, nor does inability to void make someone a bad person.

D. *Disputes and effective new philosophy (for the scriptophobic)*:

1. Who says that I must write perfectly? What difference does it really make? Actually, there is a low probability that people will reject me if I look nervous and can't write. Even if they do, it doesn't matter. I'm still a good person. A person's worth as a human being is not dependent on one's ability to write when others are watching.

2. It would be undesirable and inconvenient if I had to stop writing my check at the checkout line in the store, but not catastrophic. So what if those people in line have to wait for me to leave? Everyone eventually has to wait in a slow line. Even if I couldn't finish my transaction, it wouldn't be terrible. I would prefer that people not think I'm weird, but I don't have to have their approval!

3. Where's the rule that says to be a good person you must be able to write a check in the store? I like myself, regardless of whether I can write or whether people think I'm a bad person. I'm not my performances, and my performances are not me!

CASE EXAMPLE: FEAR OF PUBLIC SPEAKING

Sally was a 32-year-old female lab technician who entered individual therapy for a public speaking phobia. She claimed that she would become upset when required to speak in any public setting in which prior to speaking she had sufficient time to catastrophize. She was particularly fearful of conversing with any individual, especially if she was in close proximity to the person and if she knew about the encounter in advance. In her role as a lab technician, Sally frequently had to speak with other health professionals concerning patients and their lab results, and she felt sufficiently anxious to seek individual therapy. After being diagnosed with social phobia, providing a thorough social history, and learning RET procedures, Sally identified the following irrational beliefs and self-statements:

1. I must not look nervous or foolish. *(demanding)*
2. I'll become so upset that I'll have to gasp for air. *(overgeneralizing, fortune-telling)*
3. It would be terrible if I gasped, blushed, or perspired. *(catastrophizing)*
4. It would be terrible if I forgot what I wanted to say. *(catastrophizing)*
5. What if the nurses and doctors at work think I'm an incompetent lab technician? *(catastrophizing, rating of self)*
6. If people reject me or think that I'm incompetent, that means I'm a bad person. *(rating of self)*

Soon, the client was able to challenge these irrational beliefs and endorse the following rational replies:

1. I have no reason to believe, given my past experiences, that I'll look foolish, weird, or incompetent, or choke, gasp for air, blush, perspire, or forget what I wanted to say.
2. Even if people perceive me as less than perfect, my self-worth is not dependent on their acceptance or opinions.
3. I'm a good person and a competent lab technician regardless of what others think of me.

Sally chose as her first exposure walking up to a lab colleague and telling him a joke. She prepared herself by identifying and challenging her irrational beliefs and mentally rehearsing prior to entering the situation. After she completed the exposure, Sally wrote down and disputed all of the irrational beliefs that occurred to her during the exposure. She followed this process over the next 12 weeks of therapy, as she continued to dispute these and other irrational cognitions while seeking out new situations in which to practice speaking in the presence of others. For example, a turning point in the therapy for Sally occurred when she joined a local Toastmasters group in which she gave weekly speeches in front of the members. Over the course of therapy,

Sally was able to engage in increasingly difficult and potentially humiliating performance-based exposures.

During a recent follow-up phone call, Sally described continued relief from her previous anxiety symptoms and expressed great thanks for being taught the means with which to face her fears.

Chapter 5
Simple Phobia

Simple phobics typically present with intense fear and avoidance associated with one or more specific objects and/or settings. Although the average person at some time in his or her life is apt to experience exaggerated fear, the simple phobic's fear is usually debilitating enough to prompt avoidance of the fear or endurance of it with great difficulty and eventual location of professional services. Thus, the primary difference between simple phobia and mere exaggerated fears is the persistence of the phobic's fear, along with avoidance and significant interference in the activities of daily life. For example, the person who fears snakes but lives in the city and never encounters snakes is unlikely to be troubled enough to seek professional counseling, while the person who fears elevators but must travel to the top floor of a city building each day for work is much more likely to become involved in therapy.

Although the term *phobia* has been used since antiquity to describe general irrational and debilitating fear (Thyer, 1987), today the DSM-III-R (American Psychiatric Association, 1987) describes three types of phobias: simple phobia, social phobia, and agoraphobia (as a separate category and as a subtype of panic disorder). DSM-III-R defines simple phobia as "a persistent, irrational fear of, and compelling desire to avoid, an object or a situation other than being alone or in public places away from home (Agoraphobia), or of humiliation or embarrassment in certain social situations (Social Phobia)" (p. 243). In addition, simple phobics differ from social phobics and agoraphobics in that they usually are less neurotic and may not be depressed or anxious except when confronted with the anxiety-provoking stimulus (Taylor & Arnow, 1988). When confronting the anxiety stimulus, the simple phobic's physiological arousal, which is symptomatic of increased ANS activity, can be

82

virtually identical to that of other anxiety sufferers, including the sensations experienced by panic-disordered persons. Physiological symptoms when confronted with a phobic stimulus include increase in heart rate and skin conductance fluctuation (Watson, Gaind, & Marks, 1972), as well as forearm bloodflow, blood pressure, and electromyogram (Taylor & Arnow, 1988). However, in contrast to clients with other anxiety disorders, simple phobics do not differ from normals in terms of baseline arousal (Barlow, 1988). Although some phobics will describe fears of fainting, going crazy, or dying when in feared situations, these responses are unlikely. For example, a fainting response is typical only of blood and injury phobics. Nor is it likely that a phobic reaction will lead to a psychotic break (i.e., going crazy) or death.

Although childhood phobias, particularly animal phobias, are common and usually disappear as the child matures, simple phobia may develop as the fear carries over into adulthood. Otherwise, a phobia can occur at most any age; however, the typical age of onset varies from a mean age of 7 for animal phobics to a mean age of 9 for blood phobics, 12 for dental phobics, 16 for social phobics, 20 for claustrophobics, and 28 for agoraphobics (Ost, 1987).

Simple phobia is one of the most commonly diagnosed mental disorders and is more often diagnosed in women than men (American Psychiatric Association, 1987; Thyer, Parrish, Curtis, Cameron, & Nesse, 1985). Epidemiological studies (Myers et al., 1984) of the prevalence rate of this disorder have yielded figures ranging from 4.5% to 11.8% for the general population (Barlow, 1988). Other epidemiological researchers studying specific, intense fears and phobias according to category found that (a) intense fears range from 10% (fear of being alone) to 25% (fear of snakes), and (b) phobias range from 0.4% (height phobia) to 3% (injury and illness phobia) for the general population (Agras, Sylvester, & Oliveau, 1969). Agras et al. (1969) also summarized their findings by noting the prevalence of phobias in the general public to be 7.7% and the prevalence of severely disabling phobias to be 0.2%. These authors also noted that less than 1% of those interviewed had sought treatment for the disorder and that only 6% of those seeking treatment obtain freedom from their fears (Agras, Chapin, & Oliveau, 1972).

SIMPLE PHOBIA CATEGORIES

A unique characteristic of phobias is the layperson's emphasis placed on listing individual phobias by name. One need only pick up a popular text to discover the multitude of names given to focal fears (e.g., amathophobia = fear of dust; xenophobia = fear of strangers). Thyer

(1987) criticized this practice as being an unfortunate one, as it tends to encourage the creation of additional categories with an emphasis on the differences instead of the similarities between the various phobias.

Taylor and Arnow (1988) divided simple phobias in several useful categories: (a) animal phobias, which include fear of small animals and/or insects; (b) blood and injury phobias, which include fear of seeing or having blood drawn, injuries, and/or deformities; (c) dental phobias; (d) flying phobias; (e) driving phobias, which may include fear of driving on highways; (f) sexual phobias, which can include fear and avoidance of any aspect of sex; and (g) other phobias, which include such fears as fear of heights (acrophobia) and fear of closed spaces (claustrophobia). Certain of the foregoing types of phobias (e.g., fear of flying) may actually involve a combination of separate fears (claustrophobia + fear of a crash; Freund, 1989). Finally, those individuals who fear small animals, closed spaces, blood and injury, and dental visits are the most likely to seek mental health services (Barlow, 1988)

ETIOLOGY OF SIMPLE PHOBIA

Barlow's (1988) etiological model of the development of simple phobia appears comprehensive, incorporating previously accepted models and suggesting some additional mechanisms of acquisition and maintenance. Biologically and psychologically vulnerable individuals may acquire simple phobias via direct experience, vicarious experience, or informational transmission. Life stress and the nature of the phobic object or situation (i.e., prepared stimuli) further raise the likelihood of phobia development. Either true or false alarms may occur on direct or vicarious contact with the phobic object or situation. Learned alarms subsequently develop, and when anxious apprehension regarding future contact with the relevant stimuli also develops, a simple phobia is created.

As described in previous chapters, evidence suggests that certain biological factors (e.g., labile ANS) may render individuals more susceptible to developing anxiety disorders. Regarding simple phobias, such biological vulnerability may interact with stimuli that are biologically more likely to trigger fear. Thus, Seligman's (1971) "preparedness theory" (McNally, 1987) suggests that phobias develop more easily when the provoking stimulus belongs to a class of objects or situations biologically more harmful or dangerous to humans (e.g., bees) than other stimuli (e.g., houses). It has been experimentally shown, for example, that it is easier to develop fear in reaction to pictures of snakes than to pictures of flowers (Ohman et al., 1975).

As previously noted, the various forms of contact with the (eventual) phobia stimulus may be accompanied by a true or false alarm. True alarms refer to panic in response to stimuli that may actually be life threatening or harmful (e.g., snakebite or car wreck), while false alarms refer to panic in response to objects or situations that are perceived as dangerous or threatening but in actuality present no likelihood of direct physical harm (e.g., being trapped in an elevator for a short period of time).

Recent empirical evidence supports the hypothesis that alarm reactions may contribute to the development and/or maintenance of simple phobias. For example, Munjack (1984) noted in a study of 30 driving phobics that 20% reported developing a phobia following a traumatic accident (true alarm), whereas 40% reported no such incident but instead reported developing a phobia following spontaneous panic attacks (false alarms) when driving. Similarly, in terms of maintenance of phobias, McNally and Steketee (1985), after interviewing 22 outpatient animal phobics, found that clients were more fearful of panic and the consequences of panic than an attack from the feared animal. Preliminary evidence (Rygh & Barlow, 1986; Zarate, Rapee, Craske, & Barlow, 1988) suggests that panic control treatment may be an important component of treatment for simple phobia in which panic is a feature. Finally, anxious apprehension may serve as both a preexisting tendency, making the initial occurrence of alarms and phobic reactions more likely, and as a solidifier of simple phobia development and maintenance. As Barlow (1988) explained,

> It is this anxious aprehension that occasions widespread and intense vigilance or attention narrowing in regard to upcoming potential encounters with phobic objects or situations. This, in turn, guarantees relatively widespread avoidance. Without anxious apprehension, the fear reaction would presumably fall into the category of normal fears experienced by over half the population, which cause some mild distress during direct confrontation but are otherwise ignored or forgotten. (p. 481)

As for modes of acquisition, Öst and Hugdahl (1981, 1983) provided empirical data on the various pathways by which different groups of phobias are learned. Overall, for subjects who could recall, most fears were acquired through conditioning (e.g., a dog bite), followed by modeling (e.g., watching a parent panic when seeing a spider), and then by instruction and information transmission (e.g., reading about the horror of snakes). These findings are, however, at odds with other studies that provide evidence that many phobias and most fears are not learned through a direct traumatic experience but more often through vicarious or verbal means (e.g., Rimm, Janda, Lancaster, Nahl, & Dittmar, 1977; Murray & Foote, 1979). Barlow (1988) attempted a reconcil-

Table 5.1. DSM-III-R Diagnostic Criteria for Simple Phobia

A. A persistent fear of a circumscribed stimulus (object or situation) other than fear of having a panic attack (as in Panic Disorder) or of humiliation or embarrassment in certain social situations (as in Social Phobia).

Note. Do not include fears that are a part of Panic Disorder with Agoraphobia or Agoraphobia without History of Panic Disorder.

B. During some phase of the disturbance, exposure to the specific phobic stimulus (or stimuli) almost invariably provokes an immediate anxiety response.

C. The object or situation is avoided, or endured with great anxiety.

D. The fear or the avoidant behavior significantly interferes with the person's normal routine or with usual social activities or relationships with others, or there is marked distress about having the fear.

E. The person recognizes that his or her fear is excessive or unreasonable.

F. The phobic stimulus is unrelated to the content of the obsessions of Obsessive Compulsive Disorder or the trauma of Post-traumatic Stress Disorder (pp. 244–245).

Note. Reprinted with permission from the *Diagnostic and Statistical Manual of Mental Disorders, Third Edition, Revised.* Copyright 1987 American Psychiatric Association.

iation of these divergent findings by suggesting that the traumatic experiences leading to conditioning, as described by Öst and Hugdahl (1983), were false alarms (panics) that occurred in the phobic situation.

DSM-III-R DIAGNOSTIC CRITERIA FOR SIMPLE PHOBIA

The DSM-III-R diagnostic criteria for simple phobia (300.29) are presented in Table 5.1.

Mental health professionals should remember that simple phobics, although often otherwise emotionally healthy (Taylor & Arnow, 1988), may present with numerous other anxiety and/or affective disorders (Barlow, 1988). The most probable complication, however, is likely to be a form of substance abuse, particularly self-medication with alcohol, to deal with anticipatory anxiety (Thyer, 1977). In such a case, the substance abuse disorder should be the initial focus of treatment. Thus, clinicians, particularly during the assessment phase of treatment, will want to be alert to the possibility of coexisting conditions, as an accurate and complete decision concerning the primary diagnosis is vital to the type of therapeutic intervention eventually chosen.

REVIEW OF ASSESSMENT INSTRUMENTS

The ADIS-R (Di Nardo et al, 1985) provides a structured assessment of the most common simple phobias (Barlow, 1988). In addition, a variety of self-report and behavioral measures are available. One of the most widely used and accepted measures is the FQ (Marks and Mathews, 1979) a brief measure of an individual's general level of fear and avoidance, along with a blood/injury subscale. Other fear assessment measures include Walk's (1956) Fear Thermometer, Lang and Lazovik's (1963) Fear Survey Schedule-I, Geer's (1965) Fear Survey Schedule-II, and Wolpe and Lang's (1969) Fear Survey Schedule-III. Wolpe and Lang's (1977) Fear Survey Schedule has been shown to have good normative data (Tomlin et al., 1984). There also exist a variety of specific fear assessment instruments, including ones for fear of heights (Baker, Cohen, & Saunders, 1973) and snakes and spiders (Lang, Melamed, & Hart, 1970).

In addition to subjective and cognitive assessment, Sturgis and Scott (1984) recommended measurement of fear along behavioral and physiological dimensions. Given a biopsychosocial description of simple phobia, this approach to assessment would seem to be a logical one, although other authors (e.g., Taylor & Arnow, 1988) have suggested that behavioral and physiological measures of simple phobia are of limited use in most clinical settings.

REVIEW OF NON-RET
TREATMENTS

Rather than reviewing the numerous simple phobia treatment studies, in this section we briefly review (a) sources that have reviewed treatments for simple phobia, (b) studies that have evaluated the contribution of cognitive procedures to exposure therapy, (c) initial attempts to match form of treatment with individual fear response patterns, (d) one study that has tested the utility of matching treatment with the mode of phobia acquisition, (e) recent studies that have applied innovative cognitive-behavioral treatments for clinically prevalent simple phobias, and (f) psychopharmacological treatment of simple phobia.

Sturgis and Scott (1984) reviewed studies that have evaluated behavioral treatment of snake, spider, and rat phobias, acrophobia, claustrophobia, blood, illness, and injury phobia, and mixed phobias. Sturgis and Scott (1984) noted that the majority of studies reviewed could be classified as analogue. They concluded that active, in vivo exposure of long duration plus encouragement for self-exposure appears to be the treatment of choice for simple phobia.

Last (1987) examined the effect of adding cognitive procedures to various forms of exposure treatment of simple phobia and concluded as follows:

In interpreting findings on the efficacy of cognitive treatment procedures, it is clear that results are discrepant for merely fearful as opposed to truly phobic clients. Whereas the analogue investigations cited earlier tend to support the utility of cognitive restructuring with fearful populations, results from clinical investigations show purely cognitive interventions to be inferior to behavioral treatment (*in vivo* exposure) (Biran & Wilson, 1981), and to be of no additional therapeutic value when combined with behavioral techniques (Ladouceur, 1983). (p. 183)

Biran and Wilson (1981) found participant modeling superior to cognitive restructuring only with patients with either height, elevator, or darkness phobias. Ladouceur (1983) found that the inclusion of self-instructional training actually detracted from participant modeling of treatment of dog and cat phobics. Last (1987) discussed possible reasons for the lack of benefit of cognitive procedures in existing studies and suggested further exploration of the addition of cognitive techniques to exposure therapy. Last concluded,

Although empirical findings have not supported the addition of cognitive treatment to standard behavioral treatment, clinical observations suggest that cognitive therapy may aid in prompting clients to "self-exposure" between therapy appointments, and to remain exposed to phobic situations for sufficient periods of time. (p. 188)

Not included in Last's (1987) review were two studies with height phobics who did appear to show some benefit from the addition of cognitive procedures. Marks (1987), in his review of cognitive approaches to simple phobia, found Marshall (1985) to be one of six studies to find that cognitive intervention (i.e., coping self-statements) enhanced exposure. Marks (1987) designated Emmelkamp and Felten's (1985) study as a slightly positive one. Emmelkamp and Felten, who also treated height phobics, found that training in adaptive thinking (i.e., relabeling anxiety, substituting favorable anticipations for fearful ones, and task-relevant self-instructions) plus exposure was superior to exposure only on subjective anxiety and cognitions during a behavioral test. The cognitive intervention did not influence performance.

Öst and his colleagues initiated investigations examining the utility of matching form of treatment with simple phobics' individual response patterns. For example, Jerremalm, Jansson, and Öst (1986b) divided dental phobics into two groups based on more intense responding in either the physiological system (e.g., heart rate) or cognitive system (i.e., catastrophic cognitions). Results indicated no benefit from matching applied relaxation and exposure with physiological responders and self-instructional training and exposure with cognitive responders. Matching treatment with predominant response system did lead to superior results with claustrophobics (Öst, Johansson, & Jerremalm, 1982).

According to Barlow (1988), applied relaxation was slightly better than exposure for physiological reactors (p. 488). Although Barlow (1988) noted several factors that weakened confidence in these findings, he noted that there was clinical wisdom in tailoring specific treatments to individuals' specific response profiles.

Öst (1985) also explored the utility of matching treatment to mode of phobia acquisition (e.g., behavioral and physiological treatments when conditioning was the onset and cognitive treatment when mode of onset was misinformation). Barlow (1988) concluded that Öst's (1985) analysis of 370 phobics revealed results suggestive of benefit for matching treatments according to mode of phobia onset.

Several studies have evaluated what we consider to be the most up-to-date approaches to clinically relevant simple phobias, including Öst's (1989) one-session simple phobia treatment, Öst's (e.g., Öst & Sterner, 1987) applied tension treatment for blood and injury phobia, interoceptive exposure for simple phobia, treatment of fear of flying, and treatment of dental phobia.

A variety of cognitive-behavioral techniques have been used to treat simple phobia, the most common being systematic desensitization (Goldfried & Davison, 1976), which includes deep muscular relaxation, construction of a hierarchy, and graded presentation of imaginal stimuli; in vivo exposure, which has been shown to be the treatment of choice for phobias (e.g., Curtis, Nesse, Buxton, Wright, & Lippman, 1976); and participant modeling (Bandura, 1977), which includes having the therapist model appropriate behaviors with the client rehearsing the behaviors. Howard, Murphy, and Clarke (1983) successfully treated 56 flying phobics with a combination of relaxation, systematic desensitization, implosion, and flooding therapies, and Sturgis and Scott (1984) discussed the value of using implosive, flooding, and reinforced practice therapies in treating simple phobia. Furthermore, Thyer (1987) noted that several studies (e.g., Emmelkamp & Wessels, 1975) point to a therapeutic preference for performance-based desensitization over imaginal desensitization.

After reviewing a number of cognitive-behavioral treatments, Sturgis and Scott (1984) concluded that the most efficacious procedure for treatment of simple phobia involves a combination of long-duration exposure and encouragement to engage in the exposure. Similarly, Thyer (1987) concluded, "the status of empirical research at the present time indicates that real-life exposure therapy is the treatment of choice for most clients with simple or social phobias" (p. 41). Furthermore, Stern and Marks (1973) demonstrated that longer exposure sessions are more efficacious than shorter ones. Thyer (1987), however, listed the following as being contraindications for the use of exposure: the presence of

(a) a physical condition that is incompatible with severe anxiety, (b) an acute psychosis or paranoid disorder, (c) substance abuse, and (d) severe depression.

Zarate et al. (1988) discussed the therapeutic value of treating via interoceptive exposure certain simple phobics who primarily experience panic attacks in response to interoceptive (internal) cues rather than situational cues. This type of exposure involves having the client perform a variety of exercises (e.g., like those described in chapter 3) to desensitize to and gain control over the internally induced fear. In their preliminary report, the authors recommended that clients be assessed for sensitivity to interoceptive cues to decide whether interoceptive exposure is the preferred intervention. In a case example later in this chapter, we illustrate the use of panic management as part of treating an individual with fear of flying.

Öst (1989) reported on the development of a one-session treatment protocol for simple phobias in which a combination of in vivo exposure and modeling is utilized. Öst (1989) identified two different goals for this one-session treatment. The first goal is the client's goal concerning what he or she would like to be able to manage in his or her environment as a result of treatment. The second goal is the therapist's goal as to what he or she would like the client to accomplish during the single therapy session. Exposure tasks designed to obtain this second goal involve overlearning, as clients assist in accomplishing tasks that go significantly beyond their actual goals. For example, in one of the case examples presented later, the client's goal was to be able to carry out military duties without undue fear in a geographic location known to be frequented by snakes. In contrast, the therapist's goal during the one-session treatment was to have the client ultimately hold a snake and allow it to move over her arms and shoulders. Öst suggested not informing clients of this second goal at the outset of treatment, as he predicted that 90% of his patients would have refused treatment if they had been informed about this aspect of treatment. Öst (1989) reported that after treatment clients were "pleased that I had helped them to discover that they could manage much more than they had dared to dream of in their 'wildest imagination' " (p. 3).

For details concerning Öst's (1989) treatment, we recommend consulting the original article. However, to describe briefly the treatment, the in vivo exposure component includes having the patient systematically approach the phobic stimulus and engage in the exposure until anxiety decreases, at which point further approach and exposure are continued. The therapy session is terminated when anxiety has decreased by 50%. Modeling involves having the therapist demonstrate to the patient how to interact with the phobic object or situation, and then having the client repeat the therapist's actions. To facilitate maintenance and enhancement of therapeutic gains, the therapist instructs patients to view a videotape of the one-session treatment. According to Öst (1989), this last component helps to convince the client that the therapeutic accomplishments actually occurred. Clients then are reminded of the importance of welcoming opportunities to continue to confront in the future their former phobic object.

In terms of the effectiveness of this one-session approach, in a recent clinical study of 20 clients with either injection, spider, rat, cat, bird, or dog phobias, the mean treatment time was just over 2 hours. Moreover, 90% of the clients continued to maintain therapeutic gains at 4-year follow-up. Öst (1989) conceptualized his extended single-session treatment as a beginning for the client, who must always actively confront the phobic situations when encountered in daily life.

Öst and his colleagues (e.g., Öst & Sterner, 1987; Öst, Sterner, & Fellenius, 1989) also developed what appears to be the treatment of choice for blood and injury phobia, which is one of the most common of the simple phobias. In contrast to other phobics, blood and injury phobics frequently faint, which is associated with a fall in blood pressure following an initial increase in heart rate and blood pressure, when confronted with fear-evoking stimuli. Öst's treatment includes learning to prevent the fall in blood pressure and potential fainting response via (a) instruction and practice in muscle tension, (b) application of tension while being shown slides depicting wounds and mutilation, (c) observation with therapist of others donating blood at a blood donor center, (d) donation of blood by the client, and (e) observation of thoracic surgery by the client. The treatment is brief (five sessions) with 73% to 77% clinical improvements noted (Öst et al., 1989).

Barlow and his colleagues (Rygh & Barlow, 1986; Zarate et al., 1988) presented an innovative conceptualization of the etiology, maintenance, and treatment of certain simple phobias. Zarate et al. (1988) indicated that the experience of an unexpected panic attack may be etiologically related to the development of simple phobia in about 30% of individuals with this disorder (Öst, 1985). Rygh and Barlow (1986) and Zarate et al. (1988) presented reports about initial case studies providing preliminary evidence that interoceptive exposure (described in chapter 3) is an effective intervention for automobile driving phobias with panic-related etiology and/or maintenance. Zarate et al. (1988) recommended that simple phobics who experience panic attacks be assessed for phobic responsivity to interoceptive cues, and that responders may benefit from panic management procedures.

Another treatment shown to be effective with driving phobia is guided mastery, which was found to be more effective than exposure alone

(Williams et al., 1984). Guided mastery is based on self-efficacy theory (Bandura, 1977; Williams, 1987), which predicts that treatments alleviate phobia by conveying information that increases people's perceptions that they can cope effectively with specific activities (Williams, 1987, p. 175). In vivo performances, as indicated in chapter 1, powerfully increase self-efficacy. Therefore, guided mastery involves directly assisting clients in accomplishing fear-related activities in the most efficient manner possible. Thus, driving phobics might be coached in the application of diaphragm breathing, task-relevant self-talk, deliberate relaxation of arms when holding rigidly to the steering wheel, and so on. Near completion of treatment, the therapist gradually withdraws his or her assistance until the client is performing independently.

A few studies have tested programs for the fear of flying. Given the frequency of this fear, with estimates ranging between 10% and 20% of the general population (Agras et al., 1969; Howard et al., 1983), it is surprising that additional controlled studies have not been conducted. Girodo and Roehl (1978) found coping self-statement training and preparatory information training useful in self-ratings of anxiety during actual flights. Howard et al. (1983) found systematic desensitization, implosion, flooding, and relaxation equally effective in reducing self-reported fear. Flooding appeared most promising, and participation in a graduation flight was predictive of better outcomes. In addition, this study found that fear of flying is not a unitary phenomenon, but rather consists of fears of crashing, heights, confinement, instability, panicking, or losing control.

Similarly, in a sample of 39 fearful flyers, Freund (1989) found that aviaphobia was usually accompanied by acrophobia (43%), claustrophobia (13%), agoraphobia (25%), and GAD, social phobia, and other (8%). In an uncontrolled study, Freund (1989) found a three-system approach, including relaxation, slow breathing, thought stopping, positive imagery, imaginal exposure, and in vivo exposure (i.e., a graduation flight) effective in reducing self-reported fear of flying and increasing actual number of flights. Related fears also improved.

Forgione & Bauer (1980) developed cognitive-behaviorally oriented self-help books and audiocassettes for fearful flyers. Although designed for the consumer, the materials can be useful as therapist guides and homework assignments. Ellis's (1972a) *How to Master Your Fear of Flying* illustrates the RET approach to treatment.

Another phobia of clinical relevance is dental phobia. Marks (1987) described this problem as pervasive and indicated that most people have at least mild dental fear. Forty percent of adults delay or avoid visits to the dentist, and 5% have a dental phobia (Gale & Ayer, 1969;

Kleinknect, Klepac, & Alexander, 1973). A Swedish study (Hallstrom & Halling, 1984) found a 13% point prevalence for dental phobia.

Melamed's (1979) review suggested that dental anxiety may be multifacited, including fear of criticism for poor oral hygiene, loss of control, pain, anesthetic injection, or the sensations of drilling. Taylor and Arnow (1988) suggested that some dental phobias may involve blood and injury phobia. We suggest that dental phobics be assessed for the presence of PD and social phobia.

Melamed's (1979) review included systematic desensitization, modeling, cognitive rehearsal, and reinforcement treatments of dental fears. More recently, Kent (1989) reviewed cognitive aspects of the maintenance and treatment of dental anxiety. In addition to exposure and cognitive interventions, increasing pain tolerance (Klepac, 1975) and reducing hypersensitivity of the gag reflex (Marks, 1987) may be useful with some dental phobics.

Finally, in terms of psychopharmacological therapy for simple phobia, Barlow (1988) reviewed several research studies and concluded that there is a virtual unanimous opinion among researchers that medications do not facilitate treatment procedures. Hence, little research exists concerning the therapeutic value of adding to the treatment regimen a variety of drugs, probably either the benzodiazepines or beta blockers. In fact, there is accumulating evidence that such drugs may hinder exposure (Barlow, 1988) by interfering with the habituation process that is necessary for these procedures to have a therapeutic effect. Nonetheless, some clinicians support pharmacological treatment of simple phobia. For example, Noyes (1982) recommended the use of a beta blocker, instead of sedatives, for those clients who experience undue somatic symptoms as part of the phobic response, whereas Gold (1989) recommended exposure but prescribed beta blockers (e.g., propranolol) for stubborn cases.

A RET MODEL FOR SIMPLE PHOBIA

Our RET model for the etiology and maintenance of simple phobia follows the models of Barlow (1988) and Öst and Hugdahl (1981, 1983) summarized in this chapter, as well as Foa and Kozak's (1985, 1986) analyses of fear structures, described in chapter 1. From a RET perspective, we emphasize the phobic's preexisting tendencies to engage in anxious apprehension, either as a rather general approach to potential risks and dangers or as a more specific approach to specific objects or situations.

Due to biological vulnerability (e.g., an overactive ANS) and psychological vulnerability (e.g., a tendency to worry or engage in anxious apprehension), individuals develop phobic reactions to objects or situations to which individuals are biologically prepared to develop fears (McNally, 1987).

As suggested in chapter 3, we often, but not always, conceptualize worry as involving four ideational components: (a) "I must not incur the physical danger or discomfort associated with various objects or situations"; (b) to experience such danger or discomfort is awful, terrible, or catastrophic, which often means such danger or discomfort is unbearable and that one cannot cope with it or be happy at all in spite of its occurrence; (c) "If I experience extreme discomfort or anxiety, or if I avoid it, my self-worth decreases"; and (d) avoidance is the best solution to coping with danger and/or discomfort.

Individuals who hold such beliefs or related beliefs are likely to develop the cognitive biases of interpreting ambiguous information as threatening, overestimating the likelihood of the occurrence of phobia-related events, and rating the awfulness of such events as higher than would nonphobic individuals (Butler & Mathews, 1983; Ellis, 1980b; see chapter 3).

Thus, people with the biological vulnerabilities noted previously and the psychological vulnerabilities just described would be more susceptible to developing and maintaining phobic reactions. Consistent with our view, Borkovec (1985), in a discussion of worry, stated the following:

> Simple classical aversive conditioning may provide a foundation for unrealistic fear responses, but how the individual mentally reacts after the establishment of a conditioned fear response will determine whether it rapidly extinguishes or develops into a persistent neurotic condition. Thus, worrisome, catastrophizing thoughts, in strengthening fear structure by contiguous association, can contribute to anxiety maintenance. Moreover, the extent to which an individual develops a worrisome cognitive style may influence either the ease with which aversive events create new conditioned fear responses or the extent to which the world is seen as a potentially dangerous place. (p. 467)

Compared to panic-disordered individuals whose fear structures contain information that responses (e.g., anxiety, body sensations) are harmful, fear structures of simple phobics contain information that stimuli elements (e.g., snakes, heights) are potentially harmful (Foa & Kozak, 1985). However, as data reported by McNally and Steketee (1985) suggests, simple phobics often fear their reactions (i.e., panic and its consequences) as much as or more than actual danger from their feared object. Thus, the fear structures of simple phobics may also contain information that responses are dangerous or at least too uncomfortable to tolerate.

In RET terms, then, simple phobics catastrophize concerning both potential dangers and related discomfort. Avoidance behavior is designed to alleviate the potential danger or discomfort. As indicated previously, the tendency to catastrophize is both biologically and psychologically influenced.

TREATMENT OF SIMPLE PHOBIA: A RET PERSPECTIVE

When treating simple phobia, the clinician will first want to introduce the client to the basics of RET, including explanations of the nature of irrational beliefs and methods of disputing and modifying these beliefs. Use of the RET Self-Help Form is recommended as part of this process. The clinician will then discuss the behavioral component of changing beliefs (e.g., the mechanisms of exposure, the extended length of sessions, debriefing after exposure), as well as the physiological component (e.g., relaxation exercises). The cognitive component of treatment will focus on helping the client to identify irrational beliefs, challenge them, and eventually replace them with rational responses. This part of the therapy should be most effective when introduced both before and during exposures. The clinician may also wish to instruct the client in the use of other behavioral techniques, including assertion skills, rational-humorous songs, risk taking, and REI, depending on the specific needs of the client, as RET endorses the use of vigorous behavioral disputes. The Biographical Information Form and Personality Data Form—Part 1 are recommended for gathering pertinent background information (e.g., family history of anxiety disorders, medical conditions) that may relate to the client's current anxiety problems.

GUIDELINES FOR EXPOSURE THERAPY

Overview of Treatment

Treatment includes (a) summarizing interview and assessment information and providing a social learning explanation for the development and maintenance of the phobia; (b) describing treatment alternatives and the rationale for their use; (c) ascertaining previous self-help or therapy-based attempts to overcome the phobia; (d) discussing ways in which the present treatment might differ from what has already been tried; (e) delineating the roles and expectations for therapist and client, including the role of homework assignments, in vivo practice, necessary time and energy commitments, and projection of length and spacing of therapy sessions.

Length and Spacing of Sessions

Simple phobics are typically seen once each week, although more or less frequent sessions may be needed, as long as the client engages in regular and frequent exposure practice, preferably on a daily basis. Chambless (1990) recently provided evidence that ten 90-minute sessions conducted either daily or once weekly were equally effective. Öst's one-session treatment for simple phobias, described earlier, has a mean session time of 2.1 hours. Thus, the therapist and client have considerable flexibility when developing a treatment plan most appropriate for client's individual needs.

Self- Versus Therapist-Administered Exposure

Ghosh, Marks, and Carr (1988) provided evidence that motivated clients can successfully administer exposure without direct therapist accompaniment. We typically decide on the amount of self-administered versus therapist-assisted exposure according to client motivation and economic factors. In most cases, we find it useful to accompany clients on at least one or two exposure exercises so that we can coach clients on the use of coping skills and make sure that their method of approach is in accord with effective principles of exposure (e.g., engagement versus disengagement, prolonged versus brief exposure) and likely to foster a sense of mastery (Williams et al., 1985).

Graded Exposure

Exposure is practically performed in a hierarchical fashion. The primary function of the hierarchy is to provide a systematic, orderly approach to therapeutic exposure. In addition, as clients work their way up the hierarchy, they can more clearly monitor their progress and reinforce themselves for their accomplishments. The hierarchy is not a mechanism to make exposure so gradual that the client does not have to experience discomfort. We agree with Ellis that such an approach may reinforce low frustration tolerance or discomfort anxiety. As Dryden (1985) suggested, exposure may be most efficient when designed in such a way as to be challenging but not overwhelming.

There are variety of ways to assist clients in constructing hierarchies. The method we prefer consists of (a) initially brainstorming a number of fear-related situations, based on the client's stated goals and motivation; (b) rating items from 0 to 100 in terms of how much anxiety would be expected to occur in each situation; and (c) ordering items according to the ratings with approximately 10 points occurring between items, although the exact number is not crucial. Five to 12 items are often included, with this number varying according to the individual's particular circumstances.

Type of Exposure

In vivo exposure is generally believed to be superior to imaginal exposure (Foa & Kozak, 1985), although imaginal exposure may also be effective for treating simple phobias (Marks, 1987). Barlow (1988), in reviewing in vivo exposure, noted that "the few studies in the literature reveal no particular advantage for one type of exposure over another" (p. 486). In support of this position, Bourque and Ladouceur (1980) found no significant differences among five different exposure treatments for height phobia. Öst (1978) obtained similar results with thunder and lightning phobics.

Duration and Functions of Exposure

It is now clear that prolonged exposure yields superior outcomes to shorter exposure (Foa & Kozak, 1985). The optimal length of exposure is closely related to the time necessary for the client to habituate physiologically to the phobic stimuli and varies across the anxiety disorders. Typically, simple phobics habituate more quickly (often within 30 minutes) than do agoraphobics and obsessive-compulsives (Foa & Kozak, 1985).

As Williams et al. (1985) argued, other mechanisms besides habituation may be operating during exposure. Thus, as clients observe themselves performing effectively in the phobic situation, perceived self-efficacy may increase and anxiety may decrease. The length of this process may vary not only between individuals but also from one exposure exercise to another. For example, a client who was phobic of certain rides at Disneyland reported an abrupt decrease in anxiety during a particular ride when he serendipitously discovered that he felt more in control when he moved his body in particular ways in response to turns. This reported ability "to lean toward the turns" appeared to result more from an increased sense of self-control and mastery rather than a passive habituation process.

Exposure may also work, of course, because it allows the individual to disconfirm specific danger-related predictions (e.g., Clark & Salkovskis, 1990). Thus, the driving phobic who resumes driving may eventually master his or her fear when his or her prediction that becoming anxious while driving will lead to loss of control and a resulting accident is not confirmed.

Whether conceptualized as habituation, mastery, or disconfirmation of danger-related predictions, clients should, in general, prolong exposure until significant reductions in anxiety are noted. However, as Rachman, Craske, and Tallman (1986) noted, it does not appear to be necessary for clients always to stay in the phobic situation until fear subsides. Agoraphobics who were allowed the option to escape when their anxiety reached a certain level (70 or above) and then return when the fear had decreased did as well as those who did not escape. Contrary to Mowrer's (e.g., 1960) theory, escape did not strengthen avoidance behavior. Rachman et al. (1986) suggested that the option of escaping and then returning to confront the feared situation may contribute to a sense of safety and self-control, thereby facilitating fear reduction.

Functional versus Apparent Exposure

It is not uncommon for phobic patients to claim that they have already tried exposing themselves to feared situations but that fear continues to exist. In such cases, it is often helpful to explore whether clients have been disengaging (i.e., cognitively and emotionally avoiding the feared stimuli), even though behaviorally they have put themselves in phobic situations. Thus, disengagement and other forms of dissociation prevent functional exposure and its attendant emotional processing of fear cues (Borkovec, 1982; Foa & Kozak, 1986; Marks, 1987). As Butler (1989) recommended,

> Dwell on the aspects of the situation that really bother you, so that you face up to them fully. If you ignore them, then the practice will not be nearly so useful. In fact, it would be rather like trying to get used to heights by standing at the top of some steps with your eyes shut. (p. 113)

Use of Anxiety Management Procedures

Although relaxation procedures are not essential in the treatment of simple phobia, they are often useful in facilitating exposure. We usually teach cue-controlled relaxation, diaphragm breathing, and rational self-talk (Butler et al., 1984) as coping skills to increase the client's general sense of mastery and control as well as specific tools to facilitate exposure to the phobic object or situations. We typically do not advocate the use of traditional systematic desensitization as a relaxation exposure procedure. Compared to in vivo exposure, systematic desensitization appears less efficient, more time-consuming, and, as Ellis (1983) hypothesized, a possible contributor to LFT. With systematic desensitization, clients may get the message that it is possible actually to be relaxed (which is unlikely) in the presence of their phobic object, that they should not have to experience discomfort, or that discomfort might be dangerous. In discussing the treatment of agoraphobia, Foa and Kozak (1985) similarly suggested that:

> the maintenance of certain disorders is mediated by a general attitude that arousal should be avoided. If agoraphobics generally avoid arousal, the effort to minimize anxiety in systematic desensitization would reinforce this attitude. On the other hand, flooding, in which high arousal is prompted, would contradict this attitude. (p. 448)

COGNITIVE INTERVENTIONS

Some additional, specific RET treatment interventions for simple phobia are described next.

Probability versus Possibility Thinking

In certain cases, it is useful to dispute irrational beliefs by showing the client that the probability of the occurrence of the feared event is minimal. For example, the height phobic who fears fainting while climbing stairs is taught that it is possible that he or she might faint, although this response is improbable. Information concerning the nature of the fight or flight response (i.e., during arousal one's blood pressure increases so that fainting is unlikely; the only exception being the blood phobic whose blood pressure actually drops) is useful in such a case. In sum, RET assists the client in making more accurate estimates of the probability of negative events while decatastrophizing the worst possible scenarios.

Coping with Depression and LFT

While simple phobics as a rule are the most psychologically healthy of patients with anxiety disorders, when simple phobics seek treatment it is not uncommon for some degree of depression to be present. As an illustration of severe depression accompanying simple phobia, a report by Pegeron and Curtis (1986) entitled "Simple Phobia Leading to Suicide: A Case Report" appeared in *The Behavior Therapist* and was followed by reactions from others (e.g., Giles, 1988). Pegeron and Curtis (1986) described a client (Mrs. A.) with a lifelong insect phobia that had been unresponsive to previous treatment. The authors reported the following:

> During sessions with her therapist, she would occasionally talk about "feeling depressed" about her fear, and about wishing she were dead at times. . . . After the fourth session of exposure therapy, Mrs. A. terminated further treatment because she "dreaded coming and facing bugs." Six weeks later we learned of her suicide by an overdose of aspirin. (p. 135)

The authors noted that Mrs. A. had previously reported that she would commit suicide if her husband died before she did, which did occur. Pegeron and Curtis (1986) acknowledged that Mrs. A. suffered from a number of other problems, including unresolved grief over the death of her husband. Nevertheless, they concluded that "her insect phobia was severe, and we believe it was the primary pathology which led her to suicide" (p. 135).

In response to this report, Giles (1988) suggested that "from the authors' description of the case, it seems reasonable to hypothesize that the trauma of the treatment itself may have influenced Mrs. A.'s decision to attempt suicide" (p. 26). Giles (1988) went on to caution against the "movement of behavior therapists towards 'performance-based' interventions and away (perhaps) from subtler interventions having fewer side effects of emotional trauma" (pp. 26, 42) and suggested systematic desensitization as such an alternative.

From a RET perspective, neither Mrs. A.'s insect phobia nor the exposure treatment led to her suicide. Rather, her beliefs about the discomfort of her phobic condition and the exposure treatment would be the more powerful contributor to Mrs. A.'s decision to commit suicide. It is impossible to know just how much Mrs. A.'s other problems (e.g., her husband's death) and her beliefs about them may have contributed. In any case, the example of Mrs. A. tragically illustrates the RET concept of second-level problems or "problems about problems." Specifically, it illustrates LFT or DA at its worst. Thus, when a simple phobic believes, "I mustn't experience the discomfort and inconvenience of this phobia and its treatment. It is terrible to be so affected by it. I can't stand it any longer!" depression is thereby created. Further contributing to depression may be other irrational beliefs related to self-downing because of having a problem in the first place.

Thus, we encourage practitioners to be aware of clients' possible depression about their phobias and to look for the aforementioned kinds of beliefs. Not only does the secondary depression add another level of misery for the client, it may also deplete energy reserves necessary for engaging in treatment and may interfere with habituation to phobic stimuli (Foa & Kozak, 1986).

Dealing with Noncompliance

Noncompliance for simple phobics usually centers around failure to engage in consistent exposure to the source of their fear. When this occurs, we find it useful to examine clients' efficacy and outcome expectations as well as frustration tolerance issues. Using claustrophobics as an example, let us assume that failure to ride elevators consistently has occurred. Efficacy expectations refer to clients' confidence that they can in fact learn to tolerate elevator rides. Outcome expectations refer to the beliefs clients have about whether repeatedly riding elevators will eventually lead to overcoming claustrophobia. Thus, clients may have low outcome expectations if they believe that to conquer their fear they must understand the underlying conflicts for which claustrophobic fears are only symbolic. Or clients may accept the social learning model of fear reduction but have low efficacy expectations and believe that they cannot tolerate the discomfort of riding elevators. Interventions for low outcome expectations could include further education about exposure principles and examples of others (e.g., case examples, talks with former clients, research studies). For low efficacy expectations, reviewing with clients other similar situations that they handled but previously thought they could not is often helpful. In addition, directly addressing the costs and benefits of tolerating the discomfort of exposure and confronting various LFT beliefs may be indicated. Developing self-rewards for engaging in the exposure exercises and penalties for avoidance may also be appropriate with certain clients (Ellis & Dryden, 1987).

Dealing with Self-Rating

RET can be used to help clients avoid self-berating for having a phobia in the first place. The following transcript illustrates this point.

Therapist: So you feel that you're a worthless person for being afraid to go to the dentist?

Client: Right! I can't even get up enough courage to make an appointment for a cleaning. I'm such a wimp! I really don't like being this way.

Therapist: I can understand that you're not happy with the way things are at the moment, but on logical grounds, where's the rule that says people who are afraid of dentists are wimps or worthless human beings? I'm not aware of any sort of rule like that, how about you?

Client: Well, I don't really believe that there is a rule about being a wimp. It just seems that I'm much less of a person for not being as brave as I would like to be.

Therapist: Why do you have to be brave? Where's the rule? And what is really so bad about being afraid to go to the dentist?

Client: But I thought that men are supposed to be brave.

Therapist: Society would like you to believe that, but we both know that you can't always believe what others tell you. So why must you get down on yourself and worry so much that society would disapprove of you having a phobia?

Client: Well, I know from our other talks that I don't have to get down on myself. I guess this principle applies here, too.

Therapist: Exactly.

Client: Is it really possible to overcome this kind of problem?

Therapist: Yes, I believe it is. But I also believe that the healing starts when you refuse to get down on yourself for having a problem in the first place. It's much healthier to let go of those unrealistic expectations and worries while accepting yourself as a worthwhile, although fallible, human being.

Client: I'll keep working on it.

SAMPLE ABCS

The following ABCs apply to an individual who is fearful of small, enclosed spaces (i.e., claustrophobia):

A. *Activating event:*
   1. The need to ride in a crowded elevator to get to a business appointment.
B. *Beliefs:*
   1. I can't get in the elevator. What if it gets stuck and I can't get out? I'll surely pass out, look stupid in front of everyone, or go crazy! And that would be really terrible!
   2. I'm certain that I'll die in that elevator! There won't be enough air, and I'll probably suffocate to death. What an awful way to die!

The claustrophobic may also adhere to any of the following three types of irrational beliefs:
   1. *Demanding:* I must be totally in control of my fears and feelings, otherwise I'm worthless.
   2. *Catastrophizing:* It is terrible if I can't ride in the elevator. Becoming trapped in the elevator would be really horrible! I can't stand such discomfort!

3. *Rating of self and others:* Any normal person can tolerate elevators. There is something wrong with my mind. My inability to ride in an elevator makes me a worthless and awful person.

C. *Consequences:*
1. Extreme anxiety and discomfort.
2. Major inconvenience (e.g., walking up multiple levels of stairs, and then being late or exhausted).
3. Losing a business account or restricting one's business to people working in small buildings.

The following disputes apply to the claustrophobic client:

D. *Disputes:*
1. What's the actual likelihood that the elevator is going to get stuck? Even if it did, where's the evidence that I couldn't tolerate the discomfort?
2. How likely is it that I will die or suffocate in a stuck elevator?
3. How does my riding elevators determine my self-worth?

E. *Effective new philosophy:*
1. I choose whether I enter the elevator, and I can tolerate the discomfort even if it gets stuck. That certainly would be uncomfortable and inconvenient, but it wouldn't be terrible.
2. There's very little chance that I would pass out, look stupid, or go crazy. Even if I did, I don't need others' approval or acceptance. Anyway, it would be a great shame-attacking exercise!
3. There's very little chance that I would die or suffocate in the elevator. Elevators always have an escape hatch in the top, so there's always plenty of air. If for some reason I did die, everyone's got to go sometime, and I know that I could tolerate the discomfort of dying.
4. I'm a worthwhile person, regardless of whether I choose to ride in elevators.

The following ABCs apply to the spider phobic who wants to avoid exposure therapy:

A. *Activating event:*
1. During the next exposure session, the therapist wants the client to handle a jar containing a spider.

B. *Beliefs:*
1. Having to hold that jar will be really awful! Just thinking about looking at that spider makes me want to faint. I'm sure I'll faint if I have to do more exposure. I've really had enough exposure. Therapy doesn't work, anyway!
2. I'm a rotten person. I can't even stay in therapy.

C. *Consequences:*
1. Avoidance of necessary therapy.
2. Continuation of the client's phobia.

   3. Self-berating for not complying with the therapy, quitting, and continuing to have a phobia.
D. *Disputes:*
   1. What's so awful about holding a jar with a spider in it?
   2. How likely is it that I'll really faint, and if I did, where's the evidence that I couldn't stand it if I did?
   3. Why can't I stand the discomfort of exposure?
   4. How does my success in therapy determine my worth as a human being?
E. *Effective new philosophy:*
   1. Exposure is uncomfortable and anxiety provoking. But that's one of the reasons it really works! I can tolerate anything, including discomfort during exposure.
   2. I don't have to discontinue therapy. Even if I choose to do so, I still like myself. I can never be a rotten person no matter what I fail at or how often I fail!

CASE EXAMPLE: ONE-SESSION TREATMENT OF A SNAKE PHOBIA

The first author (Warren) used Öst's (1989) one-session treatment for specific phobias. Linda was a 36-year-old married nurse with a life-long snake phobia. Linda had managed to avoid snakes throughout her life, although she often experienced intense anxiety when accidently seeing snakes on television or in movies. Linda sought therapy when her military reserve position required that she spend time during the upcoming summer in a part of Texas inhabited by snakes.

After the initial assessment, Linda was presented with a social learning analysis of the development and maintenance of her snake phobia. Her mother also had a snake phobia, although interestingly she had overcome it at the time Linda sought treatment. Next, Linda was presented with the option of a gradual exposure program or a one-session treatment. Pros and cons of each were reviewed, including the intense but less protracted discomfort she would likely experience during the one-session treatment. Linda chose the latter, and the therapist rented a baby boa constrictor snake from a pet store.

On the morning of treatment, the therapist saw Linda in the parking lot of the office building, and she was clearly agitated and upset. When she came into the office, where the snake was residing in a small glass rectangular box covered with a towel, Linda immediately hurried to the other side of the office and turned her back to the snake. At this point,

Linda was in tears, asking, "Why am I doing this? I must be stupid!" The therapist empathized with her fear and doubts but expressed confidence that she could conquer her fear in spite of her doubts.

Exposure then proceeded with Linda turning toward the covered snake box, looking toward the uncovered snake box, looking directly at the snake, and progressively moving closer to the snake. When the client was about 10 feet from the snake, the therapist, wearing gloves, took the snake out of the glass cage and held it. Linda then retreated back to the other side of the office, but she soon returned. Eventually the therapist handled the snake without wearing gloves. Linda put on the gloves and then touched the therapist while he held the snake. Soon they held the snake together, and then Linda alone briefly held the snake. Therapy concluded with Linda holding the snake without wearing gloves and allowing it to crawl over her neck and shoulders.

Linda attempted at first to bargain for stopping short of actually holding the snake while not wearing gloves, but at the conclusion of the 3.5-hour treatment, Linda stated that she was glad she had completed the treatment. By this time, Linda was smiling triumphantly as she described her feelings about her accomplishments. As recommended by Öst (1989), the session was videotaped so that Linda could gain additional exposures at home, allowing her accomplishments to become more real. The therapist stressed the importance of Linda continuing to expose herself to snakes (e.g., at the zoo) following the one-session treatment.

Linda phoned the therapist about a month later and reported that on her trip to Texas she had in fact seen two snakes, and although it was not a pleasant experience, she was not upset by them. It was the therapist's impression that Linda had not only successfully conquered her snake phobia but also learned a method for coping with other fears and tolerating immediate discomfort for long-term benefits.

CASE EXAMPLE: FEAR OF INSECTS

John, a self-referred 34-year-old divorced mechanic, sought assistance at the Anxiety Disorders Clinic for his intense fear of insects, particularly wasps and yellow jackets. John had suffered from this fear since childhood, but it had worsened during recent years. John's insect phobia became debilitating when he changed jobs and began working in an open-air auto shop next to a large field. As wasps, bees, and yellow jackets are plentiful in Oregon during the spring and summer months, these insects, among others, frequently found their way into the shop and built nests in the rafters. Although the owner of the shop sprayed on a seasonal basis, the insects were too plentiful to get rid of completely. Other than occasionally annoying the other mechanics, the pests when left alone posed no particular problem. The presence of the wasps, however, was too much for John, who found his fears significantly interfering with his concentration and performance on the job. After 2 months of "emotional torture" and a stern warning from his boss, John entered into therapy at the Anxiety Disorders Clinic.

After an initial session in which simple phobia was diagnosed and a thorough psychosocial history gathered, John was presented with several therapeutic alternatives (e.g., Ost's one-session treatment). John decided that he preferred a combination of exposure and RET, and with the therapist proceeded to set up such a program. After being introduced to the principles of RET, John identified the following irrational beliefs:

1. I'm sure I'm going to be attacked by a bee, and that would be horrible. (catastrophizing)
2. I must not appear to be afraid, otherwise I'll look stupid and unmanly in front of the other mechanics. (demanding, rating of self)
3. It would be awful if a bee stung me; I'm sure I'd die from an allergic reaction. (catastrophizing)
4. Bee stings are extremely painful; I wouldn't be able to stand the pain, and that would mean I'm a rotten person. (catastrophizing; rating of self)

Shortly thereafter, John was able to dispute the foregoing cognitive distortions and voice the following rational statements:

1. Actually, there's little probability that I'll be stung. Even if I'm stung, there's an excellent chance that I'd survive.
2. It's OK to be afraid! Even if people see me as less than perfect, I still accept myself. I don't need others' approval.
3. If a bee stings me, which is unlikely, it wouldn't be awful. Instead, a bee sting simply would be an inconvenience. And there is little chance that I'd have an allergic reaction.
4. Even though bee stings are painful, I can stand the pain! I can stand just about anything! There's no reason for me to think of myself as a rotten person. I'm a good person who's less than perfect sometimes.

The exposure component of therapy first included systematic, imaginal desensitization, in which John constructed an anxiety heirarchy, learned relaxation techniques, and gradually imagined increasingly anxiety-provoking scenes from his hierarchy while relaxing. This proved to be useful for John, as he initially experienced great anxiety at the thought of approaching a bee but later became comfortable with the idea. The next component of exposure included in vivo desensitization procedures in which John once again constructed a hierarchy and gradually approached his feared object, this time in real life. The therapist was able to obtain dead and live specimens from a local biology lab supply house. In vivo exposure first involved having John look at photos of wasps and bees, then handling a jar containing a dead specimen, and finally handling a jar containing a live specimen. Over a period of eight exposure sessions, John was able to progress from barely being able to think about a bee to handling a jar containing a live bee. At 6-month follow-up, John reported both continued freedom from his previous phobia and great satisfaction at being able to function at work without distraction.

CASE EXAMPLE: FEAR OF FLYING

Sam, a 42-year-old married male grocery clerk, contacted the Anxiety Disorders Clinic for help with his fear of flying. Sam reported that he recently had flown from Portland to Seattle to make connections with a flight to Maui, where he and his wife were to spend a long-awaited vacation. Unfortunately, Sam was unable to continue on from Seattle, and he caught the flight back to Portland and cancelled the trip. In addition to preflight anticipatory apprehension concerning the plane's crashing (rather than fear of being anxious on the plane), Sam described a severe panic attack on this initial flight. He reported that as he waited for the plane to take off, his fear increased to the point that he began to experience intense physical symptoms (e.g., nausea). As the plane lifted off the ground, he had such thoughts as, "I can't go back until it lands; I must continue with these feelings and the motions of the plane. It is not normal for the plane to be having this up and down motion." Soon he noticed his heart was beating rapidly, and he felt as if he were going to lose control. This attack culminated in the flight attendants giving him a paper bag in which to breathe, followed by oxygen. During his evaluation at the Anxiety Disorders Clinic, Sam indicated that his primary fear at the time involved that of the plane crashing, as opposed to fear of losing self-control.

Sam's report of pounding heart, breathlessness, dizziness, trembling and shaking, leg rigidity, hot and cold flashes, and fear of dying from a heart attack confirmed the occurrence of a DSM-III-R panic attack. He stated that while his apprehension had been steadily rising from the beginning of the flight to being in the air, where he had his panic attack, the symptoms occurred rapidly, probably within a minute following the point when the plane dipped unexpectedly.

Assessment for previous panic attacks indicated that Sam had experienced a recent attack (3 months prior to the flight), also meeting DSM-III-R criteria, while at the dentist's office during a regular cleaning. He was tilted back in his chair and felt vulnerable and out of control, experienced a faint feeling, and became concerned about his gums bleeding and various items flowing down his throat, preventing him from being able to swallow. Sam recalled one additional attack, which met DSM-III-R criteria, 1.5 years prior during a relaxation training session with a therapist. Sam reported suddenly feeling numb and faint, in addition to various other physiological and cognitive symptoms. He stated that he did not have continuing fear of having future panic attacks following these early attacks. However, he did fear having an attack while on another airplane, in deep water, or in a high place of approximately 10 or more stories.

Several of Sam's fears appeared related to his upbringing following the death of his father when Sam was 9 years old. Sam lived with his mother, who also was fearful of heights, deep water, and flying. He also described childhood memories of having polyps removed from his nasal passages and gagging after substances flowed down his throat. Furthermore, he remembered that on his first flight at age 14 with his grandmother, he became frightened when he discovered that the plane was low on fuel.

As part of the assessment, Sam was administered the FQ, the Spielberger Trait Anxiety Inventory, the MI, an expanded version of the ACQ, the BSQ, the BDI, Belief scale, and the EPQ-N. Most of his scores were within or slightly above normal, except for the BSQ, which was significantly above normal. The body sensations listed as most fearful were numbness in arms or legs, dizziness, and shortness of breath. On the ACQ, the thoughts most likely to occur during times of anxiety were, "I'm going to pass out," "I'll have a heart attack," and "I'll choke to death."

Although Sam exhibited a symptom constellation suggestive of PD, a diagnosis of simple phobia was given instead. Factors that argued against a diagnosis of PD included (a) lack of fear of having future attacks, (b) overall low frequency of attacks, and (c) a predominant pattern of attacks being cued by phobic situations (e.g., dentist's office). Sam did acknowledge, however, significant fear of panic in the phobic situations. Thus, panic management was included as part of the overall treatment program. Finally, in assessing the specific nature of Sam's fear of flying, it appeared that neither fear of heights nor of closed spaces played significant roles. Rather, the primary fear reported was that of the plane crashing, this fear being precipitated in flight by unexpected movements of the plane, which in turn triggered negative, catastrophic cognitions. Nevertheless, Sam did experience significant fears concerning loss of self-control that appeared to be related to certain unpleasant physical sensations (e.g., dizziness).

Therapy, the primary goal of which was to help Sam feel comfortable flying in airplanes, lasted for 13 sessions. The treatment program consisted of education regarding the nature of panic attacks and the fight or flight response, cue-controlled relaxation and diaphragm breathing, interoceptive assessment and exposure, imaginal exposure to a taped flight, homework assignments, and bibliotherapy (e.g., Ellis's *How to Master Your Fear of Flying*, 1972a; Ellis and Harper's *A New Guide to Rational Living*, 1975). Therapy also included a practice flight from Portland to Seattle with the therapist. Additional assignments (e.g., swinging on swings, driving rapidly down hills in an automobile, watching chase scenes in movies) were given to stimulate unpleasant body sensations related to fear of loss of self-control. Sam used his panic management skills (e.g., breathing exercises, rational self-statements) to cope with his feared body sensations.

Sam demonstrated significant improvements, as evidenced by pre- and posttest scores and by increased comfort in being able to face phobic situations. Of course, the nature of this uncontrolled case study does not permit us to attribute the effects of Sam's improvement unequivocally to treatment. He made four flights within a 5-month period, and he phoned the therapist after the fourth flight to inform him that although he was not as comfortable with flying as he would like to be, he did feel that he had reached his therapy goals and would call the clinic should he need additional help in the future.

The most direct RET intervention in this case involved processing Sam's fear of dying. Exploration into his fears uncovered the belief that when he died he would feel sad when looking back on the people whom he had left. In accordance with Ellis's (1972a) *How to Master Your Fear of Flying*, the therapist and Sam discussed the likelihood of his looking back after death and being conscious of and concerned about that which he had missed. Also, on philosophical grounds, Sam made good efforts to work at accepting the low probability of actually being involved in a plane crash. He began to see death from a plane crash as not being more terrible than death by some other means (e.g., from health complications late in life). Cognitive therapy allowed Sam to confront his demand for a guarantee that he would live to old age, which he believed was the best time to die.

Chapter 6
Obsessive Compulsive Disorder

Compared to the other anxiety disorders, obsessive compulsive disorder (OCD) is associated with the greatest amount and most pervasive pattern of fear (Turner & Beidel, 1988; Turner, McCann, Beidel, & Mezzich, 1986). As Barlow (1988) suggested, if a patient with an anxiety disorder needs hospitalization, is referred for psychosurgery when previous psychological and pharmacological treatments have failed, or reports severe generalized anxiety, recurrent panic attacks, debilitative avoidance, and major depression, the diagnosis is likely to be OCD. While issues of control and predictability are implicated to various degrees throughout the anxiety disorders, OCD clients often are the seemingly most helpless and hopeless along these dimensions and thus resort to "magic and rituals in a vain attempt to re-establish a small haven of safety" (Barlow, 1988, p. 598).

According to Steketee and Foa (1985), the clinical syndrome now labeled OCD was first identified by Esquirol (1838) and has changed little since that time. OCD is characterized by various combinations of obsessions and compulsions, with the DSM-III-R definition of obsessions being "persistent ideas, thoughts, impulses or images that are experienced . . . as intrusive and senseless" and the definition of compulsions being "repetitive, purposeful, and intentional behaviors that are performed in response to an obsession, according to certain rules, or in a stereotyped fashion" (p. 245). This traditional, behavioral definition of obsessions and compulsions, however, has not satisfactorily accommodated OCD clinical phenomena nor served as a useful guide for behavioral treatments. Foa and her colleagues (e.g., Steketee & Foa, 1985) proposed an alternative model of obsessions and compulsions that includes covert or cognitive events as compulsions. In oversimpli-

Table 6.1. Obsessions and Related Compulsions

Obsession	Compulsion
1. *Contamination:* What if I spread cancer germs to my children?	Avoids objects or locations thought to be contaminated
	Washes ritualistically
2. *Harm:* Did I run over someone with my car?	Turns car around and looks for body
Did I turn off the stove?	Repeatedly checks stove
3. *Religion:* Christ is the devil.	Repeats "Christ is Lord. Praise the Lord."
4. *Sex:* What if I'm a homosexual?	Avoids looking at pictures of men in magazines for fear of arousal
5. *Symmetry:* Both of my eyebrows must look the same.	Spends hours trimming eyebrows
6. *Hoarding:* I can't throw this away.	Refuses to throw away anything

fied terms, obsessions increase anxiety, while either cognitive compulsions, which may take forms similar to obsessions, or behavioral compulsions, which typically include washing and checking rituals, obsessional slowing of activity ("primary obsessional slowness"), and counting rituals, are attempts to decrease anxiety. For example, a client may have the anxiety-producing thought, "What if I threw my baby out the window?" (obsession) followed by the anxiety-neutralizing thought, "I love my baby; Christ is my savior" (cognitive compulsion), which serves to reduce the anxiety. Table 6.1 contains examples of obsessions and related compulsions.

Obsessions have been delineated according to both content and form. As Barlow noted (1988) and as is shown in Table 6.1, studies consistently demonstrate that the most common themes reflected in obsessions are contamination, aggression and violence, religion, sex, somatic concerns, and the need for symmetry. Salkovskis and Kirk (1989) suggested that the content of obsessions reflects central concerns of the time (e.g., work of the devil, contamination by radiation, or fear of contracting acquired immunodeficiency syndrome [AIDS]). Carr (1974) noted that obsessional content typically includes exaggerations of normal concerns held by most people (Steketee & Foa, 1985). As for form, the DSM-III-R delineation of obsessions as ideas, thoughts, images, or impulses covers this domain, as various combinations of different content and form comprise OCD obsessional phenomena. For example, "What if I get cancer germs from touching that dollar bill?" combines content (contamination) with form (thought).

Concerning prevalence of the disorder, DSM-III-R states that "although the disorder was previously thought to be relatively rare in the general population, recent community studies indicate that mild forms of the disorder may be relatively common" (p. 246). Although prevalence was most often estimated at 0.05% (Runch, 1983), the ECA survey recently revealed lifetime rates of 2% to 3%, which is 40 to 50 times greater than figures estimated from earlier clinical investigations (Karno, Golding, Sorenson, & Burnam, 1988). It has also been discovered that obsessions and compulsions occur frequently in the normal population, with 80% to 90% of those surveyed reporting obsessive thoughts and impulses almost identical to those of OCD clients (Barlow, 1988; Rachman & de Silva, 1978; Salkovskis & Harrison, 1984) and 10% to 15% of a large college student sample scoring in the clinical range on the Maudsley Obsessional-Compulsive Inventory (Frost, Sher, & Geen, 1986).

As for age of onset, OCD typically begins in early adulthood and peaks from 18 to 25, although the disorder also appears in childhood and adolescence. Minichiello, Baer, Jenike, and Holland (1990) reported a mean age of onset of 22 years with males, a significantly earlier onset than females (25 years). Further, "cleaners" (27 years) reported a significantly later age of onset than did both "checkers" (18 years) and patients with mixed rituals (19 years).

ETIOLOGY OF OCD

A biopsychosocial explanation of the etiology of OCD includes behavioral, cognitive-behavioral, and biological components. Behavioral theory of OCD has usually included Mowrer's (1939) two-stage theory, as well as its elaboration by Dollard and Miller (1950), to account for the development and maintenance of OCD symptomatology. Classical conditioning accounts for the initial learning of fear via association of unconditioned with conditioned stimuli, which include concrete objects in addition to words, thoughts, and images. When the conditioned stimuli are further associated with additional neutral stimuli, higher order conditioning occurs, often obscuring the original conditioning process. Furthermore, operant conditioning accounts for the maintenance of OCD via negative reinforcement, as behaviors that result in escape or avoidance from the anxiety-evoking situation are acquired and strengthened with repetition.

Due to the wider range of generalization, which typically involves thoughts and images (e.g., harming someone, blasphemous fantasies), passive avoidance is often inadequate, so active avoidance (e.g., rituals) is initiated. Although some rituals are related to the source of fear (e.g., washing after having touched contaminated objects), other rituals may be acquired superstitiously through coincidental performance of behaviors that produce relief when in the presence of anxiety-evoking stimuli (e.g., rubbing a particular part of the body).

While the two-factor theory accounts nicely for avoidance behavior, it fares less well in attempting to explain initial fear acquisition. For example, most OCD clients do not recall conditioning events associated with symptom onset; instead, they often report preceding stressful life events (Grayson, Foa, & Steketee, 1985).

Cognitive-behavioral theories include those articulated by McFall and Wollersheim (1979), Salkovskis (1985), and Foa and her colleagues (e.g., Foa & Kozak, 1986; Kozak, Foa, & McCarthy, 1988; Steketee & Foa, 1985). McFall and Wollersheim (1979) theorized that OCs also hold unusually high negative valence for unpleasant events. Offering an initial RET analysis of OCD phenomena, McFall and Wollersheim (1979) proposed that the negative valence is partly due to irrational beliefs held by OCs.

Foa and Kozak (1986) suggested that OCs show impairment in epistemological reasoning, estimates of the probability of harm, negative valence associated with the feared harm, and rules for discrimination. Concerning epistemological reasoning, while most people operate on the assumption that a situation is safe unless there is valid evidence for danger, OCs appear to assume that situations are dangerous unless proven otherwise. Because evidence for total safety is rarely available, OCs are tormented with indecisiveness and doubt regarding safety versus danger, and they resort to compulsive rituals in an effort to guarantee safety. Moreover, as Carr (1974) and McFall and Wollersheim (1979) noted, OCs appear to overestimate the probability of danger occuring and to hold abnormally high negative valence for feared events, which may involve a disaster to oneself or another (stimuli; e.g., becoming contaminated with cancer germs and infecting a loved one) or the experience of anxiety and discomfort itself (responses).

Barlow (1988) presented a cognitive-behavioral-biological model of OCD. When individuals in the general population experience stress, as is common in response to certain life events, intrusive thoughts and images may occur. Due to biological vulnerability, certain individuals have more intense biological responses, at times including negative and/or anxious affect. Individuals, because of psychological vulnerabilities,

develop the notion that certain thoughts are dangerous or unacceptable, leading susceptible individuals to respond to such cognitive events
with false alarms. Anxious apprehension or worry over the occurrence
of future obsessions ensues, along with a hypervigilant narrowing of
focus of attention on such thoughts. Due to the inherent unpredicta-
bility, uncontrollability, and internal nature of cognitive events, cognitive avoidance is virtually impossible. Hence, feelings of helplessness
and depression are frequent reactions to this process, providing fertile
ground for intrusive thoughts. Attempts to suppress unwanted thoughts
may actually increase their frequency such that cognitive and behavioral compulsions are attempted in a desperate effort to prevent predicted danger or harm.

Salkovskis (1985) presented an approach similar to Barlow's (1988)
that uses Beck's (1976) cognitive therapy principles and procedures.
According to Salkovskis (1985), intrusive thoughts, images, or impulses
experienced by 80% to 90% of the normal population do not lead to
emotional disturbance except when the obsessive thoughts lead to negative automatic thoughts.

> In terms of Beck's model, intrusions may for some individuals on some
> occasions activate preexisting dysfunctional schemata and hence result in
> unpleasant automatic thoughts. Such automatic thoughts in response to
> intrusions appear to relate specifically to ideas of being responsible for
> damage or harm coming to oneself or to others. . . . Clearly, such ideas
> of responsibility would lead to self-condemnation in vulnerable individ-
> uals to the extent that such responsibility . . . is abhorrent to them. . . .
> They presumably regard themselves as being responsible for being a bad
> or evil person unless they take steps to ensure their blamelessness. The
> affective disturbance usually described as arising from the obsession or
> intrusion actually arises from such automatic thoughts about the intru-
> sion rather than from the intrusion itself. (p. 574)

Mood disturbance, both preexisting and resulting from automatic
thoughts, is theorized to increase both obsessions and compulsions.
Salkovskis (1985) viewed neutralization, both covert cognitive and overt
behavioral rituals, as attempts to avoid the possibility of being blamed
by self or others for causing or not preventing harm. Individuals described by Rachman and Hodgson (1980) as being of "tender conscience" (p. 252) are considered to be vulnerable both to developing
negative automatic thoughts in reaction to intrusions and also to developing rituals. Salkovskis (1985) suggested, especially in the early stages
of OCD, that the effort required for neutralization is minimal compared
to the feared catastrophic consequences of failure to neutralize. Salkovskis also argued that OCs specifically overestimate the probability of
being the agent of serious harm on oneself or others, rather than the
probability of the occurrence of harm per se. This argument is consistent with evidence that OCs, compared to phobics, are sensitive to crit-

icism from self and others (Turner, Steketee, & Foa, 1979). Salkovskis (1989) refined and expanded his 1985 formulation, responded to criticisms by Jakes (1989a, 1989b), and presented recent empirical findings consistent with certain of his hypotheses. For example, in a survey of 243 nonclinical subjects (Salkovskis & Dent, 1989), as predicted, subjects who neutralized had higher scores on ratings of attitudes concerning responsibility for harm but not on attitudes of threat or loss without a component of responsibility (Salkovskis, 1989, p. 680).

According to Klein, Rabkin, and Gorman (1985), the most widely endorsed biological etiological hypothesis for OCD involves a functional deficiency of brain serotonin (Yaryura-Tobias, 1977). Clomipramine (Anafranil), which is the most extensively evaluated medication for treating OCD and considered the pharmacological treatment of choice for the disorder, is thought to block neuronal reuptake of serotonin. Also, that clomipramine results in improvement in OCD symptomatology is often taken as support for this serotonin hypothesis. Additional support is derived from studies that have found abnormal markers for platelet serotonin in the CNS, as well as various neuroendocrine abnormalities found in OCD clients but not in normal or psychiatric controls (Insel, Mueller, Linnoila, & Murphy, 1985; Zohar & Insel, 1987). However, other research suggests that both serotonergic and noradrenergic systems are involved in OCD (Hollander et al., 1988). Finally, other neurobiological studies have attempted to isolate abnormalities specific to OCD. For example, Rappaport (1989) reported that there is now evidence from recent Positron Emission Tomography (PET) research that the caudate nucleus area of the basal ganglia and certain portions of the frontal lobes behave differently in OCD clients than in controls. EEG studies also reflect frontal lobe dysfunction during information processing (Flor-Henry, Yendall, Koles, & Howarth, 1979; McCarthy, 1986). Finally, McCarthy and Foa (1990) reviewed several evoked-potential studies and concluded that "electrocortical data suggest that a centrally based pathophysiological component exists for OCD and that the frontal lobe region is the site of the dysfunction" (p. 218).

DSM-III-R CLASSIFICATION AND DIAGNOSTIC CRITERIA FOR OCD

Table 6.2 presents the DSM-III-R diagnostic criteria for obsessive compulsive disorder (300.30). Individuals with obsessive compulsive disorder experience impairment across several areas. Among these are the person's cognitive, emotive, and behavioral response systems. Examples of impairment are persistent recurrent thoughts, heightened affect, and compulsive actions performed in response to obsessions.

Table 6.2. DSM-III-R Diagnostic Criteria for Obsessive Compulsive Disorder

A. Either obsessions or compulsions:
    Obsessions: (1), (2), (3), and (4):
    (1) recurrent and persistent ideas, thoughts, impulses, or images that are experi-enced, at least initially, as intrusive and senseless, e.g., a parent's having repeated impulses to kill a loved child, a religious person's having recurrent blasphemous thoughts
    (2) the person attempts to ignore or suppress such thoughts or impulses or to neu-tralize them with some other thought or action
    (3) the person recognizes that the obsessions are the product of his or her own mind, not imposed from without (as in thought insertion)
    (4) if another Axis I disorder is present, the content of the obsession is unrelated to it, e.g., the ideas, thoughts, impulses, or images are not about food in the presence of an Eating Disorder, about drugs in the presence of a Psychoactive Substance Use Disorder, or guilt thoughts in the presence of a Major Depression
    Compulsions: (1), (2), and (3):
    (1) repetitive, purposeful, and intentional behaviors that are performed in response to an obsession, or according to certain rules or in a stereotyped fashion
    (2) the behavior is designed to neutralize or to prevent discomfort or some dreaded event or situation; however, either the activity is not connected in a realistic way with what it is designed to neutralize or prevent, or it is clearly excessive
    (3) the person recognizes that his or her behavior is excessive or unreasonable (this may or may not be true for young children; it may no longer be true for people whose obsessions have evolved into overvalued ideas)

B. The obsessions or compulsions cause marked distress, are time-consuming (take more than an hour a day), or significantly interfere with the person's normal routine, occupational functioning, or usual social activities or relationships with others

Note. Reprinted with permission from the *Diagnostic and Statistical Manual of Mental Disorders, Third Edition, Revised.* Copyright 1987 American Psychiatric Association.

REVIEW OF ASSESSMENT INSTRUMENTS

The most practical methods for assessing OCD include the clinical interview, clinician-administered rating scales, self-report measures of OCD and related emotional distress, and self-monitoring devices. In addition, although it is unavailable to most clinicians, psychophysio-logical assessment can provide useful corroborative data (Turner & Bei-del, 1988). The clinical interview holds direct value for the clinician when establishing a DSM-III-R diagnosis, with the ADIS-R (Di Nardo et al., 1985) providing a structured, psychometrically sound format. In addition, several self-report measures are practical and useful in the clinical setting, including the Maudsley Obsessional-Compulsive Inventory (MOCI; Hodgson & Rachman, 1977), which uses a true-false format to assess cognitive and behavioral aspects of OCD although without measuring severity. The MOCI contains four subscales: wash-ing, checking, slowness, and doubting. Two instruments that measure the degree of severity of OCD symptomatology are the Compulsive-

Activity Checklist (CAC; see Freund, Steketee, & Foa, 1987) and the Yale-Brown Obsessive-Compulsive Scale (Y-BOCS; Goodman et al., 1989), a 10-item instrument that differentiates OCD symptoms from those of other anxiety disorders and depression and also measures sensitivity to changes following drug treatment. Finally, self-monitoring devices have been widely used in measuring OCD symptomatology. Barlow (1988) described self-monitoring procedures for frequency and duration of obsessive thoughts, rituals, and distress stemming from obsessions and urges to perform rituals. Turner and Beidel (1988) emphasized the importance of creating self-monitoring methods that are simple enough to increase compliance, although some accuracy may be sacrificed.

REVIEW OF NON-RET TREATMENTS

As Foa, Steketee, and Ozarow (1985) concluded, a combination of exposure and response prevention is the treatment of choice for OCD sufferers. Summarizing findings of 18 controlled studies of over 200 patients treated with these methods at centers around the world, Foa et al. (1985) found that at posttreatment, 51% of patients were either symptom free or much improved, 39% were moderately improved, and 10% failed to benefit from treatment. At follow-up, approximately 75% had maintained their gains. Failure to include either the exposure or response prevention components resulted in reduced effectiveness, as did omission of imaginal exposure to feared disasters associated with obsessions (Steketee, Foa, & Grayson, 1982). For a comprehensive review of the effectiveness of other behavior therapy procedures with OCD (e.g., systematic desensitization, thought stopping), see Foa et al. (1985).

As indicated earlier, clomipramine is the most extensively evaluated psychopharmacological treatment for OCD. Although it is not without controversy, clomipramine appears to have specific antiobsessive effects that are at least partially separate from antidepressant effects (Mavissakalian, Turner, Michelson, & Jacob, 1985). Some studies show support for the effectiveness of imipramine (Tofranil), which may also have direct antiobsessional effects (e.g., Mavissakalian et al., 1985). However, a recent placebo-controlled study (Foa, Steketee, Kozak, & Dugger, 1987) found imipramine to be superior to placebo in reducing depression, but no better than placebo in ameliorating OCD symptoms. Fluoxetine (Prozac) has also yielded encouraging results in early studies (e.g., Turner, Beidel, Stanley, & Jacob, 1988), as has fluvoxamine (Faverin; Price, Goodman, Charney, Rasmussen, & Heninger, 1987).

Pigott et al. (1990) recently found fluoxetine and clomipramine equally effective in the treatment of OCD.

While the beneficial effects of clomipramine on OCD symptomatology are well documented, several factors limit its usefulness, including negative side effects and relapse on discontinuation (Turner & Beidel, 1988). In addition, as Anath (1985) noted, "Most studies indicate that clomipramine does not eradicate obsessive disorder. The urge to perform an act may remain, but the emotional force attached to the urge goes away" (p. 191). That clomipramine does not eradicate OCD is apparent when improvement rates are observed. Rappaport (1989) noted that clomipramine appears to help about 75% of patients, a rate comparable to results achieved by behavior therapy. However, according to Foa (1990a), clomipramine is helpful with only 50% of OCD sufferers. If average degree of improvement across the patients who are helped by clomipramine is examined, Turner and Beidel (1988) noted improvement rates ranging from 28% to 34%, Steketee and Foa (1985) cited studies reporting rates ranging from 40% to 42%, and Foa (1990a) concluded that there is a 35% reduction in symptoms. When comparing these improvement rates with those reported by Foa et al. (1985), behavior therapy clearly remains the treatment of choice. For severely depressed OCD patients, a combination of behavioral and drug therapies may prove to be the most potent treatment program.

COGNITIVE THERAPY AND OCD

Salkovskis has written more extensively than anyone else on the integration of cognitive interventions into exposure and response prevention procedures (e.g., Salkovskis & Kirk, 1989; Salkovskis & Westbrook, 1987). Nonetheless, only one report of effectiveness has been reported to date (Salkovskis & Warwick, 1985).

The first controlled study evaluating the clinical efficacy of a cognitive approach in the treatment of OCD was conducted by Emmelkamp, van der Helm, Van Zanten, and Plochg (1980). Results indicated that self-instructional training (SIT) does not enhance the effectiveness of in vivo exposure; however, Steketee and Foa (1985), in response to the study, suggested that failure of SIT to enhance treatment should not necessarily be taken to mean that cognitive treatment should not be implemented with OCs. In discussing a sample therapist-client dialogue, Foa and Steketee (1987) noted that "the informal application of cognitive strategies is so embedded in the behavior of the sensitive therapist that it is difficult, if not impossible, to estimate the extent to which cognitive methods are required " (p. 103). Steketee and Foa (1985) also suggested that studies need to evaluate the effectiveness of cognitive procedures tailored to the specific cognitive deficits empirically shown to be associated with OCD.

Emmelkamp, Visser, and Hoekstra (1988) hypothesized that treatment focusing on OCs' irrational beliefs (e.g., those suggested by McFall & Wollersheim, 1979) might be more appropriate than SIT. Eighteen DSM-III–diagnosed OCs were randomly assigned to either RET or self-controlled in vivo exposure and response prevention. Both treatments resulted in significant reductions in OCD symptomatology and social anxiety. The authors found that clients who improved with RET, on their own initiative, started exposing themselves to feared situations. Emmelkamp et al. (1988) also speculated that perhaps RET was largely effective due to its adding pressure to clients to behave more rationally and to engage in exposure rather than rituals.

The effectiveness of RET in this first controlled study of OCs is encouraging of further studies that include the behavioral component of RET. Actually, it is surprising that only the cognitive part of RET was as effective as it was in Emmelkamp et al.'s (1988) study, as it is accepted that the behavioral component (i.e., exposure) of anxiety therapy is essential (Ellis, 1979b).

A RET MODEL FOR OCD

The RET model that we propose is similar to those developed by Barlow (1988), Rachman and Hodgson (1980), and Salkovskis (1985), although we emphasize the role of irrational beliefs. As outlined in Figure 6.1, we hypothesize that individuals who develop OCD are vulnerable biologically, not specifically in terms of developing OCD, but instead to developing some anxiety disorder. Rather than positing specific neuroanatomical abnormalities (e.g., serotonin deficiency), we hypothesize a nonspecific biological vulnerability, such as a labile or overactive ANS as discussed by Eysenck (1967). Our view is consistent with Barlow's (1988) hypothesis concerning an "overactive hypothalamic-pituitary-adrenocortical system and/or labile neurotransmitter systems" (p. 268).

Developmental and learning experiences include those experiences specifically related to what kinds of thoughts are acceptable versus unacceptable, and what it means to have certain thoughts as well as more general beliefs about oneself, others, and the world. We also hypothesize that biological vulnerabilities make it easier for one to develop irrational beliefs and thinking styles, and that individuals not only learn these beliefs from parents and other social sources but also create their own. The types of irrational beliefs associated with developing OCD are discussed later in this chapter.

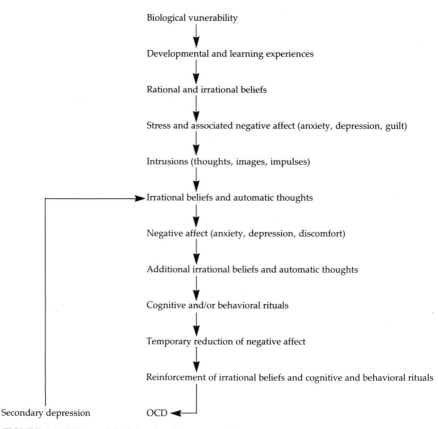

FIGURE 6.1. RET model of the development of obsessive compulsive disorder.

Stressful life events may lead to negative affect (e.g., anxiety, depression), which becomes fertile ground for developing intrusive thoughts. As Barlow (1988) noted, stress and associated negative affect seem to be antecedents to intrusive thoughts in both normals and OCs. Guilt also appears to be an antecedent to intrusive thoughts (Niler & Beck, 1989). From a RET perspective, the stress we are discussing here is also partly determined by one's beliefs, which influence both the nature and extent of events one seeks and also one's emotional responses to the beliefs (see chapter 2).

As indicated earlier, 80% to 90% of normals report the occurrence of intrusive thoughts, yet only 2% to 3% of the population develops OCD. To account for this phenomenon, we hypothesize that when intrusive thoughts are responded to with irrational beliefs and thinking styles, debilitative emotions of anxiety and depression are created. Certain behaviors (e.g., checking) then reinforce the development of rituals to alleviate the negative affect, in addition to reinforcing the belief that "I must eliminate the uncertainty and related discomfort that originally was associated with the intrusive thought." Attention narrowing occurs (Barlow, 1988) as the individual becomes hypervigilant to future unacceptable intrusions. As this cycle is continually re-created, the individual develops OCD. When the OCD patient then develops a reactive depression, he or she becomes the victim of what is known in RET as symptom stress or problems about problems. Further irrational beliefs are thus viewed as causative: "I must not have obsessions and compulsions; I can't stand the discomfort. I'll never get over this, and I'm less of a person for having this disorder."

Before discussing specific irrational beliefs associated with OCD, a review of basic personality and cognitive characteristics of these individuals is in order. As Persons (1989) recommends as a method of ascertaining underlying mechanisms (i.e., irrational beliefs) leading to depressive symptoms, cognitive and behavioral characteristics of OCD patients may suggest basic irrational beliefs from which these characteristics may emerge. Foa and Steketee (1985) reviewed several studies and concluded that OCs tend to be rigid, perfectionistic, doubting, and demanding of excessive amounts of information to make decisions. Similarly, Emmelkamp (1982) summarized literature suggesting that OCs have difficulty tolerating uncertainty and ambiguity, are reluctant to take risks, and have abnormally high estimates of the unpleasantness of making mistakes. Furthermore, OCs, compared to phobics, have a greater fear of criticism, probably both from self and others (Turner et al., 1979). Several nonempirically confirmed tendencies are also apparent, including making errors in epistemological reasoning (Foa & Kozak, 1985) and holding abnormally high estimates of being the agent of harm on others (Salkovskis, 1985). Foa and Steketee (1987) stated that "another psychopathological feature that distinguishes anxious individuals from normals is the high negative valence they attach to discomfort itself" (p. 89). Accordingly, Foa and Kozak (1985), although not specifically discussing OCD, suggested that

> the high negative valence for anxiety itself, which often characterizes individuals with anxiety disorders, will also result in increased avoidance behavior. This negative valence for anxiety may reflect a more general attitude about discomfort. One of the factors that may be involved in the development of at least certain anxiety disorders is the relative intolerance of discomfort and the belief that stress should be avoided. (p. 444)

Specifically referring to OCD, Foa and Steketee (1987) noted that "the obsessive-compulsive refrains from touching doorknobs [which produces only mild to moderate anxiety] and also manifests such oversensitivity [to discomfort]" (p. 89).

Concerning OCD-related irrational beliefs, of Ellis's three major musts (see chapter 2), the first and third account for more personally idiosyncratic derivative beliefs that lead to OCD characteristics. Hence, a person who in a global sense believes "I must perform well and/or win the approval of others or else it's awful, and I'm an inadequate or worthless person" would likely hold such specific beliefs as the following:

1. I must make the correct decision, and if I don't, it would be awful, and I would be less of a person.
2. I must have perfect certainty that I won't be the cause of harm to anyone. If I did, it would be terrible, and I would be a terrible person.
3. I must not have bizarre or unacceptable thoughts or impulses.

Each of these beliefs is typically followed by evaluations of awfulness and/or self-rating.

People who hold must 3, "My life conditions must be comfortable, or I can't be happy at all," would likely hold more OCD-relevant beliefs such as the following:

1. I can't stand the discomfort of not checking. It's horrible to experience such discomfort.
2. I can't stand the anxiety I get when I'm exposed to contaminants.
3. I can't stand the uncertainty of not having an absolute guarantee of safety for myself and others.

While the foregoing musts are considered to be central to OCD, the person who believes "others must treat me fairly and considerately; if they don't, they are rotten people," likely would hold beliefs such as the following:

1. My family must cooperate with me by helping me perform rituals.
2. My partner should clean the house so I can avoid germs.
3. Others should be understanding and accepting of my OCD condition.

As the reader reviews Ellis's (1962) original 11 irrational beliefs, it becomes apparent that most of these beliefs can be subsumed under the three musts and are relevant to OCD symptomatology. From the preceding examples, the three types of irrational thinking—demanding, catastrophizing, rating of self and others—are embedded in the more global "musturbatory ideologies," and the two basic forms of psychological disturbance posited by Ellis—ego disturbance and discomfort disturbance—also appear basically characteristic of OCD patients (e.g., "I'm a worthless person for having blasphemous thoughts, and I can't stand the discomfort of not ritualizing").

Finally, given Ellis's distinction between inferential and evaluative beliefs, the preceding examples are largely of an evaluative nature. In contrast, the dysfunctional assumptions suggested by Salkovskis (1985) as being likely to interact with intrusive thoughts (e.g., "My failing to prevent harm to self or others is the same as having caused the harm in the first place"), from a RET perspective, would be considered an inferential belief. This belief becomes evaluative when the individual concludes, "Therefore, I must prevent harm to self and others. If I don't, it's catastrophic, and I'm a bad person." For additional dysfunctional assumptions, see Salkovskis (1985) for several examples of automatic thoughts that follow intrusions and lead to behavioral consequences, similar to Ellis's ABC model.

Thus, our RET model hypothesizes evaluative beliefs as being most influential in contributing to OCD phenomena, although inferential dysfunctional assumptions, such as those described by Salkovskis (1985), would also be predicted to lead to significant negative affect and related behavioral consequences. For example, some of McFall and Wollersheim's (1979) beliefs (e.g., "One should be perfectly competent, adequate, and achieving in all possible respects in order to be worthwhile and to avoid criticism or disapproval by others or oneself") are best classified as evaluative, while others (e.g., "One is powerful enough to initiate or prevent the occurence of disastrous outcomes by magical rituals or obsessive ruminations") are classified as inferential.

In summary, our RET model of OCD views development of the disorder as resulting from the interaction of biological and psychological vulnerabilities. Central to the domain of psychological vulnerabilities are irrational beliefs, particularly evaluative ones that involve demanding, catastrophizing, and self-rating in response to issues of performance, approval, and discomfort. These irrational beliefs and thinking styles associated with intrusive thoughts lead to negative affect and cognitive and behavioral rituals designed to reduce discomfort and establish a sense of self-control. However, rather than leading to control, compulsions reinforce irrational beliefs and perpetuate intrusions, which may lead to reactive depression. Such beliefs contribute to the individual's likelihood of developing the kind of cognitive impairment noted by Foa and her colleagues (e.g., Kozak et al. 1988) as specifically characteristic of OCD clients.

TREATMENT OF OCD: A RET PERSPECTIVE

The exposure and response prevention treatment of OCD has been described elsewhere (e.g., Emmelkamp, 1982; Steketee & Foa, 1985; Turner & Beidel, 1988), and Steketee and White (1990) have recently published a detailed self-help book for OC's which also provides step-by-step guidelines useful to therapists. Rather than redescribing these procedures we allude to them when necessary to explain several RET and cognitive interventions hypothesized to enhance basic behavioral treatment of OCD.

Our treatment plan first involves, over a period of a few sessions, administering self-report measures and gathering self-monitoring data and information to create a hierarchy of anxiety-arousing cues and to target compulsive rituals for response prevention. Motivational interviewing, as described by Miller (1983) for working with problem drinkers, can be used to enhance the client's motivation for treatment, as up to 25% of patients regarded as suitable for behavior therapy refuse treatment once it is described, and up to 12% terminate prematurely (Salkovskis & Warwick, 1988).

In addition, our RET model includes the components discussed next.

Dealing with Responsibility and Reassurance Seeking

As Salkovskis and Westbrook (1987) explained, many OCs seek to avoid responsibility for potentially harming someone and seek reassurance that they will not do so. In essence, reassurance seeking becomes an anxiety-reducing ritual. Here, as with other aspects of OCD, treatment involves exposure and response prevention. For example, by having the client not repeatedly check that the stove is turned off, the OC is exposed to the low-risk possibility of being the cause of harm. Having the OC not ask others for reassurance that the stove is turned off is response prevention. Often, however, reassurance seeking can be more subtle, as when the client attributes responsibility for the consequences of not ritualizing to the therapist who provided the instructions for the assignment. Salkovskis and Westbrook (1987) recommended that to address this issue therapists ask clients to plan and execute some of the therapeutic tasks without telling anyone, including the therapist, the nature of the specific actions. Therapists can subsequently discuss the outcome and address the resulting cognitions and emotions, without knowing what exposure was undertaken.

Treatment of Obsessions with Cognitive but not Behavioral Rituals

In reviewing possible causes for the relative ineffectiveness of previous treatments for "pure" obsessions, Salkovskis and Westbrook (1989) concluded that this problem is due to failing to apply in an appropriate way exposure and response prevention. Thus, rather than applying thought stopping or other blocking procedures to obsessions, these techniques should be applied to the cognitive rituals. For example, the obsession "Christ is the devil" may be followed by the covert ritualistic thought, "Jesus is Lord." Treatment would then consist of exposure to the initial obsession and response prevention to the covert ritual. The latter may be implemented with thought-stopping or distraction techniques. Finally, for the exposure portion of treatment, Salkovskis and Westbrook (1989) and Salkovskis and Kirk (1989) provided detailed instructions for the creative use of audiotapes for exposure to the intrusive cognitions. Briefly, clients record in their own voice specific obsessions (i.e., without the covert ritualistic thought) on "looped" casettes that continuously play the intrusive thoughts.

Overvalued Ideation

One apparent risk factor for failure in OCD treatment is overvalued ideation (Foa, 1979), which refers to harm-related beliefs that the client does not easily dismiss as irrational but instead views as valid—similar to delusional processes. In fact, Foa (1990a), who originally coined the term *overvalued ideation*, now views such strongly held beliefs as delusional.

Salkovskis and Warwick (1985) described the use of cognitive therapy to weaken a client's belief that she could contract cancer from any form of ultraviolet light. This belief proved to be an obstacle to successful implementation of exposure and response prevention. Examining the evidence for and against the belief that she had cancer resulted in a reduction in the strength of the belief from 90% to 40%, a reduction in depression, and an increase in her compliance with treatment.

Chadwick and Lowe (1990) described a procedure that successfully modifies delusional beliefs in schizophrenics and that may also be useful for OCs:

1. During baseline evaluation, information concerning the nature of the belief is collected, with special emphasis on past and present evidence that helped to establish and maintain the belief.
2. The client is presented with each piece of cited evidence and is asked to rank each in order of importance to the belief system.
3. The client is encouraged to view the delusional belief as only one possible interpretation of events and is asked to consider specific alternatives. The therapist then explains the way in which already formed beliefs influence future interpretation of events.
4. After reviewing all of the evidence, the belief itself is challenged in

a nonconfrontational manner. Challenging the belief is carried out in three overlapping stages:

a. Inconsistencies and irrationalities within the belief system are discussed (i.e., "Would it make sense for things to be as you say?").
b. A viable, alternative explanation for the development of the belief is offered.
c. It is argued that the experimenter's account is a better explanation (than the delusion) of the client's experience.

5. Beliefs are submitted to reality testing via behavioral experiments.

The authors concluded that more can be done to modify delusional beliefs than traditionally assumed and that, quoting Maher (1988), "The cognitive processes whereby delusions are formed differ in no important respects from those by which nondelusional beliefs are formed" (p. 20). It appears that if delusional beliefs can be modified, one should be able to weaken overvalued ideation and thereby enhance OCD treatment with a variety of creative cognitive interventions.

Cognitive Impairment

Kozak et al. (1988) stated that both clinical and experimental evidence indicates that OCs show several areas of cognitive impairment in the rules by which they process information. Steketee and Foa (1985) suggested that "one might expect cognitive techniques to be beneficial. Such techniques, however, should be tailored to the specific deficits of the disorder" (p. 82). We propose several cognitive methods for addressing impairments in epistemological reasoning, estimates of the probability of harm, and negative valence associated with feared harm.

Epistemological Reasoning. As indicated earlier, while most people assume that situations are safe unless evidence for danger is available, OCs assume that situations are dangerous unless evidence for safety is present. Rather than operating on probabilities of safety, this reasoning process involves a demand for a guarantee of safety and leads to indecisiveness, doubt, and reliance on rituals to insure safety. We propose that therapists attempt directly to teach OCs "normal" methods of reasoning.

The following cognitive interventions are suggested to teach OCs appropriate reasoning skills:

1. Describe to clients the two contrasting types of reasoning about safety and danger.
2. Ask clients to identify what type of reasoning they typically use with respect to situations related to their particular obsessions.

Table 6.3. Dangerous-Until-Proven-Safe Rule Regarding Possibility
of Contracting Cancer Germs

Advantages	Disadvantages
If I assume it's possible to catch cancer germs, I'll be more cautious, remember to wash more, and be less likely to develop cancer.	I'll spend a lot of time worrying about getting cancer.
	Time and energy spent washing.
Therefore, I could save my life.	Inconvenience from avoiding possible cancer germs.
	Hypervigilance for danger will get in my way of being relaxed and enjoying myself.
	Constriction of activities to avoid cancer germs will limit my freedom to do things I enjoy.
	Though I might save my life with the danger rule, I would be so miserable and preoccupied with fear of dying, life would hardly be worth it.

3. Ask clients to list advantages and disadvantages of the dangerous-until-proven-safe rule (see Table 6.3).
4. Explore with clients whether they ever employ the safe-until-proven-dangerous rule in some situations.
5. Assist clients in using imaginal rehearsal to practice self-instruction for the safe-until-proven-dangerous rule.
6. Assist clients in practicing the adaptive style of reasoning during in vivo exposures.

The following dialogue illustrates several of the aforementioned points:

Client: It seems pretty clear that when it comes to contaminants, I use the rule "dangerous until proven safe."

Therapist: Can you think of any situations where you use the opposite rule, "safe until proven dangerous"?

Client: I don't think so.

Therapist: Well, let's think about it some more. What about during the day when you walk across campus to class? Which rule do you follow then?

Client: I guess "safe until proven dangerous."

Therapist: So when you walk across campus you assume you're relatively safe. What would be the effect on your walking if you followed the "dangerous until proven safe" rule?

Client: I'd probably cut a lot of classes . . . maybe even drop out of school.

Therapist: Yes, that's if you assumed the danger was life threatening. What kind of evidence would it take to suggest it was dangerous to walk across campus?

Client: If people were assaulted, or if it were printed in the school newspaper that we should avoid walking across campus. Maybe also if I personally knew someone who had been hurt or nearly hurt.

Therapist: So, if this were the case, then you would have some evidence that the situation wasn't safe, and you could decide on ways to protect yourself. At that point, you would be following the "safe until proven dangerous" rule. Now, can you see how different this is from how you think about danger from contracting cancer germs?

Client: Yes, but what would be evidence that cancer germs could be caught?

Therapist: Good question. Think about it. Any ideas?

Client: Well, doctors telling you that cancer germs exist and are contractable. Or maybe people who visited relatives with cancer and then caught it.

Therapist: Good ideas!

Client: OK, I see what you mean. But what if I were wrong and you really could contract cancer germs?

Therapist: You really do want a guarantee, absolute certainty, don't you?

Client: I do. Can I ever change that?

Therapist: It takes a lot of work and practice, but I think you can. We've looked at the advantages and disadvantages. I think you'll have to go over those a lot and continue to practice to convince yourself it's in your long-term best interest to go with the adaptive rule.

Client: It sounds really hard and scary.

Therapist: I know. Now, let's practice in your imagination. I'd like for you to close your eyes and imagine that you're visiting your aunt who has cancer at the hospital. Let yourself start to think, "This is really dangerous; I know I'll get cancer." Then say to yourself, "Stop! There's no evidence here that I can catch cancer. There's also no guarantee for safety, but I don't need one! I can go with the odds and assume things are safe until proven dangerous." Now see yourself continuing to visit with your aunt.

Overestimating the Probability of Harm. Salkovskis (1985) suggested that OCs have an inflated belief in the probability of being the cause of harm to others rather than the probability of harm per se. Assuming the soundness of Salkovskis's (1985) observation, therapists can assist clients in reducing their estimates of the likelihood of causing harm to others by the following normalizing interventions (Salkovskis & Westbrook, 1987):

1. Provide information showing that 80% to 90% of the normal population have obsessions (Rachman & de Silva, 1978; Salkovskis & Warwick, 1985), and discuss the notion that the crime rate would be much higher than it is if obsessive thoughts lead to harming others.

2. Explain Gray's (1988) concept of the checking functions of the behavioral inhibition system (BIS). According to Gray, the BIS "scans incoming sensory information for threatening or unexpected events and if they occur, brings all behavior to a halt, so as to evaluate the nature of the threat" (p. 29). Gray provided an example of someone who wants to avoid cutting himself and scans his memory to recall where he may have disposed of a razor blade. This internal scanning involves having an image of where the blade is. Gray further explained, "So a person whose greatest fear is of harming her child may imagine scenes that she has done just that" (p. 30). Thus, it appears that it is a normal protective mechanism to imagine what we do not want to have happen so that we can more successfully avoid it. Gray also described the BIS in terms of James's (1980) concept of ideomotor action to explain OC behavior: "The thought of a particular action primes the systems that produce it. Thus, checking whether one has a dangerous impulse will increase the probability of experiencing it" (p. 30). Helping clients to normalize and understand the nature of obsessions provides them with the cognitive tools necessary to correct their overestimations of the probability of their acting on these obsessions and causing harm to others.

3. Explain the concept of the availability heuristic. As Butler and Mathews (1983) explained, individuals may be considered to be using an availability heuristic when an event is judged as being likely to occur to the extent that it is readily available in memory, associated with recency, saliency, or selective exposure effects. Furthermore, increased estimates of risk can also result from internally generated representations (Warren et al., 1989). For example, research has suggested that for subjects who are asked to imagine vividly a possible outcome, probability estimates for the outcome actually occurring are increased. Thus, worry or increased frequency of catastrophic thoughts and images may lead to increased estimates of the likelihood of these events occurring (Carroll, 1978).

The availability heuristic appears to be particularly relevant to OC intrusions. Many OCs may be described as being of tender conscience (Rachman & Hodgson, 1980; Salkovskis, 1985). Thus, in such individuals, thoughts of being the cause of harm to others would be salient and easily become "figure" while other cognitions become "ground." This phenomenon, along with the frequency of intrusions, vivid images of feared disasters, and selective attention given to intrusions may lead the OC to overestimate the likelihood of the occurrence of feared disasters (e.g., hurting someone).

Non-OC-related analogies can also be presented to explain the availability heuristic concept. For example, when airplanes crash, dramatic photographs and videos of the wrecked plane, injuries, and so on often appear on the front pages of the newspapers (saliency). In addition, crashes are frequently announced on radio and television (frequency). Airplane crashes are given more exposure than other types of accidents (e.g., being hit by a car; selective attention). Just as these variables influence people to overestimate the likelihood of plane crashes, the saliency and frequency of intrusive thoughts may lead the OC to overestimate the likelihood of related disasters. As Salkovskis and Westbrook (1987) suggested, OCs can be helped to see that unpredictable intrusions becoming figure rather than ground (i.e., salient) is evidence that OCs are sensitive and of tender conscience and therefore less likely to be the cause of harm than someone whose thoughts are more consistent with their personality.

In addition, often those who are the most appalled by intrusions try harder to resist them, thereby increasing their frequency and saliency. Wegner, Schneider, Carter, and White (1987) provided empirical evidence for this phenomenon. When normal subjects were asked to try not to think of white bears, efforts directed at thought suppression apparently had the "paradoxical effect of *increasing* the frequency of occurrence of ideas of white bears" (Salkovskis, 1989, p. 680). As Salkovskis and Westbrook (1987) suggested, clients can be asked during the session to try not to have a particular intrusive thought or certain neutral thoughts (e.g., "Don't think about purple elephants"). The results of such behavioral experiments may help OCs attribute the presence of, as well as difficulty preventing, intrusive thoughts to normal rather than pathological cognitive processes. Another behavioral exercise might involve having the OC go to a grocery store, deliberately visualizing running his or her grocery cart into other shoppers, and seeing that such thoughts do not lead to actual behaviors. The results of such behavioral experiments may help OCs to attribute the presence of and difficulty preventing intrusive thoughts to normal rather than pathological cognitive processes.

Reducing Negative Valence Associated with the Feared Harm. This negative valence can also be described as having high ratings for the degree of badness assigned to negative events (Foa & Kozak, 1985), which may apply to the experience of anxiety or discomfort itself, or to the specific meanings that clients attach to the possibility of being the cause of harm. Ellis's (1979a, 1980a) concepts of ego anxiety (EA) and DA (see chapter 2) are integral aspects of OCs' fears of being responsible for harm to self or others. Furthermore, while it may be that OCs premorbidly have LFT, once having developed OCD, they may also experience higher levels of discomfort as part of OCD processes (i.e., mental anguish associated with having uncontrollable intrusive thoughts, rituals, or impulses).

Clients also may believe that harm (e.g., inability to work) will come their way in response to their having experienced anxiety or discomfort. To challenge this belief, clients can purposely expose themselves to anxiety-evoking cues without the comfort of ritualizing. During the period before the discomfort and urge to ritualize subsides, clients can practice appropriate functioning (e.g., cleaning the kitchen, reading a book). This assignment helps to disconfirm the prediction that anxiety and discomfort will continue indefinitely unless one ritualizes.

While most cognitive-behavioral therapists would help the client to reduce the negative valence associated with many negative events feared by OCs (e.g., fear of shouting obscenities), it is our impression that such interventions are not typically used for more "truly horrible" disasters. Whether such a therapeutic maneuver would be helpful or appropriate is open to empirical investigation. The following dialogue illustrates an attempt to help a client cope with a feared disaster that most people would view as catastrophic.

To help the client reduce the negative valence attached to the idea of being an agent of harm, the therapist can first explore with the client what the most awful thing about being the cause of harm to someone might be (i.e., ascertain the meaning associated with the client harming someone)—the answer likely involving ego anxiety.

Client: It would be just horrible if I ran over a pedestrian.
Therapist: What would be the most horrible thing about that for you?
Client: People would hate me.
Therapist: And if they hated you, what would be the worst thing about that?
Client: I would feel like a terrible person. I couldn't stand the guilt.

In this case, the client's horror about harming someone seems related to predicted painful feelings of guilt (DA) and associated self-condemnation (EA). The following dialogue provides an example of a means of assisting the client in reducing EA and DA.

Therapist: Now, it certainly would be tragic to run over someone, particularly if it killed or maimed them. But how would having such an accident make you a terrible person?

Client: Because I would have done such a terrible thing, to have taken a human life.

Therapist: OK, but we're assuming that if you ran over someone it would be an accident, that you didn't intentionally try to do that.

Client: Right, but I still would feel terrible, like I didn't deserve to live.

Therapist: If your best friend accidently ran over someone, would you see her as a terrible person who didn't deserve to live?

Client: No. I'd feel bad for her, knowing how guilty she would feel and that she didn't mean to run over someone.

Therapist: Sounds like you would be compassionate and feel empathy for her. You really have a double standard here, don't you? Why would you be so kind to her and so hard on yourself?

Client: I don't know. I'll have to think some more about that one.

Therapist: So, your feelings of extreme guilt would be the result of seeing yourself as a terrible person if you accidently harmed someone. If you could accept yourself as a FHB [fallible human being], allow yourself to make mistakes, even tragic ones, then your guilt feelings would change to extreme regret, which would be painful, but probably not as painful as extreme guilt and self-condemnation.

Client: I still don't know if I could stand the feeling, knowing I hurt someone.

Therapist: When other people have and cause accidents, they probably feel extremely bad about it, too. Do you think the intensity of those feelings stays at the maximum level forever, or do you think they become less intense over time?

Client: Probably over a long period of time, they wouldn't be as bad. But I might have to kill myself to blot out how horrible I would feel.

Therapist: So, you really feel like you couldn't stand those feelings?

Client: Maybe I could, but it doesn't feel like it right now.

Depression

Another risk factor for failed OCD treatment is severe depression, as the incidence of such depression among OCD clients ranges from about 17% to 60% and often is a secondary reaction (Turner & Beidel, 1988). Antidepressant medication and/or cognitive-behavioral intervention may be indicated for severe depression that exists prior to the start of OCD treatment. In addition, cognitive therapy has a well-established track record for depression, and there is some evidence for the effectiveness of RET in treating depression (e.g., Gardner & Oei, 1981;

Malouff, 1984; McKnight, Nelson, Hayes, & Jarret, 1984; Warren et al., 1988). Specifically, RET treatment of depression in OCs would focus on helping the client to change irrational thinking and self-defeating behavior related to activating events both related and unrelated to the OCD symptomatology. Treatment directly addresses irrational beliefs that having OCD and OCD-related performance impairments lowers the sufferer's self-worth. This aspect of RET theory and treatment is consistent with Kuiper and Olinger's (1986) "self-worth contingency model of depression" (p. 115). In addition, aspects of depression related to experiencing the discomfort associated with OCD is also a central focus of treatment (Ellis & Dryden, 1987). Hopelessness is frequently another essential target for intervention (Beck et al., 1979).

Criticism and Guilt

As some evidence indicates that guilt and fear of criticism are characteristic of some OCs, we usually address these issues in the RET treatment of OCD. (See Appendix E for a client handout on this topic.) Dealing with criticism and guilt is intimately connected with the concept of self-acceptance, as discussed in a later section. Burns's (1980) *Feeling Good* contains a useful chapter, "Ways of Defeating Guilt," in which he discriminates guilt from regret. A variety of Ellis's writings discuss dealing with criticism, guilt, and related issues of disapproval, as well as furthering self-acceptance (e.g., Ellis, 1988; Ellis & Becker, 1982; Ellis & Harper, 1975). Rational-emotive imagery (REI), as discussed in chapter 4, can be useful in helping clients deal with criticism and reduce their guilt.

Promoting Self-acceptance

As noted throughout this book, Ellis has championed the importance of self-acceptance in maintaining good mental health. Because many OCs find the content of their obsessions abhorrent and their rituals abnormal, they often are secretive about these problems and may be reluctant to divulge them to friends and/or therapists. In essence, OCs are often ashamed of their symptoms, seeing themselves as less worthwhile, bad, or even evil for having OCD symptoms. In addition, they berate themselves for any secondary problems (e.g., inability to work).

RET emphasizes the importance of helping OCs to accept themselves as fallible human beings while disliking their problematic OCD traits, symptoms, and secondary problems. Therapists thus encourage clients to believe that they are more than a personification of their disorder. This self-acceptance is emphasized throughout treatment. For example, asking OCs if they would see significant others as bad people if they had OCD, and exploring the reasons why they would not, often is helpful in enabling OCs to be as accepting of themselves as others. RET and general cognitive-behavioral techniques for increasing self-acceptance are presented in Warren et al. (1988).

Relapse Prevention

A variety of interventions have been suggested as effective means of maintaining treatment gains. These include booster sessions, spouse reinforcement for not ritualizing, future planning of life goals, training to identify early signs of relapse (Epsie, 1986), and social support (Steketee, 1987). Other suggested interventions include fading of session frequency, gradual shifting of responsibility for exposure and response prevention to the client, interpersonal skill training, anxiety management training, and stress management training (Turner & Beidel, 1988).

As increased stress appears to be associated with OCD onset, we recommend that clients be taught to apply RET to handle daily hassles, negative life events, and major life crises. The ability to manage one's emotional reactions will give OCs a sense of control and mastery that will make them less vulnerable to relapse. More specifically, clients who develop philosophical outlooks advocated by RET (acceptance of self, others, and world conditions; high frustration and discomfort tolerance; acceptance of uncertainty; long-range hedonism) are more likely to maintain solid emotional health and prevent a reoccurrence of OCD (Ellis & Dryden, 1987).

CASE EXAMPLE: FEAR OF CONTAMINANTS

Gary, a 42-year-old married father of three children, was referred to the Anxiety Disorders Clinic by a nurse at a local, private sexually transmitted disease (STD) clinic, as Gary frequently contacted the STD clinic for human immunodeficiency virus (HIV) testing and reassurance. He reported having engaged in washing rituals since early adolescence for fear of becoming infected by one or more contaminants. However, his primary fear at the time he sought therapy was that of contracting AIDS. His fear was related to a single experience with a prostitute 10 years ago, and although his testing was consistently negative after 10 times, he worried that the testing had failed to detect the condition. In addition, Gary complained of severe depression.

Initial evaluation yielded a BDI of 40, which was consistent with Gary's report of depression. Gary also described extreme guilt surrounding his previous experience with the prostitute and the potential of infecting his wife and children with AIDS.

Further assessment revealed a variety of passive and active avoidance patterns. Passive avoidance related to contracting AIDS included public restrooms, restaurants where gay men might be waiters and transmit AIDS to him, shaking hands, and contacting blood. Passive avoidance related to transmitting AIDS included hot tubs, swimming pools, kissing his wife and children, having sex with his wife, masturbating for fear of touching contaminated semen, and using the same drinking glass and towels as other family members. Active avoidance included frequent handwashing (about 25 times each day), contacting several local STD clinics for HIV testing and for reassurance, contacting several national STD clinics for information, frequent reading of medical journals and textbooks, and visiting the doctor for the slightest indication of colds or other minor health conditions both for himself and for family members.

Gary's depression was the first target of treatment. Irrational beliefs related to self-condemnation for past sexual behavior and the potential of infecting his family were identified and disputed. Gary, a religious man, was encouraged "to hate the sin but love the sinner"—in other words, to accept himself as a fallible human being in spite of past transgressions or future HIV status.

Following a decrease in his level of depression, Gary participated in intensive treatment for OCD, five times each week for 3 weeks. Exposure consisted of hierarchically confronting both passively and actively avoided situations. Response prevention consisted of total cessation of handwashing (except for a 10-minute shower every other day), reassurance seeking, HIV testing, and so on. Imaginal exposure to Gary's feared disaster of his family contracting AIDS was also conducted. Audiotape exposure to the obsessive thought, "What if I have AIDS" and thought stopping for the related cognitive ritual, "Christ is Lord, I am clean!" was implemented.

At the conclusion of 3 weeks of therapy, posttreatment assessment indicated that Gary had made some significant improvements. Gary was then seen in therapy on a weekly basis for 1 month, and then on a once-monthly basis for 4 months. During this time, RET was used to teach Gary general stress management skills and to reinforce attitudinal shifts that had begun earlier in the therapeutic process. Follow-up 1 year later with the STD clinic referring nurse revealed no further contact with Gary.

Chapter 7

Posttraumatic Stress Disorder

Although the existence of PTSD as an independent diagnostic category did not appear until the advent of DSM-III (APA, 1980), various diagnostic predecessors, as noted by Foa, Steketee, and Rothbaum (1989), have been described in the literature for more than 100 years, including nervous shock (Page, 1885), traumatophobia (Rado, 1942), and war neurosis (Grinker & Spiegel, 1943). Undoubtedly, a diverse array of traumatic events (e.g., genocide, wars, torture, famine, and earthquakes; Fairbank & Brown, 1987) have elicited a common constellation of symptoms, now labeled PTSD, in some individuals since the beginning of human history. According to the DSM-III-R, the PTSD-initiating trauma is typically outside the range of normal human experience. Tragically frequent traumatic events, such as rape, assault, and combat experience, raise questions about this requirement and suggest that the more central defining features of PTSD may be the ensuing stress response syndrome.

PTSD is distinctive in several ways from the other anxiety and psychiatric disorders (Foa et al., 1989). Except for the adjustment disorders, PTSD is the only disorder partly defined by etiology. In addition, the intrusive recollections, nightmares, and flashbacks so diagnostic of PTSD are atypical of the other anxiety disorders. Similarly, among the anxiety disorders, restricted affect and feelings of detachment from others also are relatively unique to PTSD. In fact, the dissociative phenomenon of PTSD has raised serious questions as to whether PTSD should be classified as an anxiety or dissociative disorder.

As noted by Keane (1989), recent epidemiological studies (e.g., Helzer, Robins, & McEvoy, 1987) have estimated the prevalence of adult PTSD to be between 1% and 2%, which amounts to about 2.4 to 4.8

million PTSD cases in the U.S. alone. In terms of the prevalence of specific types of PTSD, rape-related and combat-related PTSD have received the most recent research and clinical attention. As reviewed by Steketee and Foa (1987), estimates of the prevalence of rape in the U.S. range from 5% to 22% of adult women, making it the largest PTSD category. For example, 23% of adult women in a community-based sample reported having been a victim of completed rape, and 57% of all rape victims developed PTSD sometime after the rape. More than 75% of this sample had been crime victims (i.e., sexual assault, aggravated assault, robbery, and burglary), and 27.8% had met diagnostic criteria for crime-related PTSD at some point (Kilpatrick, Saunders, Veronen, Best, & Von, 1987). Moreover, estimates suggest that 15% to 35% of veterans who served in Vietnam meet PTSD criteria, and about 70% of Vietnam veterans in VA hospitals suffer from PTSD.

In the remainder of this chapter, we review PTSD etiological theories and pertinent victimization literature. We propose a RET model of the development of PTSD, review current treatment studies, and suggest rational-emotive interventions, including previously tested cognitive-behavioral techniques.

ETIOLOGY OF PTSD

A behavioral approach to the conceptualization of combat-related PTSD was developed by Keane, Fairbank, Caddell, Zimering, and Bender (1985). Using Mowrer's (1960) two-factor learning theory, Keane et al. (1985) accounted for the development and maintenance of PTSD psychopathology: Classical conditioning leads to fear arousal, and instrumental learning leads to avoidance. For example, the Vietnam veteran who experiences life-threatening trauma on the battlefield (UCS; unconditioned stimulus) and extreme fear (UCR; unconditioned response), cues (CS; conditioned stimulus) that were associated with the original trauma (e.g., fellow soldiers, enemy attacks) via classical conditioning comes to elicit extreme anxiety reactions comparable to those experienced during the original trauma. Higher order conditioning and stimulus generalization further increase the range of stimuli that can evoke conditioned responses (e.g., a car's backfiring, sight of Vietnamese civilians). The intrusive thoughts and nightmares characteristic of PTSD continue to present the sufferer with additional conditioned cues and associated arousal. Because these memories are short exposures to trauma-related stimuli, extinction of the emotional responses does not occur, and incubation of fear may result instead. In addition, due to the extreme aversiveness of these intrusive recollections and environmental events reminiscent of the trauma, avoidance—both cognitive

and behavioral—results and is strengthened due to the negative reinforcement of the anxiety-reducing effects. Keane et al. (1985) explained
that other PTSD behavioral disturbances such as anger and aggression,
substance abuse, and social withdrawal are learned emotional and behavioral reactions, which being incompatible with anxiety also become
further ingrained due to negative reinforcement.

Kilpatrick, Veronen, and Best (1985) presented a similar learning
theory model of rape-induced symptoms. As victims usually perceive
rape as potentially life threatening, they typically react with unconditioned responses of terror and extreme autonomic arousal. Stimuli associated with the rape situation (e.g., a man who resembles the assail-
ant, similar surroundings) become conditioned stimuli and evoke
conditioned responses of fear and anxiety. Cognitive events (e.g,
thoughts and images associated with the rape experience) also become
conditioned stimuli for anxiety so that thinking or talking about the
rape can elicit extreme anxiety. Finally, through higher order conditioning, additional stimuli associated with the conditioned stimuli acquire fear-arousing properties. Thus, situations where the rape is discussed or people with whom it is discussed may come to elicit anxiety.

Veronen and Kilpatrick (1983) expanded on this learning theory model
to include expectancies, attributions, and cognitive appraisal variables
as significant influences on victims' reactions to the rape. For example,
victims hold self-expectations for how they should have behaved during the attack and how they should later have handled their emotions.
Accepted societal myths, including the belief that a woman cannot be
forced to have sex against her will, also lead to general expectations
regarding the rape experience. Moreover, attribution and cognitive appraisal processes influence the various ways in which individuals interpret and attach meaning to events. Such interpretations include behavioral versus characterological self-blame, "just-world" hypothesis
reasoning, and in some cases viewing the rape experience as a choice
point that can be the precursor of positive as well as negative changes
(Veronen & Kilpatrick, 1983).

Victimization and Shattered Assumptions

Janoff-Bulman (1985) proposed that posttraumatic stress follows victimization due to the shattering of basic assumptions that victims hold
about themselves, others, and the world. When traumatic events are
too discrepant with preexisting assumptive worlds, the victim's experiences cannot be readily assimilated. The result is PTSD symptomatology.

According to Janoff-Bulman (1985), our assumptive world contains three major assumptions relevant to PTSD: (a) the belief in personal invulnerability, (b) the perception of the world as meaningful and comprehensible, and (c) the view of oneself in a positive light. When traumatic events seriously challenge these basic assumptions, the victim's preexisting sense of equilibrium and security become unbalanced (p. 18).

Operating on the basis of an "illusion of invulnerability," people overestimate the likelihood of experiencing positive outcomes in life and underestimate the likelihood of negative events, such as crimes, diseases, and accidents. The experience of victimization then renders one unable to say, "It can't happen to me." A sense of safety and security is replaced by feeling vulnerable, helpless, and out of control. If the trauma is of human design, interpersonal trust may be severely compromised.

One of the most common ways of making sense of the world is to view events as orderly and controllable. Such a view facilitates the belief that one will be protected against misfortune by being a good and worthy person. According to Lerner's (1970, 1980) just-world theory, people believe "they deserve what they get and get what they deserve" (p. 20). Thus, for the trauma victim who feels that he or she is a cautious and good person, the victimization violates a fundamental notion of how the world is supposed to work, leading to the question, "Why did this happen to me?" (p. 21).

According to Janoff-Bulman (1985), people generally view themselves as worthy and decent. The experience of victimization seriously challenges these perceptions, which become replaced by a self-image in which one sees oneself as weak, frightened, and no longer autonomous. Because they have been "singled out for misfortune," victims may see themselves as different from others, and this self-perception of deviance further reinforces a sense of lowered self-esteem (Coates & Winston, 1983).

Janoff-Bulman (1985) argued that the stronger the basic assumptions have been held and not previously questioned or challenged, the more likely they are to be severely shattered by the traumatic event. Similarly, individuals who feel most invulnerable and safe prior to victimization may be at greatest risk for resulting psychological disturbance (Scheppele & Bart, 1983; Wortman, 1983). Thus, the woman who is raped in an apparently safe place (e.g., home) by an apparently safe and trusted person may have more severe PTSD than a woman who is raped by a stranger when walking alone at night in a dangerous neighborhood (Foa et al., 1989).

Horowitz's Psychodynamic and Information Processing Model

Horowitz has written extensively on the theory and treatment of traumatic stress responses, well before the diagnostic category of PTSD was formally introduced in DSM-III. Horowitz's psychodynamic and information processing model accounts for both pathological and normal posttraumatic stress responses. According to Horowitz (1986), traumatic events present individuals with a situation in which "there is not an immediate good fit between new information and existing schemata," and further information processing, therefore, is instigated. "This then leads to progressive modifications of the meaning of the recently acquired information and/or to progressive modification of the preexisting models" (pp. 196–197).

In Piagetian terms (Rosen, 1989), information processing continues until the victim can somehow assimilate the meaning of the traumatic event into preexisting cognitive structures or revise preexisting cognitive structures to accommodate the new information contained in the traumatic event. Horowitz posited a completion principle that accounts for the human mind's intrinsic tendency to process information until assimilation or accommodation occurs. Thoughts, images, and emotional reactions related to the traumatic event remain in active memory until the information is transferred to long-term memory.

The aforementioned process, however, does not necessarily follow a smooth and steady course. With PTSD, the intrusive recollections and related emotional upheaval appear to threaten the individual with psychic overload, so control operations occur to cope with the state of threat. This results in responses of ideational denial, emotional numbness, and behavioral avoidance. Under favorable conditions, intrusion and denial phases will alternate until the traumatic event has been adequately processed. Superimposed on the aforementioned processes are the individual's preexisting personality styles, dormant or active conflicts, and developmental vulnerabilities.

Emotional Processing

Foa et al. (1989) recently presented an emotional processing conceptualization of PTSD. Having built on Lang's (1977, 1979) analysis of fear structures as a network in memory and Foa and Kozak's (1986) adaptation of this analysis to anxiety disorders, Foa et al. (1989) related concepts of controllability and predictability to fear structure theory.

As described in chapter 1, fear structures consist of a network in memory that includes three kinds of information: (a) information about stimuli, (b) responses (i.e., verbal, physiological, overt behavioral), and (c) meanings associated with both. The fear structure is considered a program for escape or avoidance.

Foa et al. (1989) proposed that in contrast to other anxiety disorders, in which fear structures are more circumscribed, with PTSD the fear structure is more pervasive regarding stimuli, responses, and meanings that connote danger. For example, the simple phobic who fears heights may have developed a fear structure in which a variety of high places (e.g., balconies, bridges) are associated with responses such as catastrophic thoughts (cognitive), accelerated heart rate (physiological), and avoidance of high places (behavioral), which all are associated with danger (meaning). As long as the height phobic avoids high places, the fear structure (i.e., the program for escape and avoidance) will not be activated, and the person can feel relatively safe and not generally anxious. In contrast, a woman who is raped under conditions previously associated with safety (e.g., by a trusted acquaintance in her own home) is likely to develop a fear structure wherein stimuli and responses become more pervasively associated with danger. Thus, men in general may be viewed as dangerous, and no place, not even one's home, seems safe.

According to Foa et al. (1989), traumatic events that are most likely to lead to PTSD not only are high intensity but are also, and of greater importance, of an unpredictable or uncontrollable nature. An extensive animal literature (Mineka & Kihlstrom, 1978), as well as research with human beings (e.g., Staub, Tursky, & Schwartz, 1971), documents the deleterious effects of unpredictable and uncontrollable aversive events. In short, such traumatic events shatter the victim's ability to discriminate between safety and danger, as illustrated by the aforementioned rape victim example.

In terms of the characteristic symptoms of PTSD, Foa et al. (1989) viewed intrusive thoughts, flashbacks, nightmares, and so on as due to the ready accessibility of the fear structure. In other words, fear structures are activated when an individual is presented with information that matches some of the elements of the fear structure in memory. Thus, when the Vietnam War veteran hears a car backfire or watches a war movie, these stimuli are similar to those present in the fear structure and thus may activate various parts of this structure (i.e., recollections in the forms of flashbacks, nightmares, or intrusive thoughts). Finally, PTSD symptoms of emotional numbing, depersonalization, and behavioral avoidances are viewed as attempts to escape or avoid the aversiveness of these intrusive phenomena. Behaviorally, the Vietnam veteran can avoid Fourth of July fireworks displays and war movies, while emotional numbing and other dissociative mechanisms may be used to deal with the unavoidable pain resulting from various perceptions (e.g., lack of safety, guilt, aggressive impulses).

Barlow's (1988; Jones & Barlow, 1990) model of the etiology of PTSD is based on his recent conceptualization of the process and origin of anxiety and panic as discussed in previous chapters of this book. In brief, due to biological and psychological vulnerabilities, some individuals respond to traumatic life events with intense emotions, including true alarms (i.e., panic), rage, or distress. Learned alarms occur during exposure to situations reminiscent of the trauma, and individuals subsequently avoid such situations to prevent intense fear reactions. Numbing of responsiveness serves to avoid affect associated with the possibility of experiencing disturbing emotions and panic (i.e., alarms). Anxious apprehension over the likelihood of experiencing future alarms and other intense negative emotional states maintains chronic overarousal, which in turn prompts intrusive thoughts and images. The likelihood of the aforementioned processes leading to the full development of PTSD is to some degree moderated by the individual's coping strategies and social supports. (See Jones and Barlow, 1990, for a more extensive discussion of this etiological model of PTSD, as well as a review and critical analysis of other models).

Biological Models

Biological theories of PTSD propose that extraordinary psychological trauma may prompt profound and long-lasting CNS alterations (Krystal et al., 1989). For example, norepinephrine depletion is thought to lead to the PTSD symptoms of decreased motivation and increased arousal (Fairbank & Nicholson, 1987; McFall, Murburg, Roszell, & Veith, 1989; van der Holk, Greenberg, Boyd, & Krystal, 1985). Vulnerability to recurrence of PTSD may continue due to increased sensitization of the CNS. PTSD symptoms may themselves resensitize the nervous system. In some cases, the result is a chronic psychiatric or medical morbidity (e.g., cardiac or gastric conditions; Rosen & Fields, 1988). For a more detailed discussion and critique of biological models of PTSD, see Jones and Barlow (1990).

DSM-III-R DIAGNOSTIC CRITERIA
FOR PTSD

Table 7.1 presents the DSM-III-R diagnostic criteria for PTSD (309.89). As is apparent, PTSD includes impairment across the individual's cognitive (i.e., intrusive thoughts or images of the traumatic event), emo-

Table 7.1. DSM-III-R Criteria for Posttraumatic Stress Disorder

A. The person has experienced an event that is outside the range of usual human experience and that would be markedly distressing to almost anyone, e.g., serious threat to one's life or physical integrity; serious threat of harm to one's children, spouse, or other close relatives and friends; sudden destruction of one's home or community; or seeing another person who has recently been, or is being seriously injured or killed as the result of an accident or physical violence.

B. The traumatic event is persistently reexperienced in at least one of the following ways:
    1) recurrent and intrusive distressing recollections of the event (in young children, repetitive play in which themes or aspects of the trauma are expressed)
    2) recurrent distressing dreams of the event
    3) sudden acting or feeling as if the traumatic event were recurring (includes a sense of reliving the experience, illusions, hallucinations, and dissociative [flashback] episodes, even those that occur upon awakening or when intoxicated)
    4) intense psychological distress at exposure to events that symbolize or resemble an aspect of the traumatic event, including anniversaries of the trauma

C. Persistent avoidance of stimuli associated with the trauma or numbing of general responsiveness (not present before the trauma), as indicated by at least three of the following:
    1) efforts to avoid thoughts or feelings associated with the trauma
    2) efforts to avoid activities or situations that arouse recollections of the trauma
    3) inability to recall an important aspect of the trauma (psychogenic amnesia)
    4) markedly diminished interest in significant activities (in young children, loss of recently acquired developmental skills such as toilet training or language skills)
    5) feeling of detachment or estrangement from others
    6) restricted range of affect, e.g., unable to have loving feelings
    7) sense of a foreshortened future, e.g., does not expect to have a career, marriage, or children, or a long life

D. Persistent symptoms of increased arousal (not present before the trauma), as indicated by at least two of the following:
    1) difficulty falling or staying asleep
    2) irritability or outbursts of anger
    3) difficulty concentrating
    4) hypervigilance
    5) exaggerated startle response
    6) physiologic reactivity upon exposure to events that symbolize or resemble an aspect of the traumatic event (e.g., a woman who is raped in an elevator breaks out in a sweat when entering any elevator)

E. Duration of the disturbance (symptoms in B, C, and D) of at least one month.
    Specify delayed onset if the onset of symptoms was at least six months after the trauma.

Note. Reprinted with permission from the *Diagnostic and Statistical Manual of Mental Disorders, Third Edition, Revised.* Copyright 1987 American Psychiatric Association.

tive (i.e., restricted or heightened affect), physiological (i.e., exaggerated startle response, autonomic reactivity to cues associated with trauma), and behavioral (i.e., avoidance of external situations reminiscent of the trauma) response systems (Fairbank & Brown, 1987; Foy, Resnick, Sipprelle & Carroll, 1987).

REVIEW OF ASSESSMENT
INSTRUMENTS

A variety of reliable and valid instruments for assessing PTSD and related emotional distress are available (Keane, Wolfe, & Taylor, 1987). These include structured interviews, self-report measures of PTSD symptomatology, self-report measures of related emotional distress, psychophysiological methods, and self-monitoring devices.

The ADIS-R (Blanchard, Gerardi, Kolb, & Barlow, 1986) provides a useful interview assessment device based on DSM-III-R criteria for generic PTSD, while the Jackson Structured Interview (Keane et al., 1985) specifically assesses combat-related PTSD. A useful self-report measure for evaluating the intrusive and numbing aspects of PTSD is the Impact of Event Scale (Horowitz, Wilner, & Alvarez, 1979). For assessing combat-related PTSD, the MMPI has generally proven useful in discriminating veterans with PTSD from non-PTSD combat veteran groups (Fairbank, Gross, & Keane, 1983; Fairbank, Keane, & Malloy, 1983), and Keane, Malloy, and Fairbank (1984) derived an empirically developed MMPI subscale for assessment of combat-related PTSD. The Mississippi Scale for Combat-Related PTSD is a reliable and valid 35-item self-report measure of DSM-III PTSD symptomatology.

An appropriate instrument for measuring rape-related PTSD symptomatology is the Veronen-Kilpatrick Modified Fear Survey (Veronen & Kilpatrick, 1980), a 120-item inventory of potentially fear-producing items and situations. The Derogatis Symptom Checklist (SCL-90-R; Derogatis, 1977) is a 90-item symptom checklist that generates three overall scores and nine separate symptom dimensions. Additional self-report measures of specific emotional states include the BDI (Beck et al., 1961), the STAI-T (Spielberger et al., 1970), and the EPQ-N (Eysenck & Eysenck, 1975).

Psychophysiological measures have also proven useful in the assessment of PTSD. For example, cardiac response to combat sounds (e.g., helicopter, AK-47) reliably discriminates between combat veterans with and without PTSD (Blanchard, Kolb, Gerardi, Ryan, & Pallmeyer, 1986). Veterans with PTSD also respond differently to these combat stimuli than nonveteran normal controls and nonveterans with other anxiety disorders (Gerardi, Blanchard, & Kolb, 1989). In addition, Vietnam veterans with PTSD show general heightened physiological arousal compared to veterans without combat experience (Gerardi, Keane, Cahoon, & Klauminzer, 1989).

Behavioral assessment can also be a useful and practical form of assessment of PTSD symptomatology. For example, patients can self-monitor intrusive thoughts, nightmares, and daily anxiety ratings (e.g., Becker & Abel, 1981; McCaffrey & Fairbank, 1985).

REVIEW OF NON-RET
TREATMENTS

Fairbank and Nicholson (1987), in a review of behavioral and non-behavioral treatments, concluded that all successful treatments of PTSD involved some form of exposure. Exposure via systematic desensitization, implosive therapy, flooding, and in vivo methods has been reported as successful in several case reports and a few controlled studies. Uncontrolled studies have found systematic desensitization effective in treating rape victims (e.g., Turner, 1979; Wolff, 1977). Frank, Anderson, et al. (1988) concluded that both systematic desensitization and Beck's cognitive therapy were effective in treating rape trauma, although the absence of a no-treatment control group renders the results inconclusive (Kilpatrick & Calhoun, 1988). Implosive therapy preceded and followed by relaxation for combat PTSD has been described in single-case studies (Fairbank, Gross, & Keane, 1983) and a recent controlled study (Keane, Fairbank, Caddell, & Zimering, 1989). Implosive therapy with relaxation training and self-directed exposure in vivo was successfully implemented with transportation accident-related PTSD and described in case studies of two individuals (McCaffrey & Fairbank, 1985). Another case study found relaxation and driving practice effective in treating a posttraumatic startle response subsequent to an automobile accident (Fairbank, DeGood, & Jenkins, 1981). Finally, implosive therapy was also reported effective in the treatment of an incest victim (Rychtarik, Silverman, Van Landingbam, & Prue, 1984.)

A distinctive alternative to exposure-based treatments for PTSD is the SIT comprehensive program developed by Veronen and Kilpatrick (1983) for rape-related distress and PTSD. In an uncontrolled study of SIT with six rape victims, improvement from pre- to posttreatment was noted on most self-report measures (Veronen & Kilpatrick, 1983). The effectiveness of SIT has also been tested in recent controlled studies. SIT, assertion training, supportive psychotherapy, and a naturally occurring wait-list were compared in the treatment of rape victims (Resick, Jordan, Girelli, Hunter, & Marhoefer-Dvorak, 1988). The three active treatments, but not the wait-list group, evidenced significant improvement at posttreatment, and the majority of gains were maintained at 3- and 6-month follow-ups.

Olasov and Foa (1987) compared SIT, prolonged imaginal exposure (PE), and supportive counseling (SC) for rape-related PTSD. Therapy consisted of nine 1.5-hour sessions twice each week for over a period of 4 to 5 weeks. SIT included education, breathing retraining, deep muscle relaxation, thought stopping, cognitive restructuring à la Beck and Ellis, Meichenbaum's (1974) guided self-dialogue, covert modeling, and role-playing. Exposure involved in vivo exposure to avoided situations and PE to the rape scene. SC focused on problem solving, both for rape-related and other daily problems, with no discussion of the assault (Rothbaum & Foa, in press).

At posttest, both SIT and PE were superior to SC on measures of PTSD, depression, and anxiety. Improvements were maintained at 3-month follow-up (Rothbaum & Foa, 1988), with SIT appearing to show an advantage over PE (Foa, 1990b). Future research will compare SIT, PE, and their combination in treating rape-related PTSD. Foa and Olasov (1989) hypothesized that the combined treatment may prove more effective as both major components of PTSD will be addressed. In other words, SIT targets arousal-related symptoms while PE targets cognitive and behavioral avoidance-related symptoms such as dissociation and numbing.

The controlled studies of PTSD treatments just discussed primarily included behavioral and cognitive-behavioral treatments for rape or combat-related categories. Recently, however, Brom, Kleber, and Defares (1989) reported on a large-scale controlled comparison of Horowitz's (1986) brief psychotherapy, imaginal desensitization, behaviorally oriented hypnotherapy, and a waiting-list control group with 112 people suffering from PTSD subsequent to violent crimes, traffic accidents, and loss of loved ones as a result of murder, suicide, acute illness, and chronic illness. Results indicated that clients in each of the treatment groups were significantly lower in trauma-related symptoms than the control group. Thus, in addition to the accumulating evidence for the effectiveness of behavior therapy for PTSD, it appears that Horowitz's (1986) brief psychotherapy approach may be an effective intervention. This finding is not unexpected, however, as Horowitz's intervention includes exposure to trauma-related material.

Role of Medication in the Treatment of PTSD

Finally, medications have been used in treating PTSD. Uncontrolled studies (Friedman, 1988) have suggested that both imipramine and the MAO inhibitor phenelzine reduce PTSD symptoms associated with sympathetic hyperarousal and intrusive recollections. Nevertheless, these compounds appear ineffective when used to reduce avoidance responses. Similar results were obtained in a recent controlled study (Frank, Kosten, Giller, & Dan, 1988).

A RET MODEL FOR PTSD

Table 7.2 summarizes a RET model of the development of PTSD. This model draws from previous similar person-environment interaction models (Green, Wilson, & Lindy, 1985; March, 1990; Wilson, 1989) and integrates these with RET concepts. We have tried to include variables that have been empirically associated with the development of PTSD as well as hypothesized variables that research has yet to examine.

The characteristics included under Traumatic Event are consistent with the DSM-III-R definition of trauma as "outside the range of usual human experience and that would most likely be markedly distressing to almost anyone" (p. 250). However, as traumatic as events with these characteristics are, not everyone who experiences traumatic events develops PTSD. Perhaps as the number of Traumatic Event characteristics in Table 7.2 increases, the likelihood of developing PTSD increases regardless of the victim's previous pathology. The likelihood is further increased as the risk factors under Person Variables increase. Finally, the environmental context in which the trauma occurs also affects the probability of developing PTSD.

While RET has always emphasized the role of cognitions in the creation of emotional disturbance, Dryden and Ellis (1986) acknowledged that "emotional disturbance, however, may at times stem from powerful A's—for example, from environmental disasters such as floods or wars, or from personal tragedy" (p. 140). Thus, when the characteristics in the first column of Table 7.2 are associated with such trauma as natural disaster, combat, rape, and assault, cognitive factors may play less of a role in creating Cs than when the A is of a more moderate nature. Nevertheless, individuals bring biological vulnerabilities and personality characteristics, which are influenced by prior life experiences, to the experience of the traumatic As.

In our RET model of PTSD, we hypothesize that life experiences and biological vulnerabilities influence the development of the individual's belief system, which, according to Ellis and Dryden (1987), consists of inferential and evaluative beliefs, of which the latter is considered to be more instrumental in causing sustained emotional disturbance. In Table 7.2 under the Person Variables column, basic assumptions would be considered inferential beliefs. Examples of these beliefs include (a) just-world beliefs, such as, "The world is just and fair; people get what they deserve and deserve what they get. Bad things do not happen to good people"; and (b) vulnerability and safety-related beliefs, as nonvictims appear to have an illusion of unique invulnerability and view themselves as less vulnerable to victimization than most others.

Table 7.2. Model for the Development of PTSD

Traumatic Event →	Person Variables		Posttrauma Adaptation
	Background	Immediate	Posttrauma →	

Traumatic Event	Background	Immediate	Posttrauma	Posttrauma Adaptation
Life threat	Demographics	Perception that location and/or person inflicting trauma was safe	*Cognitive:* Behavioral versus characterological self-blame	Pathological outcome: PTSD Non-PTSD anxiety and depression
Suddenness	Stressful life events	Perception of life threat	Minimization and maximization of trauma via cognitive appraisal	
Bereavement or loss of significant others	Psychiatric and substance abuse history	Perception of event as unpredictable and uncontrollable	Meaning found	
Extremely intensive combat	Previous victimization	Coping and defense mechanisms used	Unique versus universal vulnerability	
Exposure to the grotesque	Biological vulnerability	Cognitive appraisal	Activation or strengthening of irrational beliefs	
Brutality, physical harm, rape	Personality characteristics: Neuroticism Introversion Locus of control		*Behavioral:* Changing behavior to increase sense of control	
Violent loss, injury, displacement, natural disaster	Belief systems: Rational and irrational beliefs Basic assumptions about self, others, and world Vulnerability/safety Meanings of justice/order Regard for self Trust in others Strength of assumptions		Avoidance versus approach	

Environmental Factors

Positive family relationships
Other social support
Societal attitude toward event

For example, "It can't happen to me" is typical of this type of belief. Inferential beliefs become evaluative beliefs when they are escalated into demands. For example, "Bad things must not happen to good people. And bad things must not happen to me, and if they do, I must be a bad person. I must be safe and invulnerable."

The musts imply that one strongly insists that the world works in a particular way and that traumatic events cannot be accepted as part of life. Wortman (1983) discussed the issue of how one's basic assumptions about the world are developed and maintained and asked the question, "How can we explain why some people assume the world is just, while others see suffering and injustice as a normal part of life?" (p. 207). Again, RET hypothesizes that individuals who philosophically accept injustice in the world are less vulnerable to developing PTSD.

This RET hypothesis is also consistent with Janoff-Bulman's (1985) view, "To the extent that particular assumptions are held with extreme confidence and have not been challenged . . . are more likely to be utterly shattered. . . . Basic assumptions that have not been questioned may shatter most easily and lead to the greatest psychological disruption" (p. 23). In summary, RET holds that dogmatically or rigidly held negative evaluative beliefs are most likely to lead to emotional disturbance. Thus, when individuals devoutly believe in a just and fair world, unique invulnerability, trustworthiness of others, and have not challenged, even on philosophical grounds, the accuracy of such assumptions, the risk of experiencing psychological distress increases when trauma shatters these assumptions. RET holds that particular irrational beliefs, in addition to those involving safety and vulnerability and justice, increase the likelihood of one's developing and maintaining PTSD symptomatology. Examples are discussed next.

Beliefs Related to Tolerance of Discomfort and Distress

These are related to what Ellis called LFT or DA, as discussed in chapter 2 and throughout this book. Individuals who experience trauma and who previously have LFT or DA would find the trauma more aversive than someone with high discomfort tolerance. In addition, during the posttrauma period, such individuals would find it more difficult to tolerate such PTSD phenomena as intrusive recollections and anxiety. This then leads to overuse of numbing and dissociative mechanisms and avoidance of internal and environmental phobic cues, resulting in failure to extinguish conditioned stimuli or to complete processing necessary for assimilation or accommodation.

The RET view of the role of discomfort in PTSD symptomatology appears consistent with Foa et al.'s (1989) fear structure analysis. "When one associates 'badness' with the actual fear responses themselves (i.e., 'it's awful to be anxious') repeated exposure to such responses will alter the valence." The badness associated with arousal can be decreased through repeated exposure because anxiety does not persist endlessly and, therefore, comes to be perceived as less terrible. This negative evaluation of discomfort prompts avoidance, while exposure should lead to its modification (pp. 169–170).

Beliefs Related to Performance and Self-worth

Individuals who hold strongly to such beliefs would be unable to accept themselves with mistakes and fallibilities and thus are more likely to engage in characterological rather than behavioral self-blame following trauma. As Veronen and Kilpatrick (1983) discussed regarding rape trauma, victims hold expectations concerning how they should have behaved in the rape situation and how well they should cope subsequently. Victims with pretrauma perfectionistic performance beliefs would be predicted to experience more distress when holding such expectations. See Kuiper & Olinger (1986) for a discussion of the role of dysfunctional self-worth contingencies as a vulnerability factor for depression.

Beliefs Related to Approval and Self-worth

Janoff-Bulman (1985) noted that the victim often perceives herself as a deviant and singled out from others for misfortune. Thus, those with approval-irrational beliefs would be more concerned with losing approval from others, predicting they would see them as deviants. In addition, evidence indicates that victims do often receive disapproval due to their victimization. Lerner and Mathews (1967) suggested that to maintain just-world beliefs, people may blame victims for undesirable life events. In addition, victims may be ignored (Reiff, 1979) because they are seen as "losers" (Bard & Sangrey, 1979; Janoff-Bulman & Frieze, 1983).

Beliefs Related to How Other People Should Behave

RET hypothesizes that while one's preferences for others to treat them fairly and compassionately would be adaptive, when these preferences escalate into demands, anger, hostility, and bitterness result. Thus, individuals who pretraumatically adhere strongly and rigidly to beliefs regarding how others should or must behave (e.g., being understanding and supportive) would be at risk of developing anger related to interpersonal problems following the trauma. Such unrealistic expectations would be predicted to be detrimental to one's social support system and thereby increase the risk for PTSD symptoms.

RET hypothesizes that not only are specific beliefs that involve the necessity for certain events not to occur rigidly held, but also that certain individuals are characterized in general by rigidity of their cognitive structures or beliefs. Such individuals consistently and dogmatically hold to their view of themselves, others, and the world as if such views were facts, and they find it difficult to change their beliefs.

To summarize, RET hypothesizes that certain preexisting irrational beliefs, particularly those related to performance of self and others, approval, discomfort, safety, vulnerability, and fairness, may be activated by traumatic events and lead to greater likelihood of developing and maintaining PTSD symptomatology and other emotional reactions. Individuals who premorbidly hold such beliefs in a dogmatic and rigid fashion are at greater risk of developing PTSD and experiencing more difficulty coping with the resulting PTSD symptomatology.

Finally, the RET model of PTSD does not conflict with the theoretical models presented earlier in this chapter, although it does at times offer a different perspective on the various aspects of these models. For example, classical conditioning (stimulus-response [S-R] model) easily accounts for most of the PTSD symptomatology. However, RET posits that while conditioned stimuli may remind one of the trauma (stimulus-stimulus [S-S] model), the emotional response is not entirely conditioned, but rather it is mediated by one's current appraisal of these stimuli as well as by preexisting irrational beliefs. The importance of information pertaining to meanings in the fear structure is consistent with RET, and the theory that meaning, stimuli, and response information is stored in long-term memory provides an account of the mechanism by which one's beliefs are sustained and activated. Janoff-Bulman's (1985) concept of sheltered basic assumptions and Horowitz's (1986) model also appear cognitively focused and compatible with the RET model. Finally, biological theories of PTSD offer biological substrates for PTSD symptomatology and may influence how difficult it may be for PTSD victims to sustain rational thinking.

TREATMENT OF PTSD: A RET PERSPECTIVE

To date, RET has not been empirically tested as a treatment for PTSD, although aspects of RET are used as a part of some current cognitive-behavioral treatments for the disorder (e.g., Keane et al., 1985). The treatment most similar to RET that has been tested is Beck's cognitive therapy, which includes self-monitoring of mastery and pleasure activities, graded task assignments, identification and modification of automatic thoughts and basic assumptions. Frank, Anderson et al. (1988) found cognitive therapy and systematic desensitization to be equally effective with rape victims. However, the absence of a no-treatment control group renders these results inconclusive (Kilpatrick & Calhoun, 1988).

The RET approach that we outline incorporates procedures previously found to be effective in treating PTSD. We also present RET interventions that we hypothesize will be useful in treating PTSD, although without empirical confirmation.

The main treatment goals for the PTSD victim include helping him or her to cope both with the traumatic event and secondary problems stemming from his or her reaction to the event. The mechanisms of therapy are thought to involve assimilation and accommodation processes via exposure and discussion, as well as acquisition of new coping skills.

Assimilation occurs when the client cognitively appraises the traumatic event in such a way that preexisting cognitive structures or schemata become adequate to make sense of the trauma. Methods of minimizing the trauma, such as those described by Taylor, Wood, and Lichtman (1983), are relevant here. These include making social comparisons with less fortunate others, selectively focusing on personal attributes that make one appear advantaged, creating hypothetically worse worlds, construing benefit from the traumatic event, and manufacturing normative standards of adjustment that make one's own adjustment appear exceptional. Taylor et al. (1983) acknowledged that the circumstances on which such minimization processes would be adaptive versus maladaptive are important areas for research. In general, minimization may counteract catastrophization and related emotional disturbance, but it could also lead to failure to take necessary precautions against future victimization.

Accommodation involves modifying pretrauma cognitive structures and schemata so that the traumatic event can be integrated properly. We predict that the work of most PTSD victims involves accommodation more than assimilation. That is, the nature of the traumatic event is often of such magnitude and severity that one's basic assumptions regarding self, others, and the world need to be revised. In RET terms, this will involve cognitive restructuring of the preexisting inferential and evaluative beliefs discussed previously.

Education concerning the nature of PTSD is an important part of therapy. We advocate teaching clients a conceptual model that clearly explains the development of PTSD symptoms. Such a conceptual framework, in and of itself, should aid in bringing some order to the client's sense of chaos. The role of shattered basic assumptions, the classical-conditioning–related development of phobic reactions and avoidance tendencies, and the importance of perceived predictability and control are covered in the early stages of therapy.

Rules of rape avoidance and behavioral self-blame also are concepts that can be related to assimilation processes. For example, a victim might be able to retain a prior theory of reality, such as, "I can control my safety by taking proper precautions to ward off danger," if she concludes that she was not following proper precautions (e.g., locking doors, avoiding high-risk neighborhoods) but would do so in the future to ward off similar danger. On the other hand, for individuals who were already following safety rules or who see an unchangeable character flaw as responsible for the traumatic event, basic assumptions are more likely to be challenged, and the need to create revised assumptions (accommodation) would be the therapeutic target. Examples of therapeutic interventions intended to facilitate accommodation processes include cognitive restructuring of basic assumptions concerning (a) personal vulnerability; (b) meaning, fairness, and order of the world; and (c) self-worth. Thus, cognitive restructuring is achieved through both discussion and also exposure to traumatic recollections and avoided situations.

Vulnerability

As Perloff (1983) noted, nonvictims tend to underestimate their own personal vulnerability relative to others'. Perloff labeled this as the "illusion of unique invulnerability" (p. 42). This tendency to believe, "It may happen to others, but it won't happen to me," has been documented with nonvictims' perceptions of the personal invulnerability relative to others of the likelihood of cancer, heart attacks, leukemia, alcoholism, venereal disease, divorce, crime, and automobile accidents (Perloff, 1983). While such an illusion of unique invulnerability may be adaptive in increasing feelings of safety, security, and control, it may be maladaptive in facilitating less precautionary safety behavior and greater emotional distress when traumatic events do occur.

Following victimization, individuals often shift to the illusion of unique invulnerability, seeing themselves as more likely than others to experience future victimization. Perceptions of unique invulnerability are associated with poorer adjustment to trauma, lower self-esteem, harsher self-criticism, and greater depression. In contrast, victims who develop perceptions of universal vulnerability view themselves and others as equally vulnerable to future misfortunes and may adapt better to the original trauma. Why some individuals shift to unique as opposed to universal vulnerability is unclear, but therapeutically this appears to be fertile ground for cognitive intervention. Educational inputs and Socratic questioning can be used to help clients develop realistic appraisal of future vulnerability and take precautionary actions to support such views.

Meaning, Fairness, and Order

Bulman and Wortman (1977) discussed the importance of the search for meaning among individuals who were paralyzed in sudden traumatic accidents. As noted by Silver, Boon, and Stones (1983), all but one of the 29 victims in the Bulman and Wortman (1977) study had generated an answer to the question "Why me?", and the authors speculated that "the ability to place the accident in a broad, philosophical perspective influenced subjects' ability to cope effectively" (p. 83). Silver et al. (1983) in their own studies of incest victims also found that women who were able to understand why they were victimized were psychologically less distressed and socially better adjusted than those who were not able to make sense of the event (Janoff-Bulman, 1985). These findings are consistent with Victor Frankl's (1963) well-known advocation of the search for meaning as central in coping with traumatic events.

As Janoff-Bulman (1985) noted, "The problem of loss of meaning often seems to focus not on the question, 'Why did this event happen?' but on the more specific question, 'Why did this event happen to me?' " (p. 21). Embodied in this question appears to be just-world and fairness beliefs that provide a sense of order and thus controllability. RET therapists discuss these concepts with clients and assist them in their search for meaning. RET focuses on delineating clients' unrecognized specific beliefs related to fairness: (a) "If I'm a good, law-abiding, and decent person, misfortune will not occur to me"; (b) "If misfortune does occur, it is unfair"; and (c) "This unfairness should not exist."

We explain to clients that acknowledging the existence of unfairness or strongly wishing that unfairness did not occur will not lead to emotional disturbance. Rather, it is insisting or demanding that fairness should not or must not exist that leads to emotional and behavioral disturbances. Therapy focuses on helping clients accept that unfairness (and often extreme unfairness) exists and that tragedy is a part of life. In essence, the goal is to help clients philosophically accept the current trauma as well as the potential of future trauma while retaining the belief that one can still find at least some happiness and meaning in life. Thus, the question, "Why me?" may be answered by the therapist with "Why not me?" not in a flip or minimizing way, but to begin discussion concerning the fact that unfortunate events can occur to anyone.

Self-Worth

As Janoff-Bulman (1985) noted, the experience of being victimized may lead to serious questioning of perceptions of self-worth. Victims may begin to see themselves as weak, powerless, helpless, out of control, and deviant. These self-perceptions may stem from such preexisting beliefs as those discussed earlier (e.g., "Bad things only happen to those who deserve it"). Such beliefs are reinforced by others who also believe them to be true and thus may view the victim as deserving of the misfortune. Victims may accurately perceive such judgmental attitudes and then further indoctrinate themselves with thoughts of "no-goodness."

The RET therapist will explore whether the victim is engaging in behavioral self-blame, characterological self-blame, or total self-blame (self-downing). As described previously, behavioral self-blame (i.e., "I shouldn't have walked alone in that neighborhood") is associated with better adjustment than characterological self-blame (e.g., "I'm just not an assertive person, the kind that rapists prey upon"). Behavioral self-blame may increase perceived future avoidability of negative events and perceived control in general (Janoff-Bulman, 1979), while characterological self-blame is associated with feelings of passivity and helplessness.

The RET therapist assists clients in reinforcing appropriate behavioral self-blame, or more accurately, taking responsibility for one's actions, and works with them to change characterological self-blame orientations. As Wortman (1983) noted, according to Miller and Porter (1983), victims who feel they have changed the character trait in question may show no deleterious effects from a former characterological attribution.

RET theory predicts that clients usually go beyond characterological self-blame to total self-blame (e.g., "Since I'm a passive-dependent person, which made me vulnerable to assault, I'm no good"). Here, clients do an expanded overgeneralization, first by thinking, "Since I often behave dependently or naively, I'm a dependent, naive person," and then thinking, "If I'm a dependent, naive person, I'm a bad person." As discussed previously, RET has consistently focused on issues of self-worth and acceptance (Ellis & Dryden, 1987). The RET therapist who works with the PTSD self-downer would strive to help the victim achieve avoidance of self-rating and attainment of self-acceptance.

In the following transcript, the therapist attempts to assess whether a rape victim is engaging in behavioral, characterological, or total self-blame, and then to foster the former while diminishing the latter two modes of thinking.

Therapist: You say you should have taken more precautions and that you wouldn't have been raped. What do you mean?

Client: Well, I'm so naive. With my luck, I'm a perfect target. It'll probably happen again.

Therapist: So you see yourself as a naive person. And if you weren't, maybe you wouldn't have been raped?

Client: Right!

Therapist: If it were true that you generally are a naive person, would you philosophically accept yourself and think, "Well, I'm really naive, which at times could be dangerous, but I have other qualities that I like better. And I'm still a worthwhile person." Or would you think you are a pretty bad person and less worthwhile due to your naiveté?

Client: I'm not so philosophical. I feel like a real loser. I hate myself.

In this case, it appears that the client is engaging in all three types of self-blame. Normally, in RET we would go for the global self-blame and then go back and discuss behavioral self-blame (i.e., whether the client could have taken certain precautions that might have prevented the rape). However, in this case, the therapist chooses first to discuss the behavioral self-blame in a more immediate attempt to help bolster the client's sense of control so that she can take certain actions in the future to decrease the likelihood of harm.

Therapist: I think we have a lot to talk about here in terms of how you feel about yourself, but let's first talk about what precautions you think you didn't take that you should have taken.

Client: Well, I shouldn't have been walking alone at night in that part of town.

Therapist: So that's something you could be more careful about in the future?

The therapist would continue to help the client delineate actions she could take to reduce the probability of future sexual assault and to increase her perceived sense of control over future harm.

Next the therapist explores the client's view that she is a totally naive person, as evidence suggests that posttrauma adjustment may be less compromised if the client believes this destructive characterological trait is no longer characteristic of her.

Therapist: So you see yourself as a really naive person?

Client: I definitely am!

Therapist: Perhaps you're right, but let's look at that a little closer. I think it would be helpful to you if you found out that this wasn't completely the case. Then you could have more confidence that your naiveté wouldn't put you at risk for future harm.

Client: Well, that would be nice, but I really am naive.

Therapist: Again, you may be correct, but let me get a better understanding of your naiveté.

Client: Alright.

Therapist: Would you say that 100% of the time for your whole life that you've behaved in a naive manner in every situation?

Client: It seems like it.

Therapist: Yes, but if you stand back and try to be objective, perhaps ask yourself if your best friend would agree with you.

Client: (pause) Well, I don't think Judy [best friend and roommate] would say I'm naive when it comes to trusting the guys I date.

Therapist: Tell me more about that.

Client: Well, Judy has often told me that I have good intuition about guys I meet for the first time.

Therapist: Do you think she is right, or do you disagree?

Client: Well, she's probably right about that to some extent. I guess I'm not naive in that way. It's more that I don't think before I act. I just take too many risks without thinking it through.

Therapist: So maybe you're not a totally naive person, only naive in some ways and not others?

Client: Maybe.

Therapist: It sounds like you could become less naive in terms of learning to look more before you leap.

Client: Can you change that about a person?

Therapist: I think so, if you work at it. There are some skills that people can learn and practice. We could work on that at some point in the future, if you want.

Next the therapist focuses on the client's global self-blame or self-downing for being a totally naive person.

Therapist: I know we've just begun to talk about the possibility that you're not totally naive about everything, but let's assume that you were. How would that make you a bad person and less worthwhile?

Client: I don't know, it just feels that way.

Therapist: I know, I think that it feels like it's true because you believe it's true that you're a bad person if you're a naive one. But does that belief sound perfectly reasonable to you? Or do you see anything wrong with the conclusion that you're totally bad if also naive?

Client: I'm not sure.

Therapist: Do you see any similarities between the belief, "I'm bad if I'm naive" and the one we talked about earlier, "I'm totally naive"?

Client: (pause) Well, maybe it's not rational to say I'm all bad.

Therapist: Why? Can you explain it?

Client: Because there are parts of me that aren't bad, like my intuition.

Therapist: Exactly! So that's what we call an overgeneralization: generalizing from a part of you or some of your behavior to your whole worth as a human being.

Client: I think I see what you mean, but it seems so intellectual.

Therapist: Of course it does. We've just started looking at it, and that's a good start. If we keep working on it, it's possible that you will come to believe what, at least for a moment just now, seemed to be intellectually true. It takes a while to change old ways of thinking and to believe it fully on an emotional level.

The preceding dialogue is intended to give some idea of possible ways to begin exploring and challenging clients' beliefs that may have impeded adjustment, although much work and practice typically are needed for significant changes to occur.

Self-worth issues are also likely to arise when clients' PTSD symptomatology leads to perceptions of impaired functioning in daily life (e.g., increased intensity and variability of emotional and autonomic reactivity, difficulty concentrating, and phobic reactions). Clients are assisted in combating performance shoulds and subsequent self-downing. Rather than thinking, "I shouldn't get so irritable at my family members, and I'm a jerk for doing so," the client might practice thinking, "I wish I didn't get so irritable. I'll work at it, but I'm not a jerk—just a fallible human being. It's understandable that I have difficulty in this area given the trauma I experienced."

Anger

PTSD clients are often angry at themselves for somehow not avoiding the trauma, for their behavior during the trauma, and their subsequent coping with the trauma. Clients may be angry at themselves for surviving when close friends or relatives have died, which contributes to survival guilt (e.g., "I have no right to live when my buddy was killed. I should have been the one to die"). Moreover, clients may be angry at others' reactions to them or their failure to meet expectations (e.g., not being more understanding or supportive). Finally, clients understandably may be angry at the perpetrator of the trauma if it is of human design, or at God, or the world. The therapist assesses when such anger is facilitative or debilitative to client adaptation.

In typical RET fashion, the therapist assists clients in discriminating their preferences from demands on their own and others' behavior and striving to accept rather than to condemn themselves and others for their bad behaviors. Anger at God or the world is subject to similar approaches as well as philosophical and theological discussion. The following transcript presents a RET intervention for a PTSD client's anger at her spouse for not being more understanding and caring with respect to her difficulties following an automobile accident.

Therapist: So, Carol, if I understand you correctly, you feel extremely angry at Ted for not being more understanding and caring about your condition.

Client: I get so mad at him I could wring his neck!

Therapist: Would you say that your anger at Ted is helpful or is it getting in the way?

Client: I don't know, I guess it really doesn't help. Ted just withdraws and then I feel worse, like I'm really all alone.

Therapist: So it sounds like if there were some way that you could not feel so angry, and perhaps figure out some way to get Ted to be more supportive, that would be best for you.

Client: Right, that's what I really want.

Therapist: Well, perhaps if we can work on the anger first, then we can do some problem solving on how to get Ted to be more supportive.

Client: Alright.

Therapist: Fine, now remember how we've talked about how your thoughts and beliefs affect your emotions? Let's then try to figure out how your thinking might be connected to your anger at Ted. Any ideas about what goes through your mind when you're most angry at Ted?

Client: (pause) Well, I just keep thinking that if he really cared, he would be more understanding of my needs. Because he's my husband, he should understand better than anyone else how my anxiety since the accident affects me.

Therapist: So it seems that Ted more than anyone else should be able to empathize with you and realize how the accident has affected you.

Client: Right, but when I startle so easily, he just gets irritated. He doesn't understand why I now avoid driving on freeways.

Therapist: I think that you've hit on it with the belief that he *should* understand. It sounds like more than just wishing or preferring he would be more understanding.

Client: Right.

Therapist: So, I think it's the *should* that really keeps the anger going. If that's the case, what do we need to do to reduce the anger?

Client: Well, not think in terms of *shoulds,* I guess.

Therapist: Right. Now, to do that, we need to understand why the *should* may not be so reasonable. See any problems with the *should?*

Client: Well, I'm demanding that he be more understanding.

Therapist: Right, now what's the problem with that?

Client: I'm not sure.

Therapist: Well, let's look at it this way: Before the accident, if someone told you that you would be easily startled, would you have believed them?

Client: Well, it would have been hard to believe.

Therapist: And now that this really has happened to you, do you fully understand why you react the way you do?

Client: No, but since coming to therapy, I'm beginning to understand.

Therapist: Well, Ted hasn't been to therapy, so maybe it's not so surprising that he's having difficulty understanding.

Client: I guess that's right. I just wish he did understand. I could really use his support.

Therapist: Of course you do. And as long as you stick to wishing and not demanding, will you feel so angry?

Client: I suppose not.

Therapist: What would you likely feel if you only wished he understood but didn't demand it?

Client: Disappointment, I guess, maybe a little irritated.

Therapist: And that would be pretty appropriate, I'd say. Perhaps soon we can invite Ted to come in, and I'll try to explain to him the nature of PTSD reactions. Have you shared with him any of the readings I've suggested?

Client: Not yet. I suppose I should.

Therapist: Yes, it might help him to understand better.

In this interchange, the therapist's primary goal is to help the client to understand why her husband behaves as he does, which in effect goes against demanding that he behave differently. As the client's anger at her husband decreases, he is likely to be more supportive, which is the client's real desire and may help her to adjust to her PTSD.

Social Support

RET therapists advocate assessing the quality of the client's social support systems, including family, friends, public officials, and helping professionals, as well as working to enhance the client's use of such resources. In doing so, a variety of therapeutic tasks may be appropriate, including (a) social skills training for those who lack behavioral skills important for developing and maintaining relationships, (b) creating realistic expectations regarding others' capacities to be understanding and supportive, (c) developing rational thinking skills to deal with possible criticism or judgment without self-condemnation or hostility toward the other person, and (d) assisting in use of appropriate community resources (e.g., legal and health care assistance, organized support groups). As discussed earlier, the importance of support systems in the victim's adjustment is empirically well documented (Fairbank & Nicholson, 1987; Steketee & Foa, 1987).

Exposure Techniques

In addition to the aforementioned primarily cognitive interventions hypothesized to be important in rebuilding shattered assumptions and integrating the traumatic event into a revised belief system, a variety of more direct behavioral interventions are equally important in the assimilation and accommodation processes. In fact, exposure is most often effective in facilitating the types of cognitive restructuring described earlier. Keane et al.'s (1989) implosive therapy, Horowitz's (1986) gradual dosing, and Foa and Olasov's (1987) prolonged imaginal exposure are methods that help clients work through their traumatic event, discover and revise meanings, and develop more adaptive responses to the traumatic event. In RET, we incorporate imaginal exposure to the traumatic event and behavioral homework assignments to confront currently avoided phobic situations (e.g., driving automobiles in the case of a serious crash victim). These methods are adapted from Foa and Olasov (1987) and include 30- to 60-minute imaginal exposure in-session and homework assignments to listen daily to audio tapes of the exposure.

While conducting the imaginal exposure and in reviewing imagined and behavioral exposure homework assignments, we are on the lookout for clients' cognitive and emotional reprocessing of the trauma that may relate to the issues of meaning of the event, shattered assumptions, irrational beliefs, and so on. Discussion, therefore, attempts to integrate further this material with ongoing attempts to accept more fully the reality of the traumatic event and its impact on the client's life.

Increasing Self-Control

Many of the procedures described so far, although directly targeted for a variety of PTSD problems (e.g, shattered assumptions, irrational beliefs, self-blame), may have important additional effects of increasing clients' perceived sense of control of future negative events. These interventions should be conducted with this goal in mind. There are many additional cognitive-behavioral interventions that can also be used to increase perceived sense of control and address common PTSD symptomatology. The following techniques are similar to those included in stress inoculation packages for PTSD, as developed by Olasov and Foa (1987) and Veronen and Kilpatrick (1983):

1. Relaxation and breathing control for increased arousal, insomnia, and so on.
2. Thought stopping for intrusive recollections and obsessive ruminations not deemed useful as part of reprocessing the traumatic event.
3. Problem solving to devise alternative ways of coping with trauma-related difficulties ranging from emotional reactions to environmental obstacles.
4. RET for daily stresses and general emotional management.
5. Safety and danger discrimination training to develop principles that enable clients to better assess relative safety and danger in a variety of situations.

CASE EXAMPLE: PTSD
FOLLOWING AN ACCIDENT

Eva, a 60-year-old mother of four and grandmother of two, was diagnosed as suffering from PTSD following an accident that involved a truck crashing into her home. She reported that she was standing in her kitchen looking out the window when she suddenly saw a truck coming toward her. Apparently, the truck ran off the nearby highway, came through her yard, and hit her house. Although she was not actually hit by the truck, she later recalled thinking, "It's going to kill me."

Several months following this trauma, Eva sought treatment for associated depression, anxiety, and fear of a recurrence of a similar accident. Other symptoms included increased startle response (particularly in response to the sounds of trucks), decreased ability to concentrate, loss of interest in sex, general emotional numbness, withdrawal from friends and social activities, avoidance of driving where trucks would likely be present, and feelings of diminished self-worth. Eva even wanted to move from her home of 40 years, although her husband eventually convinced her to reconsider. Finally, her perception of the truck as life threatening seemed to increase the severity of the aforementioned reactions.

During the therapist's assessment, it became clear that Eva had always been strong and known for her emotional stoicism. Her house was associated with feelings of safety and security, the place where she successfully raised her family and enjoyed a stable relationship with her husband. It appeared that Eva's view of the world, others, and herself had been significantly shattered. Following the trauma, she found herself emotionally labile and feeling out of control, in sharp contrast to her previous view of herself as the rock of the family. She also questioned her religion and how God would have let this happen to her. Additionally, she felt betrayed by friends who "didn't understand" her PTSD symptomatology. She therefore withdrew from others and did not profit from an active support group.

Therapy consisted of relaxation training to decrease general heightened emotional reactivity, prolonged imaginal exposure to the traumatic event, and in vivo exposure to avoided external stimuli. RET was used to increase self-acceptance related to PTSD-impaired performances and to foster revised assumptions related to self, others, and the world. Sessions also included Eva's husband to help in understanding and coping with his wife's changed role in their relationship and the family. Couple counseling was conducted to address other conflicts that emerged due to Eva's PTSD. In addition, behavioral rehearsal and role-playing were used to prepare her for a court presentation. Eventually on her own accord, Eva and her husband decided to remodel parts of their house so that less time would need to be spent near the part of the house where the accident occurred. This appeared to increase Eva's sense of future safety.

It appeared that Eva began to feel somewhat more in control as she learned relaxation skills. Prolonged imaginal exposure to the trauma seemed associated with increased ability to concentrate and decreased emotional numbing. Even more debilitative than the phobic reactions to truck stimuli was Eva's difficulty accepting herself as more emotional, less confident, and no longer the rock of the family. RET was helpful with this secondary disturbance. At termination of therapy, however, this problem remained an ongoing challenge for Eva.

Chapter 8

Generalized Anxiety Disorder

Generalized Anxiety Disorder (GAD) refers to a pattern of chronic, pervasive anxiety or worry that significantly interferes with the individual's ability to carry on with normal daily activities. Because this worry is not consistently related to specific environmental triggers (e.g., as in phobias), it is often described as pervasive or free-floating anxiety. Although individuals with GAD are likely to experience a chronic sense of impending doom, they also may or may not experience infrequent, full, or symptom-limited panic attacks (Barlow, 1988). In addition, compared to phobics, GAD individuals are not as prone to behavioral avoidance, as there are less environmental triggers from which to hide, yet some people with GAD do evidence avoidance patterns (Barlow, 1988; Butler, Gelder, Hibbert, Cullington, & Klimes, 1987; Clark, 1989a). The moderate intensity and chronic nature of the anxiety differentiates the GAD client from the normal individual who merely worries on occasion in response to ordinary anxiety-arousing events (e.g., an upcoming IRS audit).

People with GAD experience pervasive worry (apprehension expectation) and assorted physical symptoms associated with increased ANS arousal. The DSM-III-R divides GAD arousal symptoms into the following three general categories: (a) motor tension, (b) autonomic hyperactivity, and (c) vigilance and scanning. A full listing of the DSM-III-R symptoms (e.g., trembling, palpitations, and insomnia) associated with these categories is provided later in this chapter. The distinguishing feature of GAD, however, appears to be apprehensive expectation (Barlow, 1988), as the arousal symptoms of GAD are also common to the other anxiety disorders.

Sanderson and Barlow (1986) found that people with GAD are more likely to worry about minor things and feel tense, anxious, and worried a great deal of the time. They also identified four spheres of worry most common to GAD individuals: (a) family, (b) money, (c) work, and (d) illness. These four spheres represent areas of worry for most individuals, although for the GAD sufferer the worry is excessive and persistent. This is in contrast to PD individuals, who tend to worry about the possibility of an upcoming panic attack, rather than family, money, and so on (Barlow, 1988).

Beck and Emery (1985) suggested that GAD's traditional conceptualization that focuses on the absence of specific anxiety-provoking triggers may be unfounded. Instead, GAD persons can experience worry related to specific fears, including dying, suffocating, being attacked, or losing control. There may also occur worry associated with the memory of near disaster or an actual trauma, as some cases would not meet the diagnostic criteria for PTSD or Adjustment Disorder with Anxious Mood.

Barlow, Blanchard, Vermilyea, Vermilyea, and DiNardo (1986) discussed reconceptualization issues associated with the DSM-III descriptions of GAD. The authors proposed that the disorder, according to DSM-III standards, actually was a residual category in which GAD symptoms were found in all of the other anxiety disorders. To reconceptualize GAD as a distinct disorder required several major changes with the advent of DSM-III-R, with an emphasis on the focus of the client's worry or apprehensive expectation about life problems, extension of the duration requirement to 6 months, and identification of two separate spheres of worry (Barlow, 1988).

At a recent (1990) workshop in Seattle, Washington, Barlow described upcoming changes in the GAD diagnostic criteria scheduled for DSM-IV. In short, clinicians will have the specific responsibility of deciding if the client's worry is unrealistic. Some clients do not believe that their worry is excessive, although there is significant interference in daily activities. The clinician will judge whether the client's apprehensive expectation is productive and leads to some form of constructive action. In addition, the clinician will assess issues of controllability (i.e., is the client able to stop worrying when he or she so desires?).

Given general confusion regarding the definition of GAD and changes in diagnostic criteria from DSM-III to DSM-III-R (Thyer, 1987) and beyond, studies of the prevalence of GAD are relatively rare in the literature. Reported prevalence rates include 6.4% (Uhlenhuth, Balter, & Lipman, 1978), 2.5% (Weissman, Myers, & Harding, 1978), and 2.5% (Anderson, Noyes, & Crowe, 1984). Barlow (1988) reported that 11% of 125 patients referred to the Center for Stress and Anxiety Disorders were diagnosed with GAD. Moreover, Weissman et al. (1978) found

GAD to be six times more common than PD given DSM-III criteria. Chronic anxiety, then, appears to be more prevalent than PD (Weissman et al., 1978), although there is accumulating evidence that panic attacks are indeed associated with generalized anxiety (Barlow, 1988). In fact, Barlow (1988) noted that panic attacks are more likely to develop following an extended period of generalized anxiety.

ETIOLOGY OF GAD

As with the other anxiety disorders, a biopsychosocial discussion of the etiology of GAD incorporates the physiological, cognitive, and behavioral dimensions of the disorder. Concerning the physiological component, GAD sufferers may be the victims of several possible biological mechanisms, including malfunctioning serotonergic and/or adrenergic systems, locus coeruleus and raphe, and GABA-receptor benzodiazepine-binding sites (Taylor & Arnow, 1988). Furthermore, GAD individuals differ from normals in terms of physiological measures: increased respiration, forearm blood flow, heart rate, and electromyographic activity (Taylor & Arnow, 1988). As these differences are consistent with increased autonomic activity, DSM-III-R's categorization of physical symptoms (i.e., motor tension, autonomic hyperactivity, vigilance, and scanning) is a useful one. Prolonged levels of anxiety may also predispose individuals to develop a variety of psychophysiological disorders, including migraine headaches, asthma, and ulcerative colitis (Rimm & Sommervill, 1977).

Beck and Emery (1985) suggested that GAD is largely due to social or interpersonal anxiety and stressed the importance of examining cognitive themes such as rejection, control, domination, and/or abandonment. Other cognitive-related etiological considerations include social-evaluative fears (Deffenbacher & Suinn, 1982) and dysfunctional attentional focus and shifting with increased vigilance and arousal (Barlow, 1988). GAD individuals who experience unpleasant physical symptoms are likely to interpret these as negative occurrences. For example, instead of interpreting restlessness as a sign of excitement, the GAD individual is likely to view the symptom's occurrence as uncomfortable and unbearable, although not necessarily dangerous (Hibbert, 1984), but also catastrophize concerning the outcome of the symptom as being indicative of never-ending restlessness. Such cognitive distortions can create a sense of loss of self-control and helplessness in the GAD person (Heide & Borkovek, 1984) that is exacerbated by fear of fear.

Ellis conceptualized chronic worry as resulting from the belief that various life events and circumstances will generate awful conse-quences. Irrational belief 4—the idea that it is awful and catastrophic when things are not the way one would much like them to be—and belief 6—the idea that if something is or may be dangerous or fearsome one should be concerned about it and should keep dwelling on the possibility of its occurring (Ellis, 1962)—would appear characteristic of GAD.

Concerning the behavioral component of the disorder, individuals with GAD typically do not resort to consistent circumscribed avoidance in the traditional phobic sense, as their spheres of worry do not allow ready avoidance of or escape from circumscribed phobic cues. In other words, the worry is pervasive enough that the individual is unable to hide from it. At another level, however, the GAD individual may avoid the problem-solving process necessary to gain control over the catastro-phized situation. The client might also become resistant to engaging in those therapeutic activities needed to alleviate the anxiety and restore normal life functioning, often for fear of creating more worry or losing further control. In this case, the therapist should remain alert to the possibility of negative reinforcement prompting the client's avoidance. For example, even though the therapist urges GAD patients to follow through with relaxation exercises, they may refuse to do so for fear that listening to relaxation tapes would distract them from hypervigi-lance for certain impending doom. In terms of secondary gain, these watchful clients' avoidance of listening to relaxation tapes allows them to continue to worry and thus prevent disaster, as they may irrationally believe that they must worry or disaster will result. As with the pho-bias, a never-ending cycle existing along physical, cognitive, and be-havioral dimensions is created.

Barlow's (1988) model of the etiology of GAD is similar to those pre-sented throughout previous chapters of this book. To review, due to both biological and psychological vulnerabilities, individuals have in-tense neurobiological reactions to negative stressful life events. At suf-ficient intensities, such reactions may result in false alarms (i.e., pan-ics). When various life problems appear to occur in an unpredictable, uncontrollable fashion, individuals experience intense emotional reac-tions regarding such problematic events. One's perceived ability to cope with these events further increases anxious apprehension (i.e., worry) about possible negative outcomes. Attention to tasks at hand becomes diverted to self-evaluative processes. Hypervigilance and the associ-ated narrowing of attention to the focus of one's worries or problems further increases arousal and may eventually impair performance in various life spheres (e.g., work).

Borkovec and Inz (1990) hypothesized concerning an avoidance function of worry. These investigators obtained data that indicated that the worry of GAD patients primarily involves thought as opposed to imaginal activity. Borkovec and Inz (1990) speculated that:

> the declines in imagery and increases in thought that seem to character-ize worry in the present study may represent the motivated avoidance of imaginal process. If imagery is a primary vehicle for the somatic activa-tion of emotion (Lang, 1988), then one way to learn to avoid somatic anxiety is to avoid imagery by increasing the generation of, or attentional focus on, conceptual activity. Worry may thus represent an avoidance of affect in general or anxious emotional experience in particular. Under such circumstances, triggers for worry episodes are likely to become broadly generalized to any stimulus associated with any degree of emotional elic-itation. (pp. 157–158)

Borkovec (1985) also suggested that worry may involve short, inter-rupted exposures to fear-related stimuli that may result in increases in fear rather than decreases. Finally, it may be inferred from Borkovec's hypothesis that exposure therapy creates optimal conditions for pro-cessing emotional imagery (i.e., refraining from the cognitive avoid-ance of worry and engaging in longer rather than brief exposure to feared material) and may be useful in the treatment of GAD worriers.

DSM-III-R CLASSIFICATION AND DIAGNOSTIC CRITERIA

The DSM-III-R diagnostic criteria for GAD (300.02) are listed in Table 8.1.

Unlike DSM-III, the DSM-III-R criteria point to the possible presence of additional Axis I disorders, including other anxiety or affective dis-orders. In fact, Sanderson and Barlow (1986) found that GAD was com-monly associated with social and simple phobias, as well as with PD. Barlow (1988) also described a relationship between GAD and OCD, and Taylor and Arnow (1988) cautioned mental health professionals to be alert to the possibility of coexisting depression (Taylor & Arnow, 1988).

Given the number of physical symptoms associated with GAD, the mental health professional should rule out the possibility of a medical condition generating chronic anxiety. According to Taylor and Arnow (1988), possible causes of such anxiety include various cardiovascular diseases (e.g., mitral valve prolapse, arrhythmias, coronary heart dis-ease), endocrine disorders (e.g., hyperthyroidism, hypoglycemia, hy-

Table 8.1. DSM-III-R Diagnostic Criteria for Generalized Anxiety Disorder

A. Unrealistic or excessive anxiety and worry (apprehensive expectation) about two or more life circumstances, e.g., worry about possible misfortune to one's child (who is in no danger) and worry about finances (for no good reason), for a period of six months or longer, during which the person has been bothered more days than not by these concerns. In children and adolescents, this may take the form of anxiety and worry about academic, athletic, and social performance.

B. If another Axis I disorder is present, the focus of the anxiety and worry in A is unrelated to it, e.g., the anxiety or worry is not about having a panic attack (as in Panic Disorder), being embarrassed in public (as in Social Phobia), being contaminated (as in Obsessive Compulsive Disorder), or gaining weight (as in Anorexia Nervosa).

C. The disturbance does not occur only during the course of a Mood Disorder or a psychotic disorder.

D. At least 6 of the following 18 symptoms are often present when anxious (do not include symptoms present only during panic attacks):
Motor tension
  1) trembling, twitching, or feeling shaky
  2) muscle tension, aches, or soreness
  3) restlessness
  4) easy fatigability
Autonomic hyperactivity
  5) shortness of breath or smothering sensations
  6) palpitations or accelerated heart rate (tachycardia)
  7) sweating, or cold clammy hands
  8) dry mouth
  9) dizziness or lightheadedness
  10) nausea, diarrhea, or other abdominal distress
  11) flushes (hot flashes) or chills
  12) frequent urination
  13) trouble swallowing or lump in throat
Vigilance and scanning
  14) feeling keyed up or on edge
  15) exaggerated startle response
  16) difficulty concentrating or "mind going blank" because of anxiety
  17) trouble falling or staying asleep
  18) irritability

E. It cannot be established that an organic factor initiated and maintained the disturbance, e.g., hyperthyroidism, Caffeine Intoxication (pp. 252–253).

Note. Reprinted with permission from the *Diagnostic and Statistical Manual of Mental Disorders, Third Edition, Revised.* Copyright 1987 American Psychiatric Association.

poparathyroidism), and neurologic disorders (e.g., vestibular problems, seizures).

Finally, for some individuals, substance abuse may be a complication of GAD. The clinician should be alert to the client's possible self-medication with alcohol and/or illicit drugs to reduce worry. Also, the client should be evaluated for dependence on prescription medications, such as the benzodiazepines (e.g., alprazolam, diazepam).

REVIEW OF ASSESSMENT
INSTRUMENTS

The ADIS-R (Di Nardo et al., 1985) provides a reliable structured interview for diagnosing GAD. In addition, a variety of rating scales, self-report measures, and self-monitoring procedures are available for assessment with GAD patients. Widely used instruments include the STAI (Spielberger et al., 1970) and its revised version (Spielberger, 1983), Hamilton Anxiety Rating Scale (Hamilton, 1959), EPQ-N (Eysenck & Eysenck, 1975), and the Cognitive and Somatic Anxiety Questionnaire (Schwartz, Davidson, & Goleman, 1978).

The Beck Anxiety Inventory appears particularly appropriate for assessing clinical anxiety, and unlike some previous anxiety measures (e.g., STAI) has been shown to discriminate anxiety from depression (Beck, Epstein, Brown, & Steer, 1988). The Clinical Anxiety Scale (CAS) derived largely from DSM-III diagnostic criteria for the anxiety disorders, also appears clinically useful (Thyer, 1987).

Should panic attacks be suspected, the ACQ and BSQ (Chambless et al., 1984) would be appropriate instruments, and the MI (Chambless et al., 1985) is useful in assessing possible avoidance behavior. The BDI (Beck et al., 1961) provides a measure of depressive symptomatology that is commonly associated with GAD, and the General Attitude and Belief Scale (Bernard, 1990; Di Giuseppe et al., 1988) or the briefer Belief Scale (Malouf & Schutte, 1986) are recommended for assessing irrational beliefs which may be related to generalized anxiety and worry.

The recently developed Penn State Worry Questionnaire appears to be a useful instrument for assessing the specific trait of worry characteristic of GAD (Brown, Anthony, & Barlow, 1990). The Reactions to Relaxation and Arousal Questionnaire (Heide & Borkovec, 1983) may be used to determine the presence of relaxation-induced anxiety during relaxed states.

Finally, self-monitoring devices, such as the Weekly Record of Anxiety and Depression (Barlow, 1988) and records of percentage of time spent worrying during specified time periods are also useful.

REVIEW OF NON-RET
TREATMENTS

Numerous behavioral interventions have been used to treat generalized anxiety states, although few controlled studies have evaluated treatments for actual GAD. The most common have included self-control desensitization (e.g., Goldfried, 1971), relaxation training (e.g.,

Lehrer, 1978), biofeedback (e.g., Rupert, Dobbins, & Mathew, 1981; Stoyva, 1979), and physical exercise (Gold, 1989). Anxiety management training (Suinn, 1976) has also been used with success in several clinical populations (e.g., Jannoun, Munby, Catalan, & Gelder, 1980). In addition, flooding, implosion, and modeling procedures may be used as adjunctive interventions, given the client's particular needs (Deffenbacher & Suinn, 1982; Suinn, 1984).

Pharmacological treatment of GAD has become increasingly popular, particularly with the advent of the benzodiazepines, although this class of drug appears to have only limited therapeutic effects as well as a variety of negative side effects (Barlow, 1988). Possible negative effects include physical and/or psychological dependence, cognitive impairment, and rebound anxiety following withdrawal of the drug (Barlow, 1988). Although this drug class also tends to interfere with exposure therapies, it may be useful under certain circumstances for limited periods of time (e.g., during a brief emotional crisis).

Other pharmacological agents used in treating chronic anxiety include imipramine (Kahn et al., 1986), beta blockers (e.g., propranolol; Noyes, 1985), certain antihistamines (e.g., diphenhydramine; Gold, 1989), and buspirone (Gold, 1989). Although propranolol has been shown to be little better than placebo when used to treat chronic anxiety (Hallstrom, Treasaden, Edwards, & Lader, 1981), evidence is accumulating that points to the tremendous antianxiety effects of imipramine (Kahn et al., 1986). Antihistamines may be used to avoid the addictive potential of certain other drug classifications (e.g., tranquilizers). Of course, mental health professionals will want to consider carefully a client's tendency toward substance abuse before implementing or referring for pharmacological treatment.

COGNITIVE THERAPY AND GAD

Although research on treatments for GAD has lagged behind in comparison to most of the other anxiety disorders, several well-controlled outcome studies have recently appeared. While cognitive interventions appear to play an important therapeutic role, most empirically-validated treatments are multidimensional cognitive-behavioral treatment packages. According to Wilson's (1990) recent review in "Review of Behavior Therapy," Anxiety Management like that of Gillian Butler and her colleagues at Oxford University, is "one of the most carefully studied and promising treatments for GAD" (p. 90). Wilson describes this treatment package and reviews recent related cognitive-behavioral therapy clinical outcome studies.

In the remainder of this section we will briefly describe representa-

tive studies. See Wilson (1990) for a more extensive critical review. Butler, Cullington, Hibbert, Klimes, and Gelder (1987) found anxiety management superior to a waiting list control condition at posttest, and the
clinically significant gains were maintained at six-month follow-up. Butler
et al.'s (1987) treatment package consists of: (a) information about the
nature of anxiety and what to expect from treatment, (b) a cognitive
component to address specific anxiety-producing thoughts, (c) distraction and relaxation techniques for anticipatory anxiety, (d) in-vivo exposure to avoided situations, and (e) a component focusing on increasing self-confidence, which includes identification of the client's strengths
and areas of competence and identification of and increase in enjoy-
able activities. As Wilson (1990) notes, this treatment program is described in a useful client self-help booklet and a treatment manual
which is available from Butler and her colleagues. Butler, Gelder,
Hibbert, Cullington, and Klimes (1987) found that many of the techniques included in treatment had been attempted unsuccessfully by
clients before treatment. Apparently treatment enabled clients to
use these techniques successfully with more precision and persistence. Patients also rated the self-confidence building assignments,
such as increasing social activities, particularly helpful (Wilson,
1990). Butler, Gelder et al. (1987) concluded that the findings also
supported the importance of control of anxiety-related cognitions
and exposure to cues for anxiety.

Blowers, Cobb, and Mathews (1987) compared their version of anxiety management containing brief cognitive therapy and relaxation
training, with nondirective counseling and a waiting-list control group.
At posttest and six-month follow-up anxiety management training was
superior to the waiting-list group, but not significantly better than nondirective counseling. The authors concluded that the failure to include
exposure to anxiety-arousing situations may have accounted for less
potent effects compared to Butler, Cullington et al. (1987).

Borkovec et al. (1987) found that cognitive therapy plus relaxation
training was more effective than nondirective therapy with relaxation
for a sample of undergraduate GAD clients. In a subsequent study with
older and more anxious GAD clients, Borkovec and Mathews (1988)
failed to replicate these findings. Cognitive therapy with relaxation,
nondirective therapy with relaxation, and coping desensitization (hierarchical imaginal exposure to anxiety-provoking environmental scenes
and resulting cognitive and somatic anxiety cues) were equally effective
with both GAD and PD clients. These results were maintained at 6-
and 12-month follow-ups.

Borkovec and Mathews (1988) hypothesized that common elements
among treatments and expectancies for improvement may have con-

tributed to the equal effectiveness of treatments. In addition, they noted that degree of relaxation practice and relaxation-induced anxiety were correlated with better outcome. Also, it doesn't appear that the cognitive and relaxation treatment included exposure to anxiety-arousing avoided situations as recommended by the Oxford group. Perhaps inclusion of exposure and other elements of the Oxford approach would lead to better results than nondirective counseling. It appears likely that future research will test these comparisons.

Currently, Barlow (1988) and his colleagues have obtained preliminary results from a large study in progress comparing cognitive, relaxation, combined cognitive and relaxation interventions, and waiting-list control groups. Clients receiving treatment used cognitive and/or relaxation procedures in a hierarchical manner as coping skills to deal with anxiety and anxiety-related situations. Avoidance behavior and sensitivity to somatic cues associated with anxiety are also targeted for treatment. Preliminary results suggest the effectiveness of each treatment group, with cognitive coping procedures yielding the most powerful treatment effects.

Other controlled studies also support the effectiveness of cognitive-behavioral treatments for generalized anxiety (Barlow, et al., 1984; Durham & Turvey, 1987). Only a few studies have compared cognitive behavior therapy with medication for generalized anxiety. Lindsay, Gamsu, McLaughlin, Hood, and Espie (1987) reported cognitive behavior therapy and anxiety management superior to lorazepam and a waiting-list control group at three-month follow-up, and Power, Jerrom, Simpson, Mitchell, & Swanson (1989) also reported results favoring cognitive behavior therapy over diazepam at posttreatment and twelve-month follow-up. In the most recent comparison with a larger sample of GAD patients, Power et al. (1990) found cognitive behavior therapy superior to diazepam, which was no better than medication placebo. However, the authors note that a more flexible medication dosage schedule with a higher maximum daily dose may have yielded stronger effects.

At the present time, it appears that the treatment of choice for GAD is cognitive-behavioral anxiety-management training, and exposure to avoided anxiety-arousing situations appears to be a particularly important aspect of treatment. Steps to increase compliance with relaxation practice and to reduce relaxation-induced anxiety may also prove beneficial. Whether treatments such as these are more effective in treating GAD than alternative psychological treatments, such as nondirective counseling, or medical treatments (e.g., various benzodiazepines or tricyclic antidepressants such as imipramine) remains to be determined by future research.

A RET MODEL FOR GAD

As indicated in chapter 2, anxiety neurotics are typically character-ized by cognitive bias. In other words, compared to normals they are more likely (a) to interpret ambiguous information as threatening, (b) to overestimate the probability of the occurrence of aversive events, and (c) to rate the negative events as more aversive or costly. As we discussed in chapter 3, Ellis hypothesized that this cognitive bias re-sults from underlying "musturbatory" ideologies. Thus, we, like Ellis, hypothesize that individuals who are characterized by "necessitous" thinking (Brown & Beck, 1989) with respect to performance, approval and discomfort are more likely to worry excessively about potential negative events. Likewise, GAD clients who worry about family, money, work, and/or illness (Barlow, 1988) are predicted to believe that prob-lems in these areas "must not occur, and it is terrible and unbearable if they do." The inability to cope well with such problems and beliefs may be taken as evidence of lowered self-worth.

As with RET proposed for the other anxiety disorders, we propose, as do Barlow (1988) and Taylor and Arnow (1988), that biological vul-nerabilities also play a role in the development of GAD. Thus, we pre-dict that such biologically vulnerable individuals more easily develop irrational beliefs that are activated by stressful life events and then brought to bear on life's problems. Irrational beliefs and thinking styles subsequently create emotional distress (e.g., anxiety, depression) that interferes with rather than facilitates problem solving. As this process continues, the GAD client further worries about worrying and its de-bilitative effects, which may also lead to feelings of being out of control and unable to cope, as well as damage to one's physical health.

Not only do GAD clients worry about numerous life problems, they also appear to hold any of a number of irrational beliefs about worry-ing. Such beliefs seem to be important in instigating and maintaining the worry process. Such beliefs about worrying include the following:

1. I should worry if there is a possibility that something bad might happen. Not worrying is irresponsible.
2. My worrying might ward off danger.
3. If there are bad things going on in my life, I've no right to enjoy myself. Rather, I should be worried and upset about my problems.
4. If I don't worry and remain hypervigilant for danger, it may hit me by surprise. I couldn't stand the discomfort it would create.
5. If I don't effectively manage my worrying or solve my problems, I'm less of a person.

TREATMENT OF GAD: A RET PERSPECTIVE

While RET has not been formally evaluated as a treatment for DSM-III–diagnosed GAD clients, several studies have tested the effectiveness of RET with generalized anxiety. Positive results have been reported with student volunteers (Stewart, 1983; Walsh, 1982) and older adults over 60 (Keller, Croake, & Brooking, 1975). RET has also been used to reduce trait anxiety in community mental health clinic clients (Kassinove, Miller, & Kalin, 1980; Lipsky et al., 1980) and community volunteers with clinically significant emotional distress (Warren et al., 1988). Along similar lines, Robinson (1989) found rational restructuring superior to self-control desensitization (Goldfried & Davison, 1976) and progressive relaxation in the treatment of chronic worry.

Our RET approach to treating GAD clients includes both tested and not-yet-tested interventions. Taken together, these include (a) relaxation and breathing control training for chronic hyperarousal; (b) skills training (e.g., problem solving and assertion training to increase one's awareness of options to deal with life's difficulties while fostering a sense of self-control); (c) cognitive interventions to correct probability estimates of negative events, decatastrophizing problems and feared outcomes, challenging idiosyncratic beliefs about worrying, and increasing discomfort tolerance and self-acceptance; (d) behavioral interventions to foster approach rather than avoidance behavior; and (e) thought stopping and stimulus control procedures (i.e., worrying for a specified time in a specified place).

Major Cognitive Interventions

The major cognitive interventions for GAD clients include (a) dealing with problems about problems, (b) revising probability estimates, (c) challenging shoulds and musts, (d) decatastrophizing, and (e) increasing self-acceptance.

As discussed previously, RET recommends helping clients with second- and third-level problems before dealing with first-level problems (Ellis, 1988). For GAD clients, second-level problems often involve worrying about worrying. A recent client of ours was making steady progress in decreasing worry when he began to worry about the possibility of again starting to worry uncontrollably. In this case, we helped the client to challenge the same beliefs that related to the primary worry. In essence, such beliefs often consist of, "I mustn't worry so often. It would be awful if I continued to worry so much. I can't stand the discomfort of worry! My self-worth is less if I can't control my worrying!"

The following example further illustrates the use of cognitive interventions.

CASE EXAMPLE: FEAR OF
JOB LOSS

Bill, a 50-year-old school teacher, worried constantly about losing his job, even though this appeared to be unlikely. The main evidence that Bill used to convince himself that he might be fired involved a parent complaining to the principal about Bill's discipline-focused approach to a particular child. Bill reported that he had been taught in previous cognitive therapy to examine the evidence for his prediction that he would be fired. Bill explained that while this approach initially seemed helpful, he soon began to obsess about whether he had adequately examined the evidence. Bill remarked, "I start doubting the thoroughness of my evidence [e.g., previous evaluations]. What if I've overlooked something, or what if I assign more importance to one piece of evidence than another?" Bill reported that his examination of the evidence for his prediction that he would likely lose his job had become a new source of worrying.

It appeared to us that Bill's ability to revise his probability overestimations was being compromised by more basic perfectionistic irrational beliefs. Specifically, Bill seemed to be demanding a guarantee that he would never be fired, therefore dwelling on the small possibility that he could be fired. His demand that he absolutely must not lose his job appeared to fuel his obsessive preoccupation with whether he had obtained enough evidence to insure that he would not be fired.

Exploration of what it would mean to him if his predictions came true also revealed the following beliefs:

1. Being fired would be awful, rather than unfortunate and inconvenient. (catastrophizing)
2. I couldn't stand losing my job. (catastrophizing)
3. I would be less of a person, a failure, if I lost my job. (self-rating)

In summary, we concluded that Bill's worrying about losing his job primarily stemmed from his beliefs that he must not lose his job, that this would be awful if it happened, and that losing his job would mean losing his self-worth. Bill's overestimation of the likelihood of actually losing his job (i.e., an inferential belief) was viewed as resulting from these three underlying evaluative beliefs.

Ellis's (1988) most recent self-help book, *How to Stubbornly Refuse to Make Yourself Miserable About Anything, Yes Anything,* has been well received by our GAD clients. Ellis's (1973e) *Twenty-One Ways to Stop Worrying* and his (1987) *How to Stop Worrying and Start Living* are useful audiotapes for GAD worriers.

Major Behavioral Interventions

Decreasing Avoidance. As indicated earlier, while GAD sufferers may not engage in a consistent pattern of circumscribed avoidance, as do patients meeting criteria for phobic disorders, GAD patients typically engage to varying degrees in more diffuse and subtle patterns of avoidance (Butler, Gelder, et al., 1987; Clark, 1989a). Butler et al. (1987) provided empirical support for this clinical observation, noting that 64% of a sample of GAD patients reported some form of avoidance. For example, patients with financial worries may avoid balancing the checkbook, paying bills, or reading financial sections of the newspaper. Similarly, those with worries about performing well at work may avoid certain tasks. Clark (1989a) cited an example of an academician who procrastinated with his writing for fear of not doing well.

To address GAD avoidance, we first determine specific spheres of worry (e.g., work, finances) and then probe for obvious and subtle forms of avoidance. These avoided events are woven into a hierarchy, similar to those of phobics. Clients are instructed to approach these avoided areas, using their cognitive, problem-solving, relaxation, and other relevant skills developed during treatment.

Developing Problem-Solving Skills. In discussing the treatment of GAD patients, Butler et al. (1987) stated,

> Indeed, patients gave the impression that one of the main benefits of treatment was finding that they had the resources for dealing with the problems themselves. This is one of the most important general goals of anxiety management, and of many similar treatments. (p. 521)

While all of the cognitive, behavioral, and relaxation skills may foster this sense of control or problem-solving efficacy, training in problem solving directly targets this goal. Goldfried and Davidson (1976) provided a useful clinical guide to implementing problem-solving procedures that outlines the following components, well known to most cognitive-behavioral clinicians: general orientation, problem definition and formulation, generation of alternatives, decision making, and verification. As with most skills training procedures, we usually focus on developing problem-solving skills after clients learn cognitive restructuring skills to reduce debilitative emotions (e.g., anger, depression, anxiety) that interfere with problem-solving attempts.

Client: What am I going to do to deal with my supervisor? I can't take another day at this job!

Therapist: That's an excellent question, and we'll definitely work on figuring that out. But first, let me ask you, what feelings do you have when you have contact with your supervisor? Any specific emotions?

Client: Well, I want to punch him in the face!

Therapist: So, anger is what you feel the most?

Client: Right.

Therapist: Do you think your anger is helping or interfering with figuring out how to deal with your supervisor?

Client: I guess it doesn't help. I get so angry I can't think straight.

Therapist: How about it if we work on ways for you to feel more in control of your anger, so your supervisor won't push your buttons so much? Then we can look to doing some problem solving on the best way to deal with your work predicament.

Assertiveness Training. Often, problem solving may result in a decision to try assertively to change the behavior of others or circumstances about which one has been worrying. For example, a client had been constantly worrying about how a schoolteacher was allegedly treating her daughter. Problem solving resulted in the decision to request a conference with the teacher to discuss her daughter's concerns. Behavioral rehearsal was useful in developing assertiveness skills. Examining and challenging irrational beliefs regarding needs to perform well and avoid the teacher's disapproval also proved to be helpful for the client. Alberti and Emmons's (1974) classic text and Jakubowski and Lange's (1978) *The Assertive Option: Your Rights and Responsibilities* are useful references on the topic of assertiveness.

Relaxation Procedures. Relaxation training and respiratory control procedures are indicated for GAD clients with increased muscle tension and/or autonomic reactivity. We use the same procedures as described in chapter 3 with respect to treatment of PD. These skills, once learned, are thought to facilitate clients' approach to worry-related cues and to enhance their perception of self-control.

Stimulus Control Procedures. We use the stimulus control procedures found by Borkovec et al. (1983) to be effective in reducing the amount of reported daily worry. Instructions for these procedures are as follows:

a. Learn to identify worrisome thoughts and other thoughts that are unnecessary or unpleasant. Distinguish these from necessary or pleasant thoughts related to the present moment.
b. Establish a ½-hour worry period to take place at the same time and in the same location each day.
c. When you catch yourself worrying, postpone the worry to the worry period and replace it with attending to present-moment experience.
d. Make use of the ½-hour worry period to worry about your concerns and to engage in problem-solving to eliminate those concerns. (p. 248)

Some clients seem to respond better to a more forceful interruption of worry thoughts, as well as subsequently attending to present-moment experiences. In such cases, thought-stopping procedures may be implemented. See Rimm and Masters (1979) for practical guidelines for thought stopping.

Borkovec et al. (1983) concluded that, during the half-hour worry period, it made no difference whether subjects wrote their worry thoughts or worried mentally. Neither did it matter if subjects just worried or also engaged in problem solving about their worries during the worry period.

Clinically, we often ask clients during the first month of treatment to engage daily in these stimulus control procedures. By the end of this period, clients have usually begun to use effectively the more cognitive RET interventions and can gradually fade out the daily worry periods. The basic difficulty we have encountered in having clients use the daily worry period is compliance. Clients often have difficulty getting themselves to worry purposely when they have been trying so hard to overcome worrying. However, when clients are successful at implementing the daily worry period, they are usually impressed with its effectiveness in reducing worry. While the effectiveness may be due to daily habituation of the worry thoughts and related emotions, it is also possible that the value of the procedure lies in its enhancement of the client's sense of control over mental processes.

Panic and GAD. Barlow (1988) indicated that approximately 25% of GAD patients also meet criteria for PD. In such cases, panic should be directly treated as described in chapter 3. In addition, a greater frequency of GAD patients experience periodic panic attacks. Our experience with these patients appears to be consistent with Barlow's (1988) observations that GAD patients are not particularly worried about panicking. It seems that GAD patients' particular panic episodes are typically triggered by usual GAD worries (e.g., money). Patients usually see the direct connection between these thoughts and panic reactions, and they do not appear to view these reactions as signs of immediate danger. In such cases, interoceptive exposure is probably unnecessary; rather, relaxation and breathing skills procedures provide adequate coping skills.

SAMPLE ABCS

A. *Activating event:*
  1. A minor but chronic health problem (e.g., allergies)
B. *Beliefs:*
  1. The doctor says I've got allergies, but I know he's just telling me that to avoid telling me the truth. I certainly have cancer, or at least the beginnings of it. This really scares me. Now my heart is racing, and I feel like I'll die any minute from heart failure!
  2. Maybe if I worry enough about whatever disease I have, it'll go away. Anyway, it's easier to do that than to follow up on some long, tedious, and expensive psychotherapy, like my doctor suggested.

The GAD client might engage in the following types of thinking:
  1. Demanding: I must always be perfectly calm and in control of my mind and body, otherwise life is really awful.
  2. Catastrophizing: I'm eventually going to die from a terrible illness. It'll probably be a long and painful death, and I won't be able to stand the agony!
  3. Rating of self and others: Only crazy people worry so much! That means I'm a rotten person. At best, I must have a serious mental defect.

C. *Consequences:*
  1. Chronic misery and anxiety, particularly due to fear of fear
  2. Restriction of occupational and social activities
  3. Repeated trips to the doctor
  4. Avoidance of psychotherapy
D. *Disputes and effective new philosophy:*
  1. It's unlikely that my doctor is lying to me about my allergies. So it's also unlikely that I instead have cancer. But even if I did, I could handle it. There are worse things in the world! And I don't have to be scared right now. Even if my heart does race, it doesn't mean that I'm going to die from heart failure. And even if I did die right now, then I do! Everybody has to go sometime! I'm not going to waste my life worrying!
  2. Where's the law that says worry will help solve problems? Although in the short term it's easier to avoid dealing with problems, it's better in the long run to face problems and do something about them. I'm the best person to solve my problems! And I choose to do as my doctor directed and seek psychological help for my worries.

Our RET model for treating GAD also incorporates the components discussed next.

Accepting That Worry Does Not Solve Problems. One important distinction for GAD clients versus other anxiety-disordered individuals involves a rigid, cognitive commitment to the following irrational belief: that the act of worrying is a vital and effective means of solving problems, preventing disasters, and existing in the world. For example, a GAD mother mistakenly believed that excessive, chronic worry would somehow protect her son—a cognitive process similar to magical thinking. In therapy, the GAD client must see that bad things happen to good people, regardless of how much they worry, and that the act of worry can only have a negative impact on one's life. The following dialogue illustrates a RET approach for dealing with a client's excessive worry about her son.

Therapist: So you're feeling that you *must* worry about your son while he's at school?

Client: Yeah, I just can't help myself. If I don't worry about Tommy, something terrible might happen. Like he might be hit by a car.

Therapist: What's the most terrible thing that might happen?

Client: Well . . . I guess he might be killed in some kind of freak accident.

Therapist: That sounds pretty scary for you, but tell me, what's the probability that such a tragedy would actually occur?

Client: I guess it's pretty unlikely.

Therapist: Exactly! Even if an accident were probable, could you control it by worrying or any other method?

Client: Not really.

Therapist: So how does worrying about possible accidents help things?

Client: It doesn't really. I suppose I just feel like I have to do something. So I worry about Tommy.

Therapist: Earlier, we talked about your belief that you have to control things around you.

Client: If I don't keep control, then something terrible might really happen. It just seems to me that I should worry about bad things happening. Isn't that what mothers are supposed to do? What kind of mother would I be if I didn't worry about my son?

Therapist: It is certainly normal to be concerned about your son—within reason, though. But I hear you spending a lot of time each day worrying, to the point where it has affected your life, including the fact that you almost lost your job a few months ago.

Client: Yeah, thinking about Tommy's welfare does occupy a lot of my time.

Therapist: How about working at giving up your tendency to catastrophize and instead spending some of that energy on constructive tasks, like problem solving or doing a good job at work?

Client: Sounds good, but I know it'll be really hard for me to change.

Therapist: It may take some time and effort on your part, but do you think the benefits will outweigh the negative aspects?

Accepting Responsibility. The GAD client, like many other clients, must sometimes be taught that the primary cause of his or her misery is not due to external situations but rather to an internal commitment to excessive worry. For such a person, it is often easier to externalize problems rather than to confront them. In RET, the GAD sufferer is encouraged to challenge the following irrational beliefs: that there is a perfect solution to every problem, that this solution must be found, and if it is not, the situation is uncontrollable and therefore catastrophic. The GAD client then understands that external events do not cause problems and that the fastest way to improve mental health is to accept responsibility for changing dysfunctional thinking patterns.

Depression. As mentioned earlier, GAD sufferers are at increased risk of developing coexisting depression. This depression, at least in part, is due to the client's adherence to the following irrational notion: If things are not the way in which one would like them, one should become upset (i.e., anxious and depressed). RET also conceptualizes such depression as being associated with feelings of helplessness or loss of self-control. In terms of faulty thinking patterns, GAD individuals who have worried, to no avail, for a long period of time often feel helpless and out of control in terms of their ability to alter life events. One therapeutic answer, as noted earlier, involved helping the GAD client to interrupt the negative cycle so that he or she believes that action—not worry—changes external situations. We have found that problem-solving interventions (e.g., developing a reasonable budget) are effective in assisting the client to overcome his or her GAD-related depression.

Anger. GAD clients often have unrealistic demands for people and situations. When life events do not occur as desired, the GAD sufferer is likely to become emotionally upset, which at times may include frustration and anger. Therapy assists the client in learning to overcome the tendency to demand of others and self while reacting to emotional obstacles with anger.

CASE EXAMPLE: CHRONIC WORRY

Mike was a 30-year-old single, male counselor referred by his physician (a general practitioner) to the Anxiety Disorders Clinic. Although medical records obtained from his physician indicated that Mike was in good physical health, he presented with a variety of physical symptoms apparently associated with intense worry concerning his ability to pass his national written professional counselor examinations, as well as his financial future. Just prior to coming to the Anxiety Disorders Clinic, Mike had barely missed the cutoff scores for Oregon licensure, and he became worried that he would never pass the exam. This exam "failure" further intensified his chronic anxiety and tendency to catastrophize about his situation. His chronic anxiety also began to interfere with his ability to work at a local mental health agency. He had experienced the following symptoms for several months and had been seeing his physician during that time for antianxiety medications (i.e., alprazolam): (a) motor tension: restlessness, fatigue; (b) autonomic hyperactivity: smothering sensations, sweating, dizziness, diarrhea; and (c) vigilance: feeling keyed up. The client also suffered from frequent, intense migraine headaches, possibly related to his excessive muscle tension. We also reviewed Mike's dietary and lifestyle habits and found that he consumed a large amount of sugar and caffeine on a daily basis and engaged only occasionally in physical exercise.

The first component of therapy focused on teaching Mike progressive muscle relaxation, which he quickly mastered, to deal with the chronic muscle tension. Therapy also included assertion training, problem-solving, and thought-stopping techniques. To prevent the migraine attacks, Mike began taking propranolol daily (up to 160 mg), which also seemed to help reduce his general anxiety level. He was then able to eliminate his dosage of alprazolam. We next set up a dietary and lifestyle improvement program to help Mike reduce his sucrose and caffeine intake and begin an aerobic exercise program. In 6 weeks, Mike successfully gained control over most of his anxiety symptoms by learning to relax, reducing stimulants from his diet, and jogging. He also reduced the frequency and intensity of his migraine headaches through a combination of the aforementioned lifestyle changes and appropriate use of medications.

During the 7-week therapy program, we assisted Mike in identifying the following irrational beliefs:

1. I must perform perfectly in everything I do, otherwise people won't accept me, and that would be terrible. (*demanding, catastrophizing*)

2. If I fail my exams, my colleagues will think I'm incompetent and stupid, and that would be awful. *(catastrophizing)*
3. If I fail my exams, I must really be incompetent or stupid. *(rating of self)*
4. Word will get out that I'm incompetent, and even if I eventually pass the exam (on the 39th try!), I'll never have any clients, and that would be unbearable. *(catastrophizing)*
5. I'll be in financial ruin forever and have to file multiple bankruptcies. Ten years of school and training down the drain! What a rotten person I'll be! *(catastrophizing, rating of self)*

Over a period of seven sessions, Mike was able to dispute the foregoing cognitive distortions, and he generated and accepted the following rational beliefs:

1. I'm a "FHB" (fallible human being), and it's OK to be imperfect. That's why they put erasers on the ends of pencils! I'll do the best job that I can, and if people can't accept me for who I am, that's their problem. I still can accept and like myself.

2. If I prepare properly, there's little probability that I'll fail the exam on my next try. Even if I do, I can retake it. I hope other people don't judge me, but if they do, I can stand it. I don't have to have approval to prove my worth as a person.

3. Passing or failing the exam has nothing to do with my worth as a person or competence as a professional counselor.

4. There's no reason to believe that I'll have to take the exam 39 times. Lots of competent professionals had to take the exam at least a few times. Even if I fail again, there's little chance that my scores will be published in the paper. People are busy and don't really care to focus their lives and energy around my exam scores. I'm a competent therapist and will certainly have plenty of clients. Even if I didn't, I could always go into another area of psychology (e.g., industrial consultation).

5. I have no real reason to believe that I'll be in financial ruin; I have always been able to make it. Actually, there's a good chance that I'll be successful financially! And my schooling has been immensely valuable, both professionally and personally. Even if I were to be in total poverty, my financial status has nothing to do with my self-worth.

Phone call follow-up 6 months after termination found Mike to be more relaxed and involved in studying for the upcoming national exams.

Appendix A

RET Self-help Form

Institute for Rational-Emotive Therapy
45 East 65th Street, New York, N.Y. 10021
(212) 535-0822

(A) ACTIVATING EVENTS, thoughts, or feelings that happened just before I felt emotionally disturbed or acted self-defeatingly: _____

_____

(C) CONSEQUENCE or CONDITION—disturbed feeling or self-defeating behavior—that I produced and would like to change: _____

_____

(B) BELIEFS—Irrational BELIEFS (IBs) leading to my CONSEQUENCE (emotional disturbance or self-defeating behavior). Circle all that apply to these ACTIVATING EVENTS (A).	(D) DISPUTES for each circled IRRATIONAL BELIEF. Examples: "Why MUST I do very well?" "Where is it written that I am a BAD PERSON?" "Where is the evidence that I MUST be approved or accepted?"	(E) EFFECTIVE RATIONAL BELIEFS (RBs) to replace my IRRATIONAL BELIEFS (IBs). Examples: "I'd PREFER to do very well but I don't HAVE TO." "I am a PERSON WHO acted badly, not a BAD PERSON." "There is no evidence that I HAVE TO be approved, though I would LIKE to be."
1. I MUST do well or very well!	. . . .	. . . .
2. I am a BAD OR WORTHLESS PERSON when I act weakly or stupidly.	. . . .	. . . .

(Continued)

2. (Continued)

3. I MUST be approved or accepted by people I find important!

4. I NEED to be loved by
someone who matters to me a
lot!

5. I am a BAD, UNLOVABLE
PERSON if I get rejected.

6. People MUST treat me fairly
and give me what I NEED!

7. People MUST live up to my
expectations or it is TERRIBLE!

8. People who act immorally are
undeserving, ROTTEN PEO-
PLE!

9. I CAN'T STAND really bad
things or very difficult people!

9. (Continued)

10. My life MUST have few major hassles or troubles.

11. It's AWFUL or HORRIBLE when major things don't go my way.

12. I CAN'T STAND IT when life is really unfair!

13. I NEED a good deal of immediate gratification and HAVE to feel miserable when I don't get it!

Additional Irrational Beliefs:

(F) FEELINGS and BEHAVIORS I experienced after arriving at my EFFECTIVE RATIONAL BELIEFS:

I WILL WORK HARD TO REPEAT MY EFFECTIVE RATIONAL BELIEFS FORCEFULLY TO MYSELF ON MANY OCCASIONS SO THAT I CAN MAKE MYSELF LESS DISTURBED NOW AND ACT LESS SELF-DEFEATINGLY IN THE FUTURE.

Joyce Sichel, Ph.D. and Albert Ellis, Ph.D.

Appendix B

Biographical Information Form

Date _____   Name _____

    mo.   day   yr.   (last)   (first)   (middle)

Consultation Center
Institute for Rational-Emotive Therapy
45 East 6th Street • New York, N. Y. 10021

Biographical Information Form

Instructions To assist us in helping you, please fill out this form as frankly as you can. You will save much time and effort by giving us full information. You can be sure that, like everything you say at the Institute, the facts on this form will be held in the strictest confidence and that no outsider will be permitted to see your case record without your written permission. PLEASE TYPE OR PRINT YOUR ANSWERS.

1. Date of birth: _____ Age: ____ Sex: M____ F____
                  mo.   day   yr.

2. Address: _____
          street   city   state   zip

3. Home phone: _____ Business phone: _____

4. Permanent address **(if different from above)** _____

_____

5. Who referred you to the Institute? **(check one)**

    ____(1) self ____(2) school or teacher ____(3) psychologist or psychiatrist ____(4) social

(Continued)

(Continued)

agency ＿＿(5) hospital or clinic ＿＿(6) family doctor ＿＿(7) friend ＿＿(8) relative ＿＿(9) other

(explain) ＿＿＿＿＿＿＿＿＿＿＿＿＿＿＿＿＿＿＿＿＿＿＿＿＿＿＿＿＿＿＿＿＿

Has this party been here? ＿＿Yes   ＿＿No

6. Present marital status:

＿＿(1) never married ＿＿(2) married now for first time ＿＿(3) married now for second (or

more) time ＿＿(4) separated ＿＿(5) divorced and not remarried ＿＿(6) widowed and not re-

married

Number of years married to present spouse ＿＿ Ages of male children ＿＿ Ages of female

children ＿＿

7. Years of formal education completed (circle number of years):

1 2 3 4 5 6 7 8 9 10 11 12 13 14 15 16 17 18 19 20   more than 20

8. How religious are you? **(circle number on scale that best approximates your degree of religios-**

ity):

very   average   atheist

1 2 3 4 5 6 7 8 9

9. Mother's age: ＿＿If deceased, how old were you when she died? ＿＿

10. Father's age: ＿＿If deceased, how old were you when he died? ＿＿

11. If your mother and father separated, how old were you at the time? ＿＿

12. If your mother and father divorced, how old were you at the time? ＿＿

13. Total number of times mother divorced ＿＿ Number of times father divorced ＿＿

14. Number of living brothers ＿＿ Number of living sisters ＿＿

15. Ages of living brothers ＿＿＿＿＿＿ Ages of living sisters ＿＿＿＿＿＿

16. I was child number ＿＿ in a family of ＿＿ children.

17. Were you adopted?   ＿＿Yes   ＿＿No

18. What kind of treatment have you previously had for emotional problems?

＿＿ hours of individual therapy, spread over ＿＿ years, ending ＿＿ years ago.

19. Hours of group therapy ＿＿ Months of psychiatric hospitalization ＿＿

20. Are you undergoing treatment anywhere else now? ＿＿Yes   ＿＿No

(Continued)

21. Number of times during past year you have taken antidepressants ____

22. Type of psychotherapy you have mainly had **(briefly describe method of treatment—ex., dream analysis, free association, drugs, hypnosis, etc.)** _____

    _____

23. Briefly list (PRINT) your present main complaints, symptoms, and problems: _____

    _____

    _____

    _____

24. Briefly list any additional **past** complaints, symptoms, and problems: _____

    _____

    _____

25. Under what conditions are your problems worse? _____

    _____

    _____

26. Under what conditions are they improved? _____

    _____

    _____

27. List the things you like to do most, the kinds of things and persons that give you pleasure: ___

    _____

    _____

28. List your main assets and good points: _____

    _____

    _____

29. List your main bad points: _____

    _____

    _____

30. List your main **social** difficulties: _____

(Continued)

(Continued)

_____

_____

31. List your main **love and sex** difficulties: _____

_____

_____

32. List your main **school or work** difficulties: _____

_____

_____

33. List your main life goals: _____

_____

_____

34. List the things about yourself you would most like to change: _____

_____

_____

35. List your chief physical ailments, diseases, complaints, or handicaps: _____

_____

_____

36. What occupation(s) have you mainly been trained for? _____

    Present occupation _____   ____Full time ____Part time

37. Spouse's occupation _____   ____Full time ____Part time

38. Mother's occupation   Father's occupation
    _____

39. Mother's religion   Father's religion
    _____

40. If your mother and father did not raise you when you were young, who did? _____

41. Briefly describe the type of person your mother (or stepmother or person who substituted for

    your mother) was when you were a child and how you got along with her: _____

    _____

    _____

(Continued)

42. Briefly describe the type of person your father (or stepfather or father substitute) was when you

were a child and how you got along with him: _____

_____

_____

43. If there were unusually disturbing features in your relationship to any of your brothers, briefly

describe: _____

_____

_____

44. If there were unusually disturbing features in your relationship to any of your sisters, briefly

describe: _____

_____

_____

45. Number of close male relatives who have been seriously emotionally disturbed: ____ Number

that have been hospitalized for psychiatric treatment, or have attempted suicide: ____ Number

of close female relatives who have been seriously emotionally disturbed: ____ Number that

have been hospitalized for psychiatric treatment, or have attempted suicide: ____

46. Additional information that you think might be helpful

_____

_____

_____

_____

_____

_____

_____

_____

_____

Note: Reprinted by permission of the Institute for Rational-Emotive Therapy.

Appendix C
Personality Data Form

Name _____

(last)   (first)   (middle)

Consultation Center
Institute for Advanced Study in Rational Psychotherapy
45 East 65th Street • New York, N. Y. 10021

Personality Data Form—Part 1

Instructions: Please answer all the following items as honestly as you can, so that we will be able to help you most with your problems. Read each of the items and circle after each one the word OFTEN, SOMETIMES, or SELDOM, to indicate how often you have the feeling that is described in the item. Thus, if you frequently feel quite foolish or embarrassed when you make a mistake when other people are watching, circle the word OFTEN in item 1; and if you seldom or rarely feel ashamed to do the things you really want to do if you think others will disapprove of you for doing them, circle SELDOM in item 2. Please make sure that you circle one, and only one, word in every item. DO NOT SKIP ANY ITEMS. And again, for your own good, be as honest as you can possibly be.

Acceptance

1. I feel quite foolish or embarrassed when I make a mistake and other people are watching	OFTEN	SOMETIMES	SELDOM
2. I feel ashamed to do the things I really want to do if I think others will disapprove of me for doing them	OFTEN	SOMETIMES	SELDOM
3. I feel humiliated when people discover undesirable things about my family or my background	OFTEN	SOMETIMES	SELDOM
4. I feel put down if my house, car, finances, or other possessions are not as good as are those of others	OFTEN	SOMETIMES	SELDOM
5. I feel quite uncomfortable when I am the center of people's attention	OFTEN	SOMETIMES	SELDOM
6. I feel quite hurt when a person I respect criticizes me negatively	OFTEN	SOMETIMES	SELDOM
7. I feel uneasy about my looks or about the way I am dressed when I am out in public	OFTEN	SOMETIMES	SELDOM
8. I feel that if people get to know me well they will discover how rotten I really am	OFTEN	SOMETIMES	SELDOM

(Continued)

195

(Continued)

9.	I feel terribly lonely	OFTEN	SOMETIMES	SELDOM
10.	I feel that I simply must have the approval or love of certain people who are important to me	OFTEN	SOMETIMES	SELDOM
11.	I feel dependent on others and am miserable if I cannot get their help	OFTEN	SOMETIMES	SELDOM

Frustration

12.	I feel upset when things proceed slowly and can't be settled quickly	OFTEN	SOMETIMES	SELDOM
13.	I feel like putting off things I know it would be better for me to do	OFTEN	SOMETIMES	SELDOM
14.	I feel upset about life's inconveniences or frustrations	OFTEN	SOMETIMES	SELDOM
15.	I feel quite angry when someone keeps me waiting	OFTEN	SOMETIMES	SELDOM
16.	I feel jealous of people who have better traits than I	OFTEN	SOMETIMES	SELDOM
17.	I feel terribly resentful when other people do not do my bidding or give me what I want	OFTEN	SOMETIMES	SELDOM
18.	I feel I can't stand and must change people who act stupidly or nastily	OFTEN	SOMETIMES	SELDOM
19.	I feel that I can't handle serious responsibility	OFTEN	SOMETIMES	SELDOM
20.	I resent my having to make a real effort to get what I want	OFTEN	SOMETIMES	SELDOM
21.	I feel very sorry for myself when things are rough	OFTEN	SOMETIMES	SELDOM
22.	I feel unable to persist at things I start, especially when the going gets hard	OFTEN	SOMETIMES	SELDOM
23.	I feel unexcited and bored about most things	OFTEN	SOMETIMES	SELDOM
24.	I feel that I cannot discipline myself	OFTEN	SOMETIMES	SELDOM

Injustice

25.	I feel revengeful toward others for the wrongs they have done	OFTEN	SOMETIMES	SELDOM
26.	I strongly feel like telling off wrongdoers and immoral people	OFTEN	SOMETIMES	SELDOM
27.	I get upset about the injustices of the world and feel that their perpetrators should be severely punished	OFTEN	SOMETIMES	SELDOM

Achievement

28.	I blame myself severely for my poor performances	OFTEN	SOMETIMES	SELDOM
29.	I feel very ashamed when I fail at important things	OFTEN	SOMETIMES	SELDOM
30.	I feel anxious when I have to make important decisions	OFTEN	SOMETIMES	SELDOM
31.	I feel afraid to take risks or to try new things	OFTEN	SOMETIMES	SELDOM

Worth

32.	I feel guilty about my thoughts or actions	OFTEN	SOMETIMES	SELDOM
33.	I feel that I am pretty worthless as a person	OFTEN	SOMETIMES	SELDOM
34.	I feel suicidal	OFTEN	SOMETIMES	SELDOM
35.	I feel like crying	OFTEN	SOMETIMES	SELDOM
36.	I feel that I give in too easily to others	OFTEN	SOMETIMES	SELDOM
37.	I feel hopeless about my being able to change my personality for the better	OFTEN	SOMETIMES	SELDOM
38.	I feel that I am quite stupid	OFTEN	SOMETIMES	SELDOM
39.	I feel that my life is meaningless or without purpose	OFTEN	SOMETIMES	SELDOM

Control

40.	I feel I cannot enjoy myself today because of my poor early life	OFTEN	SOMETIMES	SELDOM

(Continued)

41.	I feel that because I have failed at important things in the past I must inevitably keep failing in the future	OFTEN SOMETIMES SELDOM
42.	I resent my parents for treating me the way they did and for causing so many of my present problems	OFTEN SOMETIMES SELDOM
43.	I feel that I cannot control my strong emotions, such as anxiety or rage	OFTEN SOMETIMES SELDOM

Certainty

44.	I feel lost without some higher being or purpose on which to rely	OFTEN SOMETIMES SELDOM
45.	I feel that I should keep doing certain things over and over, even though I don't want to do them, because something bad will happen if I stop	OFTEN SOMETIMES SELDOM
46.	I feel quite uncomfortable when things are not well ordered	OFTEN SOMETIMES SELDOM

Catastrophizing

47.	I worry about what's going to happen to me in the future	OFTEN SOMETIMES SELDOM
48.	I worry about my having some accident or illness	OFTEN SOMETIMES SELDOM
49.	I am terrified at the idea of going to new places or meeting a new group of people	OFTEN SOMETIMES SELDOM
50.	I am terrified at the thought of my dying	OFTEN SOMETIMES SELDOM

Note: Reprinted by permission of the Institute for Rational-Emotive Therapy.

Appendix D

On the Receiving End
of Anger

In our work with couples, as well as individuals, difficulty responding constructively to anger is a frequent problem. Problems dealing
with anger can be divided into two main categories: (a) when your
partner is angry at someone or something else and is basically using
you as a sounding board, and (b) when your partner's anger is aimed
directly at you—you are the target!

What do you usually do when your partner expresses anger to you
about someone else? Do you tell him or her to calm down and stop
overreacting? Do you point out his or her irrational thinking or perhaps
defend the other person at whom your partner is angry? Our guess is
that we all try these methods at times and usually find them noto-
riously unhelpful. What then might be a better alternative?

First, unless your partner has directly asked you to help him or her
not feel angry, realize that you are probably not being asked to be a
problem solver. You do not have to make it all go away. Problem-
solving attempts at these times often come across as criticism—"You
shouldn't feel that way." While it is true that your partner is creating
his or her own anger by what he or she is telling himself or herself
about some external event (e.g., unfair treatment from a supervisor at
work), he or she has the right to fallibly and humanly do this. So, your
focus would be better showing understanding of your partner's feelings rather than on disputing irrational self-talk. Although individuals,
on certain occasions, may legitimately make specific requests for help
from each other in changing certain habits (e.g., chronic anger reactions), most partners rarely enjoy unsolicited therapy from their mates.

Okay, we are still suggesting what *not* to do. Here are some suggestions about what *to do*. Use your receiving communication skills—be a

good listener! By paraphrasing and perhaps asking occasional questions, you will show your partner that you understand how he or she feels and why he or she is upset. This nonjudgmental posture will usually lead your partner to feel understood, supported, and accepted, even though you do not jump in, take sides, and berate the person with whom your partner is angry. Typically, anger will soon dissipate if met with these attitudes and behaviors.

Wilbur: Damn it! That supervisor Bunker doesn't have enough brains to get out of the rain. And he had the nerve to point out an error I made in front of the whole crew! It took all of my restraint not to tell him where to get off!

Lisa: Oh, Wilbur, you're just overreacting again. He was probably just trying to be helpful. You know, you're doing this to yourself with your stupid thinking. Just get a hold on yourself!

Do you think Wilbur's anger is likely to increase or decrease after Lisa's response? How understood, accepted, and close to Lisa do you think he would feel? Consider the following alternative response Lisa could make to Wilbur's same expression of anger.

Lisa: Wow, Wilbur, it sounds like you really resent someone with power over you who seems so ignorant and insensitive. Really embarrassing to be criticized right in front of your friends! So hard to just stand there and take it!

Here, Lisa realizes her purpose is not to teach Wilbur how to not upset himself, but rather to be supportive and understanding.

Now, if your partner happens to be chronically angry, and you have paraphrased until you are blue in the face and are becoming weary, we suggest this be brought up for problem solving so that possibilities for change can be systematically explored.

Here comes the hardest part. What if you happen to be the one toward whom your partner is expressing his or her anger? The aforementioned process is recommended, but this is usually more of a challenge.

Let us assume that your partner is mad at you for displeasing him or her in some way, and he or she is expressing anger forcefully. The following steps can be taken:

1.   Nondefensively accept your influence or contribution, but realize your partner is largely creating his or her own anger. Your partner is responsible for his or her own emotional reactions. Resist your initial impulse to counterattack, cross-complain, or justify your position.

2.   Accept your partner's right to be angry, even though it is caused by his or her own irrational thinking. Avoid thinking, "He *shouldn't* be

irrational and angry." Otherwise, you will make yourself angry at your partner for being angry at you!

3. Realize that this anger toward you does not make you less of a person. It in no way belittles you or robs you of your self-worth. You may have done something your partner does not like or failed to do something that he or she really wanted you to do. Or you may have made, in your opinion, a big mistake you sincerely regret. This is evidence that you also are a fallible human being. Neither disappointing your partner, making a big mistake, nor being yelled at makes you less of a person. Remember—you do not need your partner's love and approval at all times to be a worthwhile person.

4. Paraphrase what you think your partner is saying and feeling. Try your best not to be defensive, but admit it if you are.

Tanya: Every time I think about what you said to me last night I feel so angry, just furious! I can't believe you could be so cruel!

Ben: I feel a little defensive. This is hard for me to handle, but I hear you, Tanya. You're just boiling mad at me.

5. When your partner's anger has subsided, consider the options of apologizing or negotiating a way to make it less likely that similar events, about which your partner was angry, will occur in the future.

If you have trouble following this approach, systematically practice rational-emotive imagery. Here is how you do it: (a) Make a list of about five things your partner most frequently gets angry about at you; (b) rank these situations in order from least to most difficult for you to handle; (c) get reasonably relaxed if you like, and starting with the first item on your list, close your eyes and vividly imagine yourself coping constructively, in the manner just suggested, with your partner's anger. Then vigorously dispute your irrational self-talk. Here's what Kristine said to herself, "It's not *awful* but just *unfortunate* that my spouse is expressing anger at me. I *wish* he wouldn't do this, but there is no evidence that he *should* or *must* be more calm. It's *unpleasant* but *not catastrophic* to have anger expressed to me. It doesn't make me less of a person. I'm not a bad person for disappointing or frustrating him. I don't *make* him angry. He makes himself angry by telling himself it's *awful* and that I *shouldn't* displease him or make mistakes"; (d) see yourself paraphrasing and nondefensively acknowledging it if you make a mistake.

Practice this exercise for 10 to 20 minutes each day. Research has shown that mental rehearsal can often be as effective as real-life practice. In that regard, however, real-life practice of the foregoing procedures is also strongly recommended. That means, instead of avoiding or withdrawing when your partner is angry at you, literally force yourself to stay in there and show yourself that you *can stand* his or her anger. You could probably think of other things that are more fun, but in the long run you and your relationship will benefit from learning to respond effectively to anger.

Appendix E

How to Handle Criticism and Guilt

Being able to tolerate criticism without "coming unglued" is a worthwhile goal to pursue. It can significantly help you to avoid feeling bad about yourself while at the same time preventing destructive quarrels and conflicts with others (e.g., your spouse). Dealing constructively with criticism requires knowing both what to think and what to do when criticized.

Let us first consider the thinking part. Dr. Albert Ellis has explained a useful way to think about criticism. First, when criticized by someone, ask yourself, "Is this criticism basically true or false?" For example, if Mary tells John that she thinks he is irrationally fearful of germs, John would ask himself, "Am I irrationally fearful of germs?" If he takes an honest look at himself and comes up with the answer, "Yes, I am," there is no reason to upset himself, because he (like everyone else) is a fallible human being who has the right to be imperfect and make mistakes. He does not need to feel guilty or shameful. On the other hand, if John can honestly conclude that he is basically not irrationally fearful of germs, he still does not need to upset himself. In this case, Mary, a fallible human being, is wrong, but she too has the right to have mistaken opinions.

While it may be impossible to prove who is right or wrong about John's fearfulness, both John and Mary are entitled to their different opinions. Adopting this way of thinking about criticism, of course, takes practice. Because criticism from those who are closest to us is often the most difficult to handle, the following material uses one's spouse as an example.

It is important to challenge two particular irrational beliefs that make handling criticism difficult. The first is the belief that one must be per-

203

fect and competent in everything to be a worthwhile person. The second is the belief that one must be loved and approved of (by one's spouse, in this case) to be a worthwhile person. Conquering the first belief allows you to accept both yourself and your spouse, whether or not the criticism is valid. Conquering the second enables you to tolerate without anxiety those times when your spouse is not feeling or acting in a loving or approving manner. Also, remember that while particular criticisms may seem like attacks on you as a person, they are usually related to specific behaviors. So do not overgeneralize. Remember, although your behavior may have been bad, that does not mean that you as a whole person are bad. You still remain a fallible human being—nothing more, nothing less. So after working on thinking constructively about criticism, what is the best thing to say or do when actually criticized by your spouse? The following steps may prove to be useful for you.

1. Paraphrase your partner's expression of criticism. *Do not counterattack or cross-complain,* even though this may be your initial impulse. By paraphrasing, you convey empathy and demonstrate your interest in what your partner has to tell you. You can show respect, although you may disagree with the other person's point of view.

Laura: I'm really angry with you for being so selfish. You only think of yourself!

Bob: You're angry at me for being selfish and self-centered (paraphrasing) *versus*

Bob: Me selfish? What about you? I'm the one who takes the kids to baseball practice, washes dishes, and runs all the errands. What have you done lately for me? (cross-complaining)

2. If you are unclear about exactly what your partner is unhappy with, ask for some specific details. When you receive this feedback, paraphrase again.

Bob: You're angry at me for being selfish and self-centered. (paraphrasing) What kinds of things have I done that seem really selfish? (asking for specific details)

Laura: Well, mainly this last week, you haven't asked me anything about how my day went. You just come home, read the paper, and work in the shop.

Bob: It sounds like you've been neglected, like I've been focusing just on me and leaving you out.

3. If your spouse's criticism is true or valid, accept the criticism and acknowledge your error, but do not put yourself down for being fallible. If you do not think the criticism is valid, perhaps it is too broad.

Try to find a grain of truth in the criticism with which you can agree. If the problem is not a major one, tell your partner what you will do differently in the future. Ask for suggestions.

Bob: You're right. I've been in my own world lately, and it was selfish not to give you much attention. I love you, and I'm interested in how your day goes. I'll make a better effort to show you that. Are there other ways I can show you I care?

Note that Bob could have argued that overall he is unselfish, that Laura is unappreciative, and that she is really the selfish one for wanting so much attention. We all can imagine the outcome of that scenario. Instead, Bob found some truth in Laura's criticism, nondefensively acknowledged that her criticism was valid, and stated his intention to be more attentive. He also asked Laura if she could think of other ways he could demonstrate his interest in her.

If the criticism you receive is a major one or is one that is frequently pointed out, it would be important to discuss this in problem-solving sessions (e.g., perhaps with a counselor).

4. If you conclude that there is not even a grain of truth to the criticism, after following steps 1 and 2, state your disagreement, acknowledge that you could be wrong, and offer your willingness to be on the lookout for this in the future.

Laura: I really think that you have a lot of hostility toward me and that you were trying on purpose to hurt me when you didn't call to tell me you were going to be late.

Suppose that Bob paraphrases, shows empathy for her complaint and point of view, but honestly believes he is not guilty of the accusation. Here is a constructive reply.

Bob: Laura, I don't blame you for feeling hurt and angry if it seemed to you that I'm really hostile and trying deliberately to hurt you. It's possible that I'm unaware of my real intentions, but I honestly believe the last thing in the world I wanted to do was hurt you. I really love you very much.

Here, Bob stated his disagreement with Laura's criticism but acknowledged his fallibility and reassured her that he loves her.

5. If your partner is often critical, perform steps 1 through 4 and attempt to discuss this with your partner at an appropriate time.

References

Agras, W. S., Chapin, H. N., & Oliveau, D. C. (1972). The natural history of phobia. *Archives of General Psychiatry, 26,* 315–317.

Agras, W. S., Sylvester, D., & Oliveau, D. (1969). The epidemiology of common fears and phobia. *Comprehensive Psychiatry, 10,* 151–156.

Alberti, R., & Emmons, M. (1974). *Your perfect right.* San Luis Obispo, CA: Impact.

Alden, L. (1989). Short-term structured treatment for avoidant personality disorder. *Journal of Consulting and Clinical Psychology, 57,* 756–764.

Alden, L., & Cappe, R. (1981). Nonassertiveness: Skill deficit or selective self-evaluation? *Behavior Therapy, 12,* 107–114.

American Psychiatric Association. (1980). *Diagnostic and statistical manual of mental disorders* (3rd ed.). Washington, DC: Author.

American Psychiatric Association. (1987). *Diagnostic and statistical manual of mental disorders* (3rd ed., revised). Washington, DC: Author.

Amies, P. L., Gelder, M. G., & Shaw, P. M. (1983). Social phobia: A comparative clinical study. *British Journal of Psychiatry, 142,* 174–179.

Ananth, J. (1985). Pharmaco therapy of obsessive compulsive disorder. In M. Mavissakalian, S. M. Turner, & L. Michelson (Eds.), *Obsessive-compulsive disorder; Psychological and pharmacological treatment* (pp. 167–211). New York: Plenum Publishing.

Anderson, D. J., Noyes, R., Jr., & Crowe, R. R. (1984). A comparison of panic disorder and generalized anxiety disorder. *American Journal of Psychiatry, 141,* 572–575.

Anderson, L. T. (1977). Desensitization *in vivo* for men unable to urinate in a public facility. *Journal of Behavior Therapy and Experimental Psychiatry, 8,* 105–106.

Arnkoff, D. B., & Glass, C. R. (1989). Cognitive assessment in social anxiety and social phobia. *Clinical Psychology Review, 9,* 61–74.

Arnow, B. A., Taylor, C. B., Agras, W. S., & Telch, M. J. (1985). Enhancing agoraphobic treatment outcome by changing couple communication patterns. *Behavior Therapy, 16,* 452–467.

Baker, B. L., Cohen, D. C., & Saunders, J. T. (1973). Self-directed desensitization for agoraphobia. *Behaviour Research and Therapy, 11,* 79–89.

Ballenger, J. C., Burrows, G. D., DuPont, R. L., Lesser, I. M., Noyes, R., Pecknold, J. C., Rifkin, A., & Swinson, R. P. (1988). Alprazolam in panic disorder and agoraphobia: Results from a multicenter trial: I. Efficacy in short-term treatment. (1988). *Archives of General Psychiatry, 45,* 413–422.

Bandura, A. (1977). Self-efficacy: Toward a unifying theory of behavioral change. *Psychological Review, 84*, 191–215.

Bandura, A. (1986). *Social foundations of thought and action: A social cognitive theory.* Englewood Cliffs, NJ: Prentice-Hall.

Bandura, A. (1988). Self-efficacy conception of Anxiety. *Anxiety Research, 1*, 77–98.

Bard, M., & Sangrey, D. (1979). *The crime victim's book.* New York: Basic Books.

Barlow, D. H. (1985). The dimensions of anxiety disorders. In A. H. Tuma & J. D. Maser (Eds.), *Anxiety and the anxiety disorders* (pp. 479–500). Hillsdale, NJ: Lawrence Erlbaum Associates.

Barlow, D. H. (1986). Behavioral conception and treatment of panic. *Psychopharmacology Bulletin, 22*, 802–806.

Barlow, D. H. (1988). *Anxiety and its disorders.* New York: Guilford Press.

Barlow, D. H. (1990, April). *Anxiety disorders: Assessment and treatment.* Workshop presented at the University of Washington, Seattle.

Barlow, D. H., Blanchard, E. B., Vermilyea, J. A., Vermilyea, B. B., & DiNardo, P. A. (1986). Generalized anxiety and generalized anxiety disorder: Description and reconceptualization. *American Journal of Psychiatry, 143*, 40–44.

Barlow, D. H., Cohen, A. S., Waddell, M., Vermilyea, J. A., Klosko, J. S., Blanchard, E. B., & Di Nardo, P. A. (1984). Panic and generalized anxiety disorders: Nature and treatment. *Behavior Therapy, 15*, 431–449.

Barlow, D. H., & Craske, M. G. (1989). *Mastery of your anxiety and panic.* Albany, NY: Graywind Publications; Center for Stress and Anxiety Disorders, State University of New York at Albany.

Barlow, D. H., Craske, M. G., Cerny, J. A., & Klosko, J. S. (1989). Behavioral treatment of panic disorder. *Behavior Therapy, 20*, 261–282.

Barlow, D. H., Hayes, S. C., & Nelson, R. O. (1984). *The scientist-practitioner: Research and accountability in clinical and educational settings.* Elmsford, NY: Pergamon Press.

Beck, A. T. (1976). *Cognitive therapy and the emotional disorders.* New York: International Universities Press.

Beck, A. T. (1988). Cognitive approaches to panic disorder: Theory and therapy. In S. Rachman & J. D. Maser (Eds.), *Panic: Psychological perspectives* (pp. 91–109). Hillsdale, NJ: Lawrence Erlbaum Associates.

Beck, A. T., & Emery, G. (1985). *Anxiety disorders and phobias: A cognitive perspective.* New York: Basic Books.

Beck, A. T., Epstein, N., Brown, G., & Steer, R. A. (1988). An inventory for measuring clinical anxiety: Psychometric properties. *Journal of Consulting and Clinical Psychology, 56*, 893–897.

Beck, A. T., Rush, A. J., Shaw, B. F., & Emery, G. (1979). *Cognitive therapy of depression.* New York: Guilford Press.

Beck, A. T., Ward, C. H., Mendelsohn, M., Mock, J., & Erbaugh, J. (1961). An inventory for measuring depression. *Archives of General Psychiatry, 4*, 561–571.

Becker, J. V., & Abel, G. G. (1981). Behavioral treatment of victims of sexual assault. In S. M. Turner, K. S. Calhoun, & H. E. Adams (Eds.), *Handbook of clinical behavioral therapy* (pp. 347–379). New York: John Wiley & Sons.

Beidel, D. C., Borden, J. W., Turner, S. M., & Jacob, R. G. (1989). The Social Phobia and Anxiety Inventory: Concurrent validity with a clinic sample. *Behaviour Research and Therapy, 27*, 573–576.

Beidel, D. C., Turner, S. M., & Dancu, C. V. (1985). Physiological, cognitive, and behavioral aspects of social anxiety. *Behaviour Research and Therapy, 23*, 109–117.

Beidel, D. C., Turner, S. M., Stanley, M. A., & Dancu, C. V. (1989). The Social Phobia and Anxiety Inventory: Concurrent and external validity. *Behavior Therapy, 20*, 417–427.

Beitman, B. D., DeRosear, L., Basha, I., Flaker, G., & Corcoran, C. (1987). Panic disorder in cardiology patients with atypical or non-anginal chest pain: A pilot study. *Journal of Anxiety Disorders, 1,* 277–282.

Bernard, M. E. (1990, June). *Validation of General Attitude and Belief Scale.* Paper presented at the World Congress on Mental Health Counseling, Keystone, CO.

Bernard, M. E., & DiGiuseppe, R. (Eds.). (1989). *Inside Rational-Emotive Therapy: A critical appraisal of the theory and therapy of Albert Ellis.* San Diego, CA: Academic Press.

Bernstein, D. A., & Borkovec, T. D. (1973). *Progressive relaxation training.* Champaign, IL: Research Press.

Berotti, D., Heimberg, R. G., Holt, C. S., & Liebowitz, M. R. (1990). *Irrational beliefs among social phobics: An examination of the validity of the Belief Scale.* Paper presented at the annual meeting of the Association for Advancement of Behavior Therapy, San Francisco.

Biran, M., Augusto, F., & Wilson, G. T. (1981). In vivo exposure vs. cognitive restructuring in the treatment of scriptophobia. *Behaviour Research and Therapy, 19,* 525–532.

Biran, M., & Wilson, G. T. (1981). Treatment of phobic disorders using cognitive and exposure methods: A self-efficacy analysis. *Journal of Consulting and Clinical Psychology, 49,* 886–899.

Blanchard, E. B., Gerardi, R. J., Kolb, L. C., & Barlow, D. H. (1986). The utility of the Anxiety Disorders Interview Schedule (ADIS) in the diagnosis of post-traumatic stress disorder (PTSD) in Vietnam veterans. *Behaviour Research and Therapy, 24,* 577–580.

Blanchard, E. B., Kolb, L. C., Gerardi, R. J., Ryan, P., & Pallmeyer, T. P. (1986). Cardiac response to relevant stimuli as an adjunctive tool for diagnosing post-traumatic stress disorder in Vietnam veterans. *Behavior Therapy, 17,* 592–606.

Blowers, C., Cobb, J., & Mathews, A. (1987). Generalized anxiety: A controlled treatment study. *Behaviour Research and Therapy, 25,* 493–502.

Bonn, J. A., Readhead, C. P. A., & Timmons, B. H. (1984). Enhanced adaptive behavioral response in agoraphobic patients pretreated with breathing retraining. *Lancet, ii,* 665–669.

Borkovec, T. D. (1982). Functional CS exposure in the treatment of phobics. In J. Boulougouris (Ed.), *Learning theory approaches to psychiatry* (pp. 95–102). Wiley, N.Y.

Borkovec, T. D. (1985). The role of cognitive and somatic cues in anxiety and anxiety disorders: Worry and relaxation-induced anxiety. In A. H. Tuma & J. D. Maser (Eds.), *Anxiety and the anxiety disorders* (pp. 463–478). Hillsdale, NJ: Lawrence Erlbaum Associates.

Borkovec, T. D., & Inz, J. (1990). The nature of worry in generalized anxiety disorder: A predominance of thought activity. *Behaviour Research and Therapy, 28,* 153–158.

Borkovec, T. D., & Mathews, A. (1988). Treatment of nonphobic anxiety disorders: A comparison of nondirective, cognitive and coping desensitization therapy. *Journal of Consulting and Clinical Psychology, 56,* 877–884.

Borkovec, T. D., Mathews, A. M., Chambers, A., Ebrahimi, S., Lytle, R., & Nelson, R. (1987). The effects of relaxation training with cognitive or nondirective therapy and the role of relaxation-induced anxiety in the treatment of generalized anxiety. *Journal of Consulting and Clinical Psychology, 55,* 883–888.

Borkovec, T. D., Wilkinson, L., Folensbee, R., & Lerman, C. (1983). Stimulus control applications to the treatment of worry. *Behaviour Research and Therapy, 21,* 247–251.

Bourque, P., & Ladouceur, R. (1980). An investigation of various performance-based treatments with acrophobics. *Behaviour Research and Therapy, 18,* 161–170.

Boyd, J. (1986). Use of mental health services for the treatment of panic disorder. *American Journal of Psychiatry, 143,* 1569–1574.

Boyd, J., & Grieger, R. (1982). Self-acceptance problems. in R. Grieger and I. Grieger (Eds.), *Cognition and emotional disturbance.* New York: Human Sciences Press.

Brom, D., Kleber, R. J., & Defares, P. B. (1989). Brief psychotherapy for posttraumatic stress disorders. *Journal of Consulting and Clinical Psychology, 57,* 607–612.

Brown, G., & Beck, A. T. (1989). The role of imperatives in psychopathology: A reply to Ellis. *Cognitive Therapy and Research, 13,* 315–321.

Brown, T. A., Anthony, M. M., & Barlow, D. H. (1990). *Psychometric properties of the Worry Questionnaire in a clinical anxiety disorders sample.* Paper presented at the annual meeting of the Association for Advancement of Behavior Therapy, San Francisco.

Bruch, M. A. (1989). Familial and developmental antecedents of social phobia: Issues and findings. *Clinical Psychology Review, 9,* 37–47.

Bruch, M. A., Heimberg, H. G., Berger, P., & Collins, T. M. (1987). *Parental and personal origins of social evaluative threat: Differences between social phobics and agoraphobics.* Unpublished manuscript.

Bulman, R. I., & Wortman, C. B. (1977). Attributions of blame and coping in the "real world": Severe accident victims react to their lot. *Journal of Personality and Social Psychology, 35,* 351–363.

Burns, D. D. (1980). *Feeling good: The new mood therapy.* New York: William Morrow.

Burns, D. D. (1989). *The feeling good handbook.* New York: William Morrow.

Buss, A. H. (1980). *Self-consciousness and social anxiety.* San Francisco: W H Freeman.

Butler, G. (1985). Exposure as a treatment for social phobia: Some instructive difficulties. *Behaviour Research and Therapy, 23,* 651–657.

Butler, G. (1989). Phobic disorders. In K. Hawton, P. M. Salkovskis, J. Kirk, & D. M. Clark (Eds.), *Cognitive behavior therapy for psychiatric problems: A practical guide* (pp. 97–128). Oxford: Oxford Medical Publications.

Butler, G., Cullington, A., Hibbert, G., Klimes, I., & Gelder, M. (1987). Anxiety management for persistent generalized anxiety. *British Journal of Psychiatry, 151,* 532–542.

Butler, G., Cullington, A., Munby, M., Amies, P., & Gelder, M. (1984). Exposure and anxiety management in the treatment of social phobia. *Journal of Consulting and Clinical Psychology, 52,* 642–650.

Butler, G., Gelder, M., Hibbert, G., Cullington, A., & Klimes, I. (1987). Anxiety management: Developing effective strategies. *Behaviour Research and Therapy, 25,* 517–522.

Butler, G., & Mathews, A. (1983). Cognitive processes in anxiety. *Advances in Behaviour Research and Therapy, 5,* 51–62.

Cacioppo, J. T., Glass, C. R., & Merluzzi, T. V. (1979). Self-statements and self-evaluations: A cognitive-response model of social anxiety. *Cognitive Therapy and Research, 3,* 249–262.

Carr, A. T. (1974). Compulsive neuroses: A review of the literature. *Psychological Bulletin, 81,* 311–318.

Carr, D. B., & Sheehan, D. V. (1984). Evidence that panic disorder has a metabolic cause. In J. C. Ballenger (Ed.), *Biology of agoraphobia* (pp. 99–111). Washington, DC: American Psychiatry Press.

Carroll, J. (1978). The effect of imaging an event on expectations for the event: An interpretation in terms of the availability heuristic. *Journal of Experimental Social Psychology, 14,* 88–96.

Cerny, J. A., Barlow, D. H., Craske, M., & Himadi, W. G. (1987). Couples treatment of agoraphobia: A two-year follow-up. *Behavior Therapy, 18,* 401–415.

Chadwick, P. D. J., & Lowe, C. F. (1990). Measurement and modification of delusional beliefs. *Journal of Consulting and Clinical Psychology, 58,* 225–232.

Chambless, D. L. (1990). Spacing of exposure sessions in treatment of agoraphobia and simple phobia. *Behavior Therapy, 21,* 217–229.

Chambless, D. L., Caputo, G. C., Bright, P., & Gallagher, R. (1984). Assessment of fear of fear in agoraphobics: The Body Sensations Questionnaire and the Agoraphobic Cognitions Questionnaire. *Journal of Consulting and Clinical Psychology, 52,* 1090–1097.

Chambless, D. L., Caputo, G. C., Jasin, S. E., Gracely, E. J., & Williams, C. (1985). The Mobility Inventory for Agoraphobia. *Behaviour Research and Therapy, 23,* 35–44.

Chambless, D. L., Goldstein, A. A., Gallagher, R., & Bright, P. (1986). Integrating behavior therapy and psychotherapy in the treatment of agoraphobia. *Psychotherapy: Theory, Research, and Practice, 23,* 150–159.

Chambless, D. L., & Gracely, E. J. (1989). Fear of fear and the anxiety disorders. *Cognitive Therapy and Research, 13,* 9–20.

Chambless, D. L., & Mason, J. (1986). Sex, sex-role stereotyping and agoraphobia. *Behaviour Research and Therapy, 24,* 231–235.

Cheek, J. M., & Buss, A. H. (1981). Shyness and sociability. *Journal of Personality and Social Psychology, 41,* 330–339.

Chhabra, S., & Fielding, D. (1985). The treatment of scriptophobia by *in vivo* exposure and cognitive restructuring. *Journal of Behavior Therapy and Experimental Psychiatry, 16,* 265–269.

Clark, D. M. (1986). A cognitive approach to panic. *Behaviour Research and Therapy, 24,* 461–470.

Clark, D. M. (1988). A cognitive model of panic attacks. In S. Rachman & J. D. Maser (Eds.), *Panic: Psychological perspectives.* Hillsdale, NJ: Lawrence Erlbaum Associates.

Clark, D. M. (1989a). Anxiety states: Panic and generalized anxiety. In K. Hawton, P. M. Salkovskis, J. Kirk, & D. M. Clark (Eds.), *Cognitive behaviour therapy for psychiatric problems: A practical guide.* Oxford: Oxford Medical Publications.

Clark, D. M. (1989b). *Comparative efficacy of cognitive therapy, applied relaxation, and imipramine in the treatment of panic disorder.* Paper presented at the annual meeting of the Association for Advancement of Behavior Therapy, Washington, DC.

Clark, D. M., & Beck, A. T. (1988). Cognitive approaches. In C. G. Last & M. Hersen (Eds.), *Handbook of anxiety disorders* (pp. 362–385). Elmsford, NY: Pergamon Press.

Clark, D. M., & Salkovskis, P. M. *Cognitive therapy for panic and hypochondriasis.* Unpublished Manuscript.

Clark, D. M., & Salkovskis, P. M. (1990). *Cognitive therapy for panic.* Workshop presented at the annual meeting of the Association for Advancement of Behavior Therapy, San Francisco.

Clark, D. M., Salkovskis, P. M., & Chalkley, A. J. (1985). Respiratory control as a treatment for panic attacks. *Journal of Behavior Therapy and Experimental Psychiatry, 16,* 23–30.

Clum, P. G. A. (1989). Psychological intervention vs. drugs in the treatment of panic. *Behavior Therapy, 20,* 429–457.

Coates, D., & Winston, T. (1983). Counteracting the deviance of depression: Peer support groups for victims. *Journal of Social Issues, 39,* 171–196.

Cox, B. J., Norton, G. R., Swinson, R. P., & Endler, N. S. (1990). Substance abuse and panic-related anxiety: A critical review. *Behavior Research and Therapy, 28,* 385–393.

Craske, M. G., & Barlow, D. H. (1988). A review of the relationship between panic and avoidance. *Clinical Psychology Review, 8,* 667–685.

Craske, M. G., & Barlow, D. H. (1990). *Therapist's guide for the mastery of your anxiety and panic.* Center for Stress and Anxiety Disorders, University of Albany, State University of New York.

Craske, M. G., & Krueger, M. T. (1990). Prevalence of nocturnal panic in a college population. *Journal of Anxiety Disorders, 4,* 125–139.

Craske, M. G., Street, L., & Barlow, D. H. (1989) Instructions to focus upon or distract from internal cues during exposure treatment of agoraphobic avoidance. *Behaviour Research and Therapy, 27,* 663–672.

Curran, J. P., Miller, I. W. III, Zwick, W. R., Monti, P. M., & Stout, R. L. (1980). The socially inadequate patient: Incidence rate, demographic and clinical features, and hospital and posthospital functioning. *Journal of Consulting and Clinical Psychology, 48,* 375–382.

Curtis, G. C., Nesse, R. M., Buxton, M., Wright, J., & Lippman, D. (1976). Flooding *in vivo* as a research tool and treatment method for phobias: A preliminary report. *Comprehensive Psychiatry, 17,* 153–160.

Deffenbacher, J., & Suinn, R. (1982). The self-control of anxiety. In P. Karoly & F. H. Kanfer (Eds.), *Self management and behavior change: From theory to practice.* Elmsford, NY: Pergamon Press.

De Loof, C., Zandbergen, H., Lousberg, T., Pols, H., & Griez, E. (1989). The role of life events in the onset of panic disorder. *Behaviour Research and Therapy, 27,* 461–463.

Derogatis, L. R. (1977). *SCL-90-R: Administration, scoring, and procedures manual—II.* Towson, MD: Clinical Psychometric Research.

Derogatis, L. R., Lipman, R. S., & Cove, L. (1973). The SCL-90: An outpatient psychiatric rating scale: Preliminary report. *Psychopharmacological Bulletin, 9,* 13–28.

DiGiuseppe, R., Leaf, R., Exener, T., & Robins, M. (1988, September). *The development of a measure of irrational thinking.* Paper presented at the World Congress of Behavior Therapy, Edinburgh, Scotland.

Di Nardo, P. A., Barlow, D. H., Cerny, J. A., Vermilyea, J. A., Vermilyea, D. D., Himadi, W., & Waddell, M. T. (1985). *The Anxiety Disorders Interview Schedule—Revised (ADIS-R).* Albany, NY: Phobia and Anxiety Disorders Clinic, State University of New York at Albany.

Dollard, J., & Miller, N. E. (1950). *Personality and psychotherapy: An analysis in terms of learning, thinking and culture.* New York: McGraw-Hill.

Dryden, W. (1982). *Social problems: Treatment from a rational-emotive perspective.* London: Institute for RET (UK).

Dryden, W. (1985). Challenging but not overwhelming: A compromise in negotiating homework assignments. *British Journal of Cognitive Psychotherapy, 3,* 77–79.

Dryden, W. (1987). *Counseling individuals: The rational-emotive approach.* London: Whurr Publishers Ltd.

Dryden, W., & DiGiuseppe, R. (1990). *A primer on rational-emotive therapy.* Champaign, IL: Research Press.

Dryden, W., & Ellis, A. (1986). Rational-emotive therapy (RET). In W. Dryden & W. Golden (Eds.), *Cognitive-behavioral approaches to psychotherapy.* London: Harper & Row.

Durham, R. C., & Turvey, A. A. (1987). Cognitive therapy vs. behaviour therapy in the treatment of chronic general anxiety. *Behaviour Research and Therapy, 25,* 229–234.

Ellis, A. (in press). Rational-emotive therapy of simple phobias. *Psychotherapy.*

Ellis, A. (1957a). *How to live with a neurotic.* North Hollywood, CA: Wilshire. [Rev. ed., 1975]

Ellis, A. (1957b). Outcome of employing three techniques of psychotherapy. *Journal of Clinical Psychology, 13,* 334–350.

Ellis, A. (1962). *Reason and emotion in psychotherapy.* New York: Lyle Stuart.

Ellis, A. (1967). Phobia treated with rational-emotive therapy. *Voices, 3*(3), 34–40.

Ellis, A. (Speaker). (1970). *Excerpts from 2nd to 7th sessions with a 54-year-old woman with job anxiety; and 26-year-old woman guilty about mistakes and fearful of rejection* [Cassette recording]. New York: Institute for Rational-Emotive Therapy.

Ellis, A. (1971a). *Growth through reason.* North Hollywood, CA: Wilshire.

Ellis, A. (Speaker). (1971b). *Sex therapy sessions.* [Cassette recording]. New York: Institute for Rational-Emotive Therapy.

Ellis, A. (1972a). *How to master your fear of flying.* New York: Institute for Rational Living.

Ellis, A. (1972b). Psychotherapy without tears. In A. Burton (Ed.), *Twelve therapists* (pp. 103–126). San Francisco: Jossey-Bass.

Ellis, A. (Speaker). (1973a). *Anxiety and phobias: Twenty-four-year-old male with fear of urinating in public bathrooms* [Cassette recording]. New York: Institute for Rational-Emotive Therapy.

Ellis, A. (Speaker). (1973b). *How to stubbornly refuse to be ashamed of anything* [Cassette Recording]. New York: Institute for RET.

Ellis, A. (1973c). *Humanistic psychotherapy: The rational-emotive approach.* New York: Mc-Graw-Hill.

Ellis, A. (Speaker). (1973d). *Twenty-five ways to stop downing yourself* [Cassette Recording]. Philadelphia, PA: American Academy of Psychotherapists Tape Library.

Ellis, A. (Speaker). (1973e). *Twenty-one ways to stop worrying* [Cassette recording]. New York: Institute for RET.

Ellis, A. (1976). The biological basis of human irrationality. *Journal of Individual Psychology, 32,* 145–168.

Ellis, A. (Speaker). (1977a). *Conquering low frustration tolerance* [Cassette Recording]. New York: Institute for RET.

Ellis, A. (Speaker). (1977b). *Conquering the dire need for love* [Cassette Recording]. New York: Institute for RET.

Ellis, A. (1977c). Psychotherapy and the value of a human being. In A. Ellis and R. Grieger (Eds.), *Handbook of rational-emotive therapy* (pp. 99–112). New York: Springer.

Ellis, A. (1979a). Discomfort anxiety: A new cognitive-behavioral construct, Part 1. *Rational Living, 14,* 3–8.

Ellis, A. (1979b). A note on the treatment of agoraphobics with cognitive modification versus prolonged exposure *in vivo. Behaviour Research and Therapy, 17,* 162–164.

Ellis, A. (1979c). *Theoretical and empirical formulations of rational-emotive therapy.* Monterey, CA: Brooks/Cole.

Ellis, A. (1980a). Discomfort anxiety: A new cognitive-behavioral construct, Part 2. *Rational Living, 15,* 25–30.

Ellis, A. (1980b). Rational-emotive therapy and cognitive behavior therapy: Similarities and differences. *Cognitive Therapy and Research, 4,* 325–340.

Ellis, A. (1982). Psychoneurosis and anxiety problems. In R. Grieger and I. Grieger (Eds.), *Cognition and emotional disturbance* (pp. 17–45). New York: Human Sciences Press.

Ellis, A. (1983). The philosophical implications and dangers of some popular behavior therapy techniques. In M. Rosenbaum, C. M. Franks, & Y. Jaffe (Eds.), *Perspectives on behavior therapy in the eighties* (pp. 138–151). New York: Springer.

Ellis, A. (Speaker). (1984). *Unconditionally accepting yourself and others* [Cassette Recording]. New York: Institute for RET.

Ellis, A. (1985a). Intellectual facism. *Journal of Rational-Emotive Therapy, 3,* 3–12. (Speaker).

Ellis, A. (1985b). *Overcoming resistance.* New York: Springer.

Ellis, A. (Speaker). (1987). *How to stop worrying and start living* [Cassette Recording]. Washington, DC: Psychology Today Tapes.

Ellis, A. (1988). *How to stubbornly refuse to make yourself miserable about anything, yes anything.* New York: Lyle Stuart.

Ellis, A. (1989). The history of cognition in psychotherapy. In A. Freeman, K. M. Simon, L. E. Beutler, & H. Arkowitz (Eds.), *Comprehensive handbook of cognitive therapy* (pp. 5–19). New York: Plenum Publishing.

Ellis, A. (1991). My life in clinical psychology. In C. E. Walker (Ed.), *History of clinical psychology in autobiography.* Vol. 1, pp. 1–37..Homewood, IL: Dorsey.

Ellis, A., & Becker, I. (1982). *A guide to personal happiness.* North Hollywood, CA: Wilshire.

Ellis, A., & Dryden, W. (1987). *The practice of rational-emotive therapy (RET)*. New York: Springer.

Ellis, A., & Dryden, W. (1990). *The essential Albert Ellis*. New York: Springer.

Ellis, A., & Grieger, R. (Eds.). (1977). *Handbook of rational-emotive therapy* (Vol 1). New York: Springer.

Ellis, A., & Grieger, R. (Eds.). (1986). *Handbook of rational-emotive therapy* (Vol. 2). New York: Springer.

Ellis, A., & Harper, R. A. (1961). *A guide to successful marriage*. North Hollywood, CA: Wilshire.

Ellis, A., & Harper, R. A. (1975). *A new guide to rational living*. North Hollywood, CA: Wilshire.

Ellis, A., & Knaus, W. (1977). *Overcoming procrastination*. New York: New American Library.

Ellis, A., McInerney, J. F., Di Giuseppe, R., & Yeager, R. J. (1988). *Rational-emotive therapy with alcoholics and substance abusers*. Elmsford, N.Y.: Pergamon Press.

Emmelkamp, P. M. G. (1982). *Phobic and obsessive-compulsive disorders: Theory, research, and practice*. New York: Plenum Publishing.

Emmelkamp, P. M. G., Brilman, E., Kuiper, H., & Mersch, P. (1986). The treatment of agoraphobia: A comparison of self-instructional training, rational-emotive therapy, and exposure *in vivo*. *Behavior Modification, 10*, 37–53.

Emmelkamp, P. M. G., & Felten, M. (1985). Cognitive and physiological changes during exposure *in vivo* treatment of acrophobia. *Behaviour Research and Therapy, 23*, 219–223.

Emmelkamp, P. M. G., Kuipers, A. C. M., & Eggeraat, J. B. (1978). Cognitive modification versus prolonged exposure *in vivo*: A comparison with agoraphobics as subjects. *Behaviour Research and Therapy, 16*, 33–41.

Emmelkamp, P. M. G., & Mersch, P. P. (1982). Cognition and exposure *in vivo* in the treatment of agoraphobia: Short-term and delayed effects. *Cognitive Therapy and Research, 6*, 77–90.

Emmelkamp, P. M. G., Mersch, P., & Vissia, E. (1985). The external validity of analogue outcome research: Evaluation of cognitive and behavioral interventions. *Behaviour Research and Therapy, 23*, 83–86.

Emmelkamp, P. M. G., Mersch, P., Vissia, E., & van der Helm, M. (1985). Social phobia: A comparative evaluation of cognitive and behavioral interventions. *Behaviour Research and Therapy, 23*, 365–369.

Emmelkamp, P. M. G., van der Helm, M., Van Zanten, B., & Plochg, I. (1980). Treatment of obsessive-compulsive patients: The contribution of self-instructional training to the effectiveness of exposure. *Behaviour Research and Therapy, 18*, 61–66.

Emmelkamp, P. M. G., Visser, S., & Hoekstra, R. J. (1988). Cognitive therapy vs. exposure *in vivo* in the treatment of obsessive-compulsives. *Cognitive Therapy and Research, 12*, 103–114.

Emmelkamp, P. M. G., & Wessels, H. (1975). Flooding in imagination vs. flooding *in vivo*: A comparison with agoraphobics. *Behaviour Research and Therapy, 13*, 7–15.

Epsie, C. A. (1986). The group treatment of obsessive-compulsive ritualizers: Behavioural management of identified patterns of relapse. *Behavioural Psychotherapy, 14*, 21–33.

Esquirol, J. E. D. (1838). *Des maladies mentales* [Mental Illnesses] (Vol. II). Paris: Bailliere.

Eysenck, H. J. (Ed.). (1967). *The biological basis of personality*. Springfield, IL: Charles C Thomas.

Eysenck, H., & Eysenck, S. (1975). *Eysenck Personality Questionnaire*. San Diego, CA: Educational and Industrial Testing Service.

Fairbank, J. A., & Brown, T. A. (1987). Current behavioral approaches to the treatment of posttraumatic stress disorder. *The Behavior Therapist, 3*, 57–64.

Fairbank, J. A., De Good, D. E., & Jenkins, C. W. (1981). Behavioral treatment of a persistent post-traumatic startle response. *Journal of Behavior Therapy and Experimental Psychiatry, 12,* 321–324.

Fairbank, J. A., Gross, R. T., & Keane, T. M. (1983). Treatment of posttraumatic stress disorder: Evaluating outcome with a behavioral code. *Behavior Modification, 7,* 557–568.

Fairbank, J. A., Keane, T. M., & Malloy, P. F. (1983). Some preliminary data on the psychological characteristics of Vietnam veterans with post-traumatic stress disorders. *Journal of Consulting and Clinical Psychology, 51,* 912–919.

Fairbank, J. A., & Nicholson, R. A. (1987). Theoretical and empirical issues in the treatment of post-traumatic stress disorder in Vietnam veterans. *Journal of Clinical Psychology, 43,* 44–55.

Falloon, I. R. H., Lloyd, G. G., & Harpin, R. E. (1981). Real-life rehearsal with non-professional therapists. *Journal of Nervous and Mental Disease, 169,* 180–184.

Farrell, A. D., Curran, J. P., Zwick, W. R., & Monte, P. M. (1983). Generalizability and discriminant validity of anxiety and social skills ratings in two populations. *Behavioral Assessment, 6,* 1–14.

Fischetti, M., Curran, J. P., & Wessberg, H. W. (1977). Sense of timing. *Behavior Modification, 1,* 179–194.

Fleming, D., & Faulk, A. (1989). Discriminating factor in panic disorder with and without agoraphobia. *Journal of Anxiety Disorders, 3,* 209–219.

Flor-Henry, P., Yendall, L. T., Koles, Z. J., & Howarth, B. G. (1979). Neuropsychological and power spectral EEG investigations of the obsessive-compulsive syndrome. *Biological Psychology, 14,* 119–130.

Foa, E. B. (1979). Failure in treating obsessive-compulsives. *Behaviour Research and Therapy, 17,* 169–176.

Foa, E. B. (1990a, June). *Obsessive-compulsive disorder.* Workshop presented for the Oregon Psychological Association, Portland, OR.

Foa, E. B. (1990b, June). *Post traumatic stress disorder.* Workshop presented for the Oregon Psychological Association, Portland, OR.

Foa, E. B., & Kozak, M. J. (1985). Treatment of anxiety disorders: Implications for psychopathology. In A. H. Tuma & J. D. Maser (Eds.), *Anxiety and the anxiety disorders* (pp. 421–452). Hillsdale, NJ: Lawrence Erlbaum Associates.

Foa, E. B., & Kozak, M. J. (1986). Emotional processing of fear: Exposure to corrective information. *Psychological Bulletin, 99,* 20–35.

Foa, E. B., & Olasov, B. (1989). *Treatment of post-traumatic stress disorder.* Workshop conducted at Advances in Theory and Treatment of Anxiety Disorders, Philadelphia, PA.

Foa, E. B., & Steketee, G. (1987). Behavioral treatment of phobics and obsessive-compulsives. In N. S. Jacobson (Ed.), *Psychotherapists in clinical practice* (pp. 78–120). New York: Guilford Press.

Foa, E. B., Steketee, G., Kozak, M., & Dugger, D. (1987). Imipramine and placebo in the treatment of obsessive-compulsives: Their effect on depression and on obsessional symptoms. *Psychopharmacology Bulletin, 23,* 8–11.

Foa, E. B., Steketee, G., & Rothbaum, B. O. (1989). Behavioral/cognitive conceptualizations of post-traumatic stress disorder. *Behavior Therapy, 20,* 155–176.

Foa, E. B., Steketee, G. S., & Ozarow, B. J. (1985). Behavior therapy with obsessive-compulsives: From theory to treatment. In M. Mavissakalian (Ed.), *Obsessive-compulsive disorder: Psychological and pharmacological treatment* (pp. 49–129). New York: Plenum Publishing.

Forgione, A. G., & Bauer, F. M. (1980). *Fearless flying: The complete program for relaxed air travel.* Boston: Houghton Mifflin.

Foy, D. W., Resnick, H. S., Sipprelle, C., & Carroll, E. M. (1987). Premilitary, military, and postmilitary factors in the development of combat-related post-traumatic stress disorder. *The Behavior Therapist, 10,* 3–9.

Frank, E., Anderson, B., Stewart, B. D., Dancu, C., Hughes, C., & West, D. (1988). Efficacy of cognitive behavior therapy and systematic desensitization in the treatment of rape trauma. *Behavior Therapy, 19,* 403–420.

Frank, J. B., Kosten, T. R., Giller, E. L., & Dan, E. (1988). A randomized clinical trial of phenelzine and imipramine for post-traumatic stress disorder. *American Journal of Psychiatry, 145,* 1289–1291.

Frankl, V. (1963). *Man's search for meaning.* New York: Washington Square Press.

Freund, B. (1989). *Diagnostic considerations and treatment follow-up for fearful flyers.* Paper presented at the annual meeting of the Association for Advancement of Behavior Therapy, Washington, DC.

Freund, B., Steketee, G. S., & Foa, E. B. (1987). Compulsive activity checklist (CAC): Psychometric analysis with obsessive-compulsive disorder. *Behavioral Assessment, 9,* 67–79.

Friedman, M. J. (1988). Toward rational pharmacotherapy for posttraumatic stress disorder: An interim report. *American Journal of Psychiatry, 145,* 281–285.

Frost, R. O., Sher, K. J., & Geen, T. (1986). Psychopathology and personality characteristics of non-clinical compulsive checkers. *Behavior Research and Therapy, 24,* 133–143.

Gale, E. N., & Ayer, W. A. (1969). Treatment of dental phobias. *Journal of American Dental Association, 78,* 1304–1307.

Gardner, P., & Oei, T. (1981). Depression and self-esteem: An investigation that used behavioral and cognitive approaches to the treatment of clinically depressed clients. *Journal of Clinical Psychology, 37,* 128–135.

Geer, J. H. (1965). The development of a scale to measure fear. *Behaviour Research and Therapy, 3,* 45–53.

Gerardi, J. R., Blanchard, E. B., & Kolb, L. C. (1989). Ability of Vietnam veterans to dissimulate a psychophysiological assessment for post-traumatic stress disorder. *Behavior Therapy, 20,* 229–243.

Gerardi, J. R., Keane, T. M., Cahoon, B. J., & Klauminzer, G. W. (1989). *Physiological arousal in Vietnam veterans: Hyperarousal or hyperactivity?* Paper presented at the annual meeting of the Association for Advancement of Behavior Therapy, Washington, DC.

Ghosh, A., Marks, I. M., & Carr, A. C. (1988). Therapist contact and outcome of self-exposure treatment for phobias. *British Journal of Psychiatry, 152,* 234–238.

Giles, T. R. (1988). Phobia and suicide: An influence of treatment? *The Behavior Therapist, 11,* 26–42.

Girodo, M., & Roehl, J. (1978). Cognitive preparation and coping self-talk: Anxiety management during the stress of flying. *Journal of Consulting and Clinical Psychology, 46,* 978–989.

Gitlin, B., Martin, J., Shear, M. K., Frances, A., Ball, G., & Josephson, S. (1985). Behavior therapy for panic disorder. *Journal of Nervous and Mental Disease, 173,* 742–743.

Glasgow, R. E. (1975). *In vivo* prolonged exposure therapy in the treatment of urinary retention. *Behavior Therapy, 6,* 701–702.

Glass, C. R., Merluzzi, T. V., Biever, J. L., & Larsen, K. H. (1982). Cognitive assessment of social anxiety: Development and validation of a self-statement questionnaire. *Cognitive Therapy and Research, 6,* 37–55.

Gold, D. (1989). *The good news about panic, anxiety, and phobias.* New York: Villard Books.

Goldberg, R. (1988). Clinical presentations of panic-related disorders. *Journal of Anxiety Disorders, 2,* 61–75.

Goldfried, M. (1971). Systematic desensitization as training in self-control. *Journal of Clinical and Consulting Psychology, 37,* 228–234.

Goldfried, M. R., & Davison, G. C. (1976). *Clinical behavior therapy*. New York: Holt, Rinehart & Winston.

Goodman, W. K., Price, L. H., Rosmussen, S. A., Mazure, C., Fleischmann, R. L., Hill, C. L., Herringer, G. R., & Charney, D. S. (1989). The Yale-Brown Obsessive Compulsive Scale. *Archives of General Psychiatry, 46*, 1006–1011.

Gorman, J. M., Liebowitz, M. R., Fyer, A. J., Campeas, R., & Klein, D. F. (1985). Treatment of social phobia with atenolol. *Journal of Clinical Psychopharmacology, 5*, 298–301.

Gorman, J. M., Liebowitz, M. R., Fyer, A. J., & Stein, J. (1989). A neuroanatomical hypothesis for panic disorder. *American Journal of Psychiatry, 146*, 148–161.

Gray, J. A. (1988). The neuropsychological basis of anxiety. In C. A. Last & M. Hersen (Eds.), *Handbook of anxiety disorders* (pp. 10–37). Elmsford, NY: Pergamon Press.

Grayson, J. B., Foa, E. B., & Steketee, G. (1985). In M. Hersen & A. S. Bellack (Eds.), *Handbook of clinical behavior therapy* (pp. 133–165). New York: Plenum Publishing.

Green, B. L., Wilson, J. P., & Lindy, J. D. (1985). Conceptualizing post-traumatic stress disorder: A psychosocial framework. In C. R. Figley (Ed.), *Trauma and its wake* (pp. 53–69). New York: Brunner/Mazel.

Grieger, R., & Boyd, J. (1980). *Rational-emotive therapy: A skills-based approach.* New York: Van Nostrand Reinhold.

Grinker, R. R., & Spiegel, J. P. (1943). *War neurosis in North Africa, The Tunisian Campaign, January to May 1943*. New York: Josiah Macy Foundation.

Hallstrom, C., Treasaden, I., Edwards, J., & Lader, M. (1981). Diazepam, propranolol, and their combination in the management of chronic anxiety. *Archives of General Psychiatry, 41*, 741–750.

Hallstrom, T., & Halling, A. (1984). Prevalence of dentistry phobia in an urban community sample. *Acta Psychiatrica Scandinavia, 70*, 438–446.

Hamilton, M. (1959). The assessment of anxiety states by rating. *British Journal of Medical Psychology, 32*, 50–55.

Hartman, L. M. (1984). Cognitive components of social anxiety. *Journal of Clinical Psychology, 40*, 137–139.

Hauk, P. (1973). *Overcoming depression*. Philadelphia: Westminister Press.

Heide, F. J., & Borkovec, T. D. (1983). Relaxation-induced anxiety: Paradoxical anxiety enhancement due to relaxation training. *Journal of Clinical and Consulting Psychology, 51*, 171–182.

Heide, F. J., & Borkovek, T. D. (1984). Relaxation-induced anxiety: Mechanisms and theoretical implications. *Behaviour Research and Therapy, 22*, 1–12.

Heimberg, R. G. (1989). Social phobia: No longer neglected. *Clinical Psychology Review, 9*, 1–2.

Heimberg, R. G., Acerra, M., & Holstein, A. (1985). Partner similarity mediates interpersonal anxiety. *Cognitive Therapy and Research, 9*, 436–445.

Heimberg, R. G. & Becker, R. E. (1984). *Cognitive-behavioral treatment of social phobia in a group setting*. Manual prepared under support of the National Institute of Mental Health.

Heimberg, R. G., Becker, R. E., Goldfinger, K., & Vermilyea, J. A. (1985). Treatment of social phobia by exposure, cognitive restructuring and homework assignments. *Journal of Nervous and Mental Disease, 173*, 236–245.

Heimberg, R. G., Dodge, C. S., & Becker, R. E. (1987). Social phobia. In L. Michelson & L. M. Ascher (Eds.), *Anxiety and stress disorders: Cognitive-behavioral assessment and treatment*. New York: Guilford Press.

Heimberg, R. G., Dodge, C. S., Hope, D. A., Kennedy, C. R., Zollo, L. J., & Becker, R. E. (1990). Cognitive behavioral group treatment for social phobia: Comparison with a credible placebo control. *Cognitive Therapy and Research, 14*, 1–23.

Heimberg, R. G., Hope, D. A., Dodge, C. S., & Becker, R. E. (1990). DSM-III-R subtypes of social phobia: Comparison of generalized social phobics and public speaking phobics. *The Journal of Nervous and Mental Disease, 178,* 172–179.

Heimberg, R. G., Hope, D. A., Rapee, R. M., & Bruch, M. A. (1988). The validity of the Social Avoidance and Distress Scale and the Fear of Negative Evaluation Scale with social phobic patients. *Behaviour Research and Therapy, 26,* 407–410.

Helzer, J. E., Robins, L. N., & McEvoy, L. (1987). Post-traumatic stress disorder in the general population: Findings of the Epidemiologic Catchment Area Survey. *New England Journal of Medicine, 317,* 1630–1634.

Hibbert, G. N. (1984). Ideational components of anxiety: Their origin and content. *British Journal of Psychiatry, 144,* 618–624.

Hodgson, R. J., & Rachman, S. J. (1977). Obsessional-compulsive complaints. *Behaviour Research and Therapy, 15,* 389–395.

Hollander, E., Fay, M., Cohen, B., Campeas, R., Gorman, J. M., & Leibowitz, M. R. (1988). Serotonergic and noradrenergic sensitivity in obsessive-compulsive disorder: Behavioral findings. *American Journal of Psychiatry, 145,* 1015–1017.

Holt, C. S., Heimberg, R. G., & Hope, D. A. (1990). *Avoidant personality disorder and the generalized subtype in social phobia.* Paper presented at the annual meeting of the Association for Advancement of Behavior Therapy, San Francisco.

Hope, D. A., Gansler, D. A., & Heimberg, R. G. (1989). Attentional focus and causal attributions in social phobia: Implications from social psychology. *Clinical Psychology Review, 9,* 49–60.

Horowitz, M. (1986). *Stress response syndromes* (2nd ed.). Northvale, NJ: Jason Aronson.

Horowitz, M. D., Wilner, N., & Alvarez, W. (1979). Impact of Event Scale: A measure of subjective stress. *Psychosomatic Medicine, 41,* 209–218.

Howard, W. A., Murphy, S. M., & Clarke, J. C. (1983). The nature and treatment of fear of flying: A controlled investigation. *Behavior Therapy, 14,* 557–567.

Insel, T. R., Mueller, E. A., Linnoila, M., & Murphy, D. L. (1985). Obsessive-compulsive disorder and serotonin: Is there a connection? *Biological Psychiatry, 20,* 1174–1188.

Jakes, I. (1989a). Salkovskis on obsessional-compulsive neurosis: A critique. *Behaviour Research and Therapy, 27,* 673–675.

Jakes, I. (1989b). Salkovskis on obsessional-compulsive neurosis: A rejoinder. *Behaviour Research and Therapy, 27,* 683–684.

Jakubowski, P., & Lange, A. J. (1978). *The assertive option: Your rights and responsibilities.* Champaign, IL: Research Press.

James, W. (1980). *Principles of psychology.* London: Macmillan.

Jannoun, L., Munby, M., Catalan, J., & Gelder, M. (1980). A home-based treatment program for agoraphobia: Replication and controlled evaluation. *Behavior Therapy, 11,* 294–305.

Janoff-Bulman, R. (1979). Characterological versus behavioral self-blame: Inquiries into depression and rape. *Journal of Personality and Social Psychology, 37,* 1798–1809.

Janoff-Bulman, R. (1985). The aftermath of victimization: Rebuilding shattered assumptions. In C. R. Figley (Ed.), *Trauma and its wake.* New York: Brunner/Mazel.

Janoff-Bulman, R., & Frieze, I. H. (1983). A theoretical perspective for understanding reactions to victimization. *Journal of Social Issues, 39,* 1–17.

Jansson, L., & Ost, L. G. (1982). Behavioral treatments for agoraphobia: An evaluative review. *Clinical Psychology Review, 2,* 311–336.

Jerremalm, A., Jansson, L., & Ost, L. G. (1986a). Cognitive and physiological reactivity and the effects of different behavioral methods in the treatment of social phobia. *Behaviour Research and Therapy, 24,* 171–180.

Jerremalm, A., Jansson, L., & Ost, L. G. (1986b). Individual response patterns and the effects of different behavioural methods in the treatment of dental phobia. *Behaviour Research and Therapy, 24,* 587–596.

Jones, J. C., & Barlow, D. H. (1990). The etiology of posttraumatic stress disorder. *Clinical Psychology Review, 10,* 299–328.

Jones, W. H., & Russell, D. (1982). The Social Reticence Scale: An objective measure of shyness. *Journal of Personality Assessment, 46,* 629–631.

Kagan, J., Reznick, J. S., & Snidman, N. (1988). Biological bases of childhood shyness. *Science, 240,* 167–171.

Kahn, R. J., McNair, D. M., Lipman, R. S., Covi, L., Rickels, K., Downing, R., Fisher, S., & Frankenthaler, L. M. (1986). Imipramine and cloridiazepoxide in depressive and anxiety disorders. *Archives of General Psychiatry, 43,* 79–85.

Kanter, N. J., & Goldfried, M. R. (1979). Relative effectiveness of rational restructuring and self-control desensitization in the reduction of interpersonal anxiety. *Behavior Therapy, 10,* 472–490.

Karno, M., Golding, J. M., Sorenson, S. B., & Burnam, A. (1988). The epidemiology of obsessive-compulsive disorder in five US communities. *Archives of General Psychiatry, 45,* 1094–1099.

Karno, M., Hough, R. L., Burman, M. A., Escobar, J. I., Timbers, D. M., Santana, F., & Boyd, J. H. (1987). Lifetime prevalence of specific psychiatric disorders among Mexican Americans and non-Hispanic whites. *Archives of General Psychiatry, 44,* 695–701.

Kassinove, H., & DiGiuseppe, R. (1975). Rational role reversal. *Rational Living, 10,* 44–45.

Kassinove, H., Miller, N., & Kalin, M. (1980). Effects of pretreatment with rational-emotive bibliotherapy and rational-emotive audiotherapy on clients waiting at community mental health centers. *Psychological Reports, 46,* 851–857.

Katon, W., Vitaliano, P. P., Russo, J., Jones, M., & Anderson, K. (1987). Panic disorder: Spectrum of severity and somatization. *Journal of Nervous and Mental Disease, 175,* 12–19.

Keane, T. M. (1989). Post-traumatic stress disorder: Current status and future directions. *Behavior Therapy, 20,* 149–153.

Keane, T. M., Caddell, J. M., & Taylor, K. L. (1988). Mississippi Scale for Combat-related Post-traumatic Stress Disorder: Three studies in reliability and validity. *Journal of Consulting and Clinical Psychology, 56,* 85–90.

Keane, T. M., Fairbank, J. A., Caddell, J. M., & Zimering, R. T. (1989). Implosive (flooding) therapy reduces symptoms of PTSD in Vietnam combat veterans. *Behavior Therapy, 20,* 245–260.

Keane, T. M., Fairbank, J. A., Caddell, J. M., Zimering, R. T., & Bender, M. E. (1985). A behavioral approach to assessing and treating post-traumatic stress disorder in Vietnam veterans. In C. R. Figley (Ed.), *Trauma and its wake* (pp. 255–294). New York: Brunner/Mazel.

Keane, T. M., Malloy, P. F., & Fairbank, J. A. (1984). Empirical development of an MMPI subscale for the assessment of combat-related post-traumatic stress disorder. *Journal of Consulting and Clinical Psychology, 52,* 888–891.

Keane, T. M., Wolfe, J., & Taylor, K. L. (1987). Post-traumatic stress disorder: Evidence for diagnostic validity and methods of psychological assessment. *Journal of Clinical Psychology, 43,* 32–43.

Keller, J. F., Croake, J. W., & Brooking, J. Y. (1975). Effects of a program in rational thinking on anxieties in older persons. *Journal of Counseling Psychology, 22,* 54–57.

Kendrick, M. J., Craig, K. D., Lawson, D. M., & Davidson, P. O. (1982). Cognitive and behavioral therapy for musical-performance anxiety. *Journal of Consulting and Clinical Psychology, 50,* 353–362.

Kent, G. (1989). Cognitive aspects of the maintenance and treatment of dental anxiety: A review. *Journal of Cognitive Psychotherapy, 3,* 201–222.

Kilpatrick, D. G., & Calhoun, K. S. (1988). Early behavioral treatment for rape trauma: Efficacy or artifact? *Behavior Therapy, 19*, 421–427.

Kilpatrick, D. G., Saunders, B. E., Veronen, L. J., Best, C. L., & Von, J. M. (1987). Criminal victimization: Lifetime prevalence, reporting to police, and psychological impact. *Crime and Deliquency, 33*, 479–489.

Kilpatrick, D. G., Veronen, L. J., & Best, C. L. (1985). Factors predicting psychological distress among rape victims. In C. R. Figley (Ed.), *Trauma and its wake* (pp. 113–141). New York: Brunner/Mazel.

Klein, D. F. (1964). Delineation of two drug-responsive anxiety syndromes. *Psychopharmacologia, 5*, 397–408.

Klein, D. F. (1980). Anxiety reconceptualized. *Comprehensive Psychiatry, 21*, 411–427.

Klein, D. F., Rabkin, J. G., & Gorman, J. M. (1985). Etiological and pathophysiological inferences from the pharmacological treatment of anxiety. In A. H. Tuma & J. D. Maser (Eds.), *Anxiety and the anxiety disorders* (pp. 501–532). Hillsdale, NJ: Lawrence Erlbaum Associates.

Kleinknecht, R. A., Klepac, R. K., & Alexander, L. D. (1973). Origin and characteristics of fear of dentistry. *Journal of the American Dental Association, 86*, 842–847.

Klepac, R. K. (1975). Treatment of dental avoidance by desensitization or by increasing pain tolerance. *Journal of Behavior Therapy and Experimental Psychiatry, 6*, 307–310.

Klosko, J. S., Barlow, D. H., Tassinari, R., & Cerny, J. A. (1990). A comparison of alprazolam and behavior therapy in treatment of panic disorder. *Journal of Consulting and Clinical Psychology, 58*, 77–84.

Kozak, M. J., Foa, E. B., & McCarthy, P. R. (1988). Obsessive-compulsive disorder. In C. Last & M. Hersen (Eds.), *Handbook of anxiety disorders* (pp. 87–108). Elmsford, NY: Pergamon Press.

Krystal, J. H., Kosten, T. R., Southwick, S., Mason, J. W., Perry, B. D., & Giller, E. L., Jr. (1989). Neurobiological aspects of PTSD: Review of clinical and preclinical studies. *Behavior Therapy, 20*, 177–198.

Kuiper, N. A., & Olinger, L. J. (1986). Dysfunctional attitudes and a self-worth contingency model of depression. In P. C. Kendal (Ed.), *Advances in cognitive-behavioral research and therapy* (vol. 5, pp. 115–142). New York: Academic Press.

Kushner, M. G., Sher, K. J., & Beitman, B. D. (1990). The relation between alcohol problems and the anxiety disorders. *American Journal of Psychiatry, 147*, 685–695.

Ladouceur, R. L. (1983). Participant modeling with or without cognitive treatment for phobias. *Journal of Consulting and Clinical Psychology, 51*, 942–944.

Lamontagne, Y., & Marks, I. M. (1973). Psychogenic urinary retention: Treatment by prolonged exposure. *Behavior Therapy, 4*, 581–585.

Lang, P., Melamed, B. H., & Hart, J. (1970). Psychophysiological analysis of fear modification with automated desensitization. *Journal of Abnormal Psychology, 76*, 220–234.

Lang, P. J. (1968). Fear reduction and fear behavior: Problems in treating a construct. In J. M. Shlien (Ed.), *Research in psychotherapy (Vol. 3)*. Washington, DC: American Psychological Association.

Lang, P. J. (1977). Imagery in therapy: An informational processing analysis of fear. *Behavior Therapy, 8*, 862–886.

Lang, P. J. (1978). Anxiety: Toward a psychophysiological definition. In H. S. Akiskal & W. L. Webb (Eds.), *Psychiatric diagnosis: Exploration of biological predictors* (pp. 365–389). New York: Spectrum.

Lang, P. J. (1979). A bio-informational theory of emotional imagery. *Psychophysiology, 16*, 495–512.

Lang, P. J., & Lazovik, A. D. (1963). Experimental desensitization of a phobia. *Journal of Abnormal and Social Psychology, 66*, 519–525.

Last, C. G. (1987). Simple phobias. In L. Michelson & L. M. Ascher (Eds.), *Anxiety and stress disorders* (pp. 176–190). New York: Guilford Press.

Last, C. G., Barlow, D. H., & O'Brien, G. T. (1984). Precipitants of agoraphobia: Role of stressful life events. *Psychological Reports, 54*, 567–570.

Ledwidge, B. (1978). Cognitive behavior modification: A step in the wrong direction? *Psychological Bulletin, 85*, 353–375.

Leelarthaepin, B., Gray, W., & Chesworth, E. (1980). Exersentry: An evaluation of its cardiac frequency monitoring accuracy. *Australian Journal of Sports Science, 1*, 1–11.

Lehrer, P. (1978). Psychophysiological effects of progressive relaxation in anxiety neurotic patients and of progressive relaxation and alpha feedback in nonpatients. *Journal of Consulting and Clinical Psychology, 46*, 389–404.

Lerner, M. J. (1970). The desire for justice and reactions to victims: Social psychological studies of some antecedents and consequences. In J. Macaulay & L. Berkowitz (Eds.), *Altruism and helping behavior* (pp. 205–229). New York: Academic Press.

Lerner, M. J. (1980). *The belief in a just world.* New York: Plenum Publishing.

Lerner, M. J., & Mathews, G. (1967). Reactions to suffering of others under conditions of indirect responsibility. *Journal of Personality and Social Psychology, 5*, 319–325.

Levin, A. P., Schneier, F. R., & Liebowitz, M. R. (1989). Social phobia: Biology and pharmacology. *Clinical Psychology Review, 9*, 129–140.

Ley, R. (1985). Agoraphobia, the panic attack and the hyperventilation syndrome. *Behaviour Research and Therapy, 23*, 79–82.

Liebowitz, M. R., Campeas, R., Levin, A., Sandberg, D., Hollander, E., & Papp, L. (1987). Pharmacotherapy of social phobia. *Psychosomatics, 28*, 305–308.

Liebowitz, M. R., Fyer, A. J., Gorman, J. M., Campeas, R., & Levin, A. (1986). Phenelzine in social phobia. *Journal of Clinical Psychopharmacology, 6*, 93–98.

Liebowitz, M. R., Gorman, J. M., Fyer, A. J., & Klein, D. F. (1985). Social phobia: Review of a neglected anxiety disorder. *Archives of General Psychiatry, 42*, 729–736.

Lindsay, W. R., Gamsu, C. V., McLaughlin, E., Hood, E., & Epsie, C. A. (1987). A controlled trial of treatments for generalized anxiety. *British Journal of Clinical Psychology, 26*, 3–15.

Lipsky, M., Kassinove, H., & Miller, N. (1980). Effects of rational-emotive therapy, rational-role reversal, and rational-emotive imagery on the emotional adjustment of community mental health center patients. *Journal of Consulting and Clinical Psychology, 48*, 366–374.

Lucock, M. P., & Salkovskis, P. M. (1988). Cognitive factors in social anxiety and its treatment. *Behaviour Research and Therapy, 26*, 297–302.

Lydiard, R. B., & Ballenger, J. C. (1988). Panic-related disorders: Evidence for efficacy of the antidepressants. *Journal of Anxiety Disorders, 2*, 95–108.

Maher, B. A. (1988). Anomalous experience and delusional thinking: The logic of explanations. In T. F. Oltmanns & B. A. Maher (Eds.), *Delusional beliefs* (pp. 15–33). New York: John Wiley & Sons.

Malloy, P. F., Fairbank, J. A., & Keane, T. M. (1983). Validation of a multimethod assessment of PTSD in Vietnam veterans. *Journal of Consulting and Clinical Psychology, 51*, 488–494.

Malouff, J. M. (1984). *A study of brief cognitive treatment for depressed persons who have recently experienced a marital separation.* Unpublished doctoral dissertation, Arizona State University, Tempe.

Malouff, J. M., & Lanyon, R. I. (1985). Avoidant paruresis: An exploratory study. *Behavior Modification, 9*, 225–234.

Malouff, J. M., & Schutte, N. S. (1986). Development and validation of a measure of irrational belief. *Journal of Consulting and Clinical Psychology, 54*, 860–862.

Malouff, J. M., Valdenegro, J., & Schutte, N. S. (1987). Further validation of a measure of irrational belief. *Journal of Rational-Emotive Therapy, 5,* 189–193.

March, J. S. (1990). The nosology of post-traumatic stress disorder. *Journal of Anxiety Disorders, 4,* 61–82.

Margraf, J., & Ehlers, A. (1989a). Etiological models of panic—medical and biological aspects. In R. Baker (Ed.), *Panic disorder: Theory, research and therapy* (pp. 145–203). West Sussex, England: John Wiley & Sons, Ltd.

Margraf, J., & Ehlers, A. (1989b). Etiological models of panic—psychophysiological and cognitive aspects. In R. Baker (Ed.), *Panic disorder: Theory, research and therapy* (pp. 205–231). West Sussex, England: John Wiley & Sons, Ltd.

Margraf, J., Ehlers, A., & Roth, W. T. (1986). Biological models of panic disorder and agoraphobia—review. *Behaviour Research and Therapy, 24,* 553–567.

Margraf, J., Ehlers, A., & Roth, W. T. (1989). Expectancy effects and hyperventilation as laboratory stressors. In H. Weiner, I. Florin, R. Murison, & D. Hellhammer (Eds.), *Frontiers of stress research* (pp. 395–400). Toronto: Huber.

Markowitz, J. S., Weissman, M. M., Quellette, R., Lish, J. D., & Klerman, G. L. (1989). Quality of life in panic disorder. *Archives of General Psychiatry, 46,* 984–992.

Marks, I. M. (1987). *Fears, phobias, and rituals.* New York: Oxford University Press.

Marks, I. M., & Gelder, M. C. (1966). Different ages of onset in varieties of phobia. *American Journal of Psychiatry, 123,* 218–221.

Marks, I. M., & Matthews, A. M. (1979). Brief standard self-rating for phobic patients. *Behaviour Research and Therapy, 17,* 263–267.

Marshall, W. L. (1985). The effects of variable exposure in flooding therapy. *Behavior Therapy, 16,* 117–135.

Mathews, A. M., & MacLeod, C. (1986). Discrimination of threat cues without awareness in anxiety states. *Journal of Abnormal Psychology, 95,* 131–138.

Mattick, R. P., & Clarke, J. C. (1988). *Development and validation of measures of social phobia scrutiny fear and social interaction anxiety.* Unpublished manuscript.

Mattick, R. P., & Peters, L. (1988). Treatment of severe social phobia: Effects of guided exposure with and without cognitive restructuring. *Journal of Consulting and Clinical Psychology, 56,* 251–260.

Mattick, R. P., Peters, L., & Clarke, J. C. (1989). Exposure and cognitive restructuring for social phobia: A controlled study. *Behavior Therapy, 20,* 3–23.

Mavissakalian, M. (1988a). Clinically significant improvement in agoraphobia research. *Behaviour Research and Therapy, 24,* 369–370.

Mavissakalian, M. (1986b). The Fear Questionnaire: A validity study. *Behaviour Research and Therapy, 24,* 83–85.

Mavissakalian, M., Turner, S. M., Michelson, L., & Jacob, R. (1985). Tricyclic antidepressants in obsessive-compulsive disorder: Antiobsessional or antidepressant agents? II. *American Journal of Psychiatry, 142,* 572–576.

McCaffrey, R. J., & Fairbank, J. A. (1985). Behavioral assessment and treatment of accident-related post-traumatic stress disorder; Two case studies. *Behavior Therapy, 16,* 406–416.

McCarthy, P. R. (1986). Cognitive influences on autonomic and central nervous system activity in obsessive-compulsive disorder [Doctoral Dissertation, Pennsylvania State University]. *Dissertation Abstracts International, 47,* 2378/2B.

McCarthy, P. R., & Foa, E. B. (1990). Obsessive-compulsive disorder. In M. E. Thase, B. A., Edelstein, & M. Hersen (Eds.) *Handbook of outpatient treatment of adults* (pp. 209–234). New York: Plenum Publishing.

McFall, M. E., Murburg, M. M., Roszell, D., K., & Veith, R. C. (1989). Psychophysiologic and neuroendocrine findings in posttraumatic stress disorder: A review of theory and research. *Journal of Anxiety Disorders, 3,* 243–257.

McFall, M. E., & Wollersheim, J. P. (1979). Obsessive-compulsive neurosis: A cognitive-behavioral formulation and approach to treatment. *Cognitive Therapy and Research, 3,* 333–348.

McKnight, D. L., Nelson, R. O., Hayes, S. C., & Jarrett, R. B. (1984). Importance of treating individually assessed response classes in the amelioration of depression. *Behavior Therapy, 15,* 315–335.

McNally, R. J. (1987). Preparedness and phobias: A review. *Psychological Bulletin, 101,* 283–303.

McNally, R. J., & Foa, E. B. (1987). Cognition and agoraphobia: Bias in the interpretation of threat. *Cognitive Therapy and Research, 11,* 567–582.

McNally, R. J., & Steketee, G. S. (1985). The etiology and maintenance of severe animal phobias. *Behaviour Research and Therapy, 23,* 431–435.

Meichenbaum, D. (1985). *Stress inoculation training.* Elmsford, NY: Pergamon Press.

Meichenbaum, D. H. (1974). *Therapist manual for cognitive behaviour modification.* Unpublished manuscript, University of Waterloo, Ontario, Canada.

Melamed, B. G. (1979). Behavioral approaches to fear in dental settings. In M. Hersen, R. Eisler, & P. Miller (Eds.), *Progress in behavior modification* (Vol. 7). New York: Academic Press.

Mersch, P. P. A., Emmelkamp, P. M. G., Bogels, S. M., & van der Sleen, J. (1989). Social phobia: Individual response patterns and the effects of behavioral and cognitive interventions. *Behaviour Research and Therapy, 27,* 421–434.

Meyer, T. J., Miller, M. L., Metzger, R. L., & Borkovec, T. D. (in press). Development and validation of the Penn State Worry Questionnaire. *Behaviour Research and Therapy.*

Michelson, L. (1987). Cognitive-behavioral assessment and treatment of agoraphobia. In L. Michelson & L. M. Ascher (Eds.), *Anxiety and stress disorders* (pp. 213–279). New York: Guilford Press.

Michelson, L., Marchione, K., Greenwald, M., Glanz, L., Testa, S., & Marchione, N. (1990). Panic disorder: Cognitive-behavioral treatment. *Behaviour Research and Therapy, 28,* 141–151.

Middlemist, R. D., Knowles, E. S., & Matter, C. F. (1976). Personal space invasions in the lavatory: Suggestive evidence for arousal. *Journal of Personality and Social Psychology, 33,* 541–546.

Miller, D. T., & Porter, C. A. (1983). Self-blame in victims of violence. *Journal of Social Issues, 39,* 139–152.

Miller, W. R. (1983). Motivational interviewing with problem drinkers. *Behavioural Psychotherapy, 11,* 147–172.

Mineka, S., & Kihlstrom, J. F. (1978). Unpredictable and uncontrollable events: A new perspective on experimental neurosis. *Journal of Abnormal Psychology, 87,* 256–271.

Minichiello, W. E., Baer, L., Jenike, M. A., & Holland, A. (1990). Age of onset of major subtypes of obsessive-compulsive disorder. *Journal of Anxiety Disorders, 4,* 147–150.

Mowrer, O. H. (1939). Stimulus-response analysis of anxiety and its role as a reinforcing agent. *Psychotherapy Review, 46,* 553–565.

Mowrer, O. H. (1960). *Learning theory and behavior.* New York: John Wiley & Sons.

Mueller, G., Heimberg, R. C., Holt, C. S., Hope, D. A., & Liebowitz, M. R. (1990). *A validation study of the social interaction anxiety scale and the social phobia scale.* Paper presented at the annual meeting of the Association for Advancement of Behavior Therapy, San Francisco.

Munjack, D. J. (1984). The onset of driving phobias. *Journal of Behavior Therapy and Experimental Psychiatry, 15,* 305–308.

Murray, E. J., & Foote, F. (1979). The origins of fears of snakes. *Behaviour Research and Therapy, 17,* 489–493.

Myers, J. K., Weissman, M. M., Tischler, G. L., Holzer, C. E. III, Leaf, P. J., Orvaschel, H., Anthony, J. C., Boyd, J. H., Burke, J. D., Jr., Kramer, M., & Stoltzman, R. (1984). Six-month prevalence of psychiatric disorders in three communities. *Archives of General Psychiatry, 41,* 959–967.

Nichols, K. A. (1974). Severe social anxiety. *British Journal of Medical Psychology, 74,* 301–306.

Niler, E. R., & Beck, S. J. (1989). The relationship among guilt, dysphoria, anxiety and obsessions in a normal population. *Behaviour Research and Therapy, 27,* 213–220.

Norton, G. R., Dorward, J., & Cox, B. J. (1986). Factors associated with panic attacks in nonclinical subjects. *Behavior Therapy, 17,* 239–252.

Norton, G. R., Harrison, B., Hauch, J., & Rhodes, L. (1985). Characteristics of people with infrequent panic attacks. *Journal of Abnormal Psychology, 94,* 216–221.

Noyes, R. (1982). Beta-blocking drugs and anxiety. *Psychosomatics, 23,* 155–170.

Noyes, R., Jr. (1985). Beta-adrenergic blocking drugs in anxiety and stress. *Psychiatric Clinics of North America, 8,* 119–132.

O'Banion, K., & Arkowitz, H. (1977). Social anxiety and selective attention for affective information about the self. *Social Behavior and Personality, 5,* 321–328.

Ohman, A. (1986). Face the beast and fear the face: Animal and social fears as prototypes for evaluating analyses of emotion. *Psychophysiology, 23,* 123–145.

Ohman, A., Erixon, G., & Lofburg, I. (1975). Phobias and preparedness: Phobic versus neutral pictures as conditioned stimuli for human autonomic responses. *Journal of Abnormal Psychology, 84,* 41–45.

Olasov, B., & Foa, E. G. (1987). *The treatment of post-traumatic stress disorder in sexual assault survivors using stress inoculation training (SIT).* Paper presented at the annual meeting of the Association for Advancement of Behavior Therapy, Boston, MA.

Öst, L. G. (1978). Behavioral treatment of thunder and lightning phobias. *Behaviour Research and Therapy, 16,* 197–207.

Öst, L. G. (1985). Mode of acquisition of phobias. *Acta Universitatis Uppsaliensis (Abstracts of Uppsala Dissertations from the Faculty of Medicine), 529,* 1–45.

Öst, L. G. (1987). Age of onset of different phobias. *Journal of Abnormal Psychology, 96,* 223–229.

Öst, L. G. (1988). Applied relaxation vs. progressive relaxation in the treatment of panic disorder. *Behaviour Research and Therapy, 26,* 13–22.

Öst, L. G. (1989). One-session treatment for specific phobias. *Behaviour Research and Therapy, 27,* 1–7.

Öst, L. G., & Hugdahl, K. (1981). Acquisition of phobias and anxiety response patterns in clinical patients. *Behaviour Research and Therapy, 19,* 439–447.

Öst, L. G., & Hugdahl, K. (1983). Acquisition of agoraphobia, mode of onset and anxiety patterns. *Behaviour Research and Therapy, 21,* 623–631.

Öst, L. G., Jerremalm, A., & Johansson, J. (1981). Individual response patterns and the effects of different behavioural methods in the treatment of social phobia. *Behaviour Research and Therapy, 19,* 1–16.

Öst, L. G., Johansson, J., & Jerremalm, A. (1982). Individual response patterns and the effects of different behavioral methods in the treatment of claustrophobia. *Behaviour Research and Therapy, 20,* 445–460.

Öst, L. G., & Sterner, U. (1987). Applied tension: A specific behavioural method for treatment of blood phobia. *Behaviour Research and Therapy, 22,* 205–216.

Öst, L. G., Sterner, U., & Fellenius, J. (1989). Applied tension, applied relaxation, and the combination in the treatment of blood phobia. *Behaviour Research and Therapy, 27,* 109–121.

Page, H. (1885). *Injuries of the spine and spinal cord without apparent mechanical lesion.* London: J&A Churchill.

Pegeron, J., & Curtis, G. (1986). Simple phobia leading to suicide: A case report. *The Behavior Therapist, 9,* 134.

Perloff, L. S. (1983). Perceptions of vulnerability to victimization. *Journal of Social Issues, 39,* 41–61.

Persons, J. B. (1989). *Cognitive therapy in practice: A case formulation approach.* New York: WW Norton & Company.

Pigott, T. A., Pato, M. T., Bernstein, S. E., Grover, G. N., Hill, J. L., Tolliver, T. J., Murphy, D. L. (1990). Controlled comparisons of clomipramine and fluoxetine in the treatment of obsessive-compulsive disorder: Behavioral and biological results. *Archives of General Psychiatry, 47,* 926–932.

Pollack, M. H., & Rosenbaum, J. F. (1988). Benzodiazepines in panic-related disorders. *Journal of Anxiety Disorders, 2,* 95–108.

Pollard, A., & Cox, G. (1986). *Social-evaluative anxiety in panic disorder and agoraphobia.* Paper presented at the annual meeting of the Association for Advancement of Behavior Therapy, Chicago, IL.

Pollard, C. A., Pollard, H. J., & Corn, K. J. (1989). Panic onset and major events in the lives of agoraphobics: A test of contiguity. *Journal of Abnormal Psychology, 98,* 318–321.

Power, K. G., Jerrom, D., Simpson, R., Mitchell, M., & Swanson, V. (1989). A controlled comparison of cognitive-behavior therapy, diazepam, and placebo in the management of generalized anxiety. *Behavioural Psychotherapy, 17,* 1–14.

Power, K. G., Simpson, R. J., Swanson, V., Wallace, L. A., Feistner, A. T. C., & Sharp, D. (1990). A controlled comparison of cognitive-behaviour therapy, diazepam, and placebo, alone and in combination for the treatment of generalized anxiety disorder. *Journal of Anxiety Disorders, 4,* 267–292.

Price, L. H., Goodman, W. K., Charney, D. S., Rasmussen, M. D., & Heninger, G. R. (1987). Treatment of severe obsessive-compulsive disorder with fluvoxamine. *American Journal of Psychiatry, 144,* 1059–1061.

Rachman, S. J. (1978). *Fear and courage.* San Francisco: W H Freeman.

Rachman, S. J. (1980). Emotional processing. *Behaviour Research and Therapy, 18,* 51–60.

Rachman, S. J., Craske, M., & Tallman, K. (1986). Does escape behavior strengthen agoraphobic avoidance? *Behavior Therapy, 177,* 366–384.

Rachman, S. J., & de Silva, P. (1978). Abnormal and normal obsessions. *Behaviour Research and Therapy, 16,* 233–238.

Rachman, S. J., & Hodgson, R. (1980). *Obsessions and compulsions.* Englewood Cliffs, NJ: Prentice-Hall.

Rachman, S. J., & Lopatka, C. (1986). Match and mismatched in the prediction of fear— I. *Behaviour Research and Therapy, 24,* 387–393.

Rachman, S. J., & Maser, J. D. (Eds.). (1988). *Panic: Psychological perspectives.* Hillsdale, NJ: Lawrence Erlbaum Associates.

Rado, S. (1942). Pathodynamics and treatment of traumatic war neurosis (traumatophobia). *Psychosomatic Medicine, 42,* 363–368.

Ramm, E., Marks, I. M., Yuksel, S., & Stern, R. S. (1981). Anxiety management training for anxiety states: Positive compared with negative self-statements. *British Journal of Psychiatry, 140,* 367–373.

Rapee, R. M. (1987). The psychological treatment of spontaneous panic attacks: Theoretical conceptualization and review of evidence. *Clinical Psychology Review, 7,* 427–438.

Rapee, R. M., & Barlow, D. H. (1989). Psychological treatment of unexpected panic attacks: Cognitive/behavioral components. In R. Baker (Ed.), *Panic disorder; Theory, research, and therapy* (pp. 239–259). West Sussex, England: John Wiley & Sons.

Rapee, R. M., Craske, M. G., & Barlow, D. H. (1988). *The causes of anxiety and panic attacks.* Center for Stress and Anxiety Disorders, University of Albany, State University of New York.

Rapee, R. M., Craske, M. G., & Barlow, D. H. (1990). Subject-described features of panic attacks using self-monitoring. *Journal of Anxiety Disorders, 4,* 171–181.

Rapee, R. M., Litwin, E. M., & Barlow, D. H. (1990). Impact of life events on subjects with panic disorder and on comparison subjects. *American Journal of Psychiatry, 147,* 640–644.

Rapee, R. M., Mattuk, R., & Murrell, E. (1986). Cognitive mediation in the affective component of spontaneous panic attacks. *Journal of Behavior Therapy and Experimental Psychiatry, 17,* 245–253.

Rapee, R. M., & Murrell, E. (1988). Predictors of agoraphobic avoidance. *Journal of Anxiety Disorders, 2,* 203–218.

Rappaport, J. L. (1989). *The boy who couldn't stop washing.* New York: E P Dutton.

Raulin, M. L., & Wee, J. L. (1984). The development and initial validation of a scale to measure social fear. *Journal of Clinical Psychology, 40,* 780–784.

Redmond, D. E., & Huang, Y. (1979). Current concepts. II. New evidence for a locus coeruleus—norepinephrine connection with anxiety. *Life Sciences, 25,* 2149–2162.

Reich, J., & Yates, W. (1988). A pilot study of treatment of social phobia with alprazolam. *American Journal of Psychiatry, 145,* 590–594.

Reiff, R. (1979). *The invisible victim: The criminal justice's system's forgotten responsibility.* New York: Basic Books.

Reiss, S., Peterson, R. A., Gursky, D. M., & McNally, R. J. (1986). Anxiety sensitivity, anxiety frequency and the prediction of fearfulness. *Behaviour Research and Therapy, 24,* 1–8.

Resick, P. A., Jordan, C. G., Girelli, S. A., Hutter, C. K., & Marhoefer-Dvorak, S. (1988). A comparative outcome study of behavioral group therapy for sexual assault victims. *Behavior Therapy, 19,* 385–401.

Rimm, D., & Sommervill, J. (1977). *Abnormal psychology.* New York: Academic Press.

Rimm, D. C., Janda, L. H., Lancaster, D. W., Nahl, M., & Dittmar, K. (1977). An exploratory investigation of the origin and maintenance of phobias. *Behaviour Research and Therapy, 15,* 231–238.

Rimm, D. C., & Masters, J. C. (1979). *Behavior therapy: Techniques and empirical findings* (2nd ed.). New York: Academic Press.

Robins, L. N., Helzer, J. E., Weissman, M. M., Orvaschel, H., Gruenberg, E., Burke, J. D., Jr., & Regier, D. A. (1984). Lifetime prevalence of specific psychiatric disorders in three sites. *Archives of General Psychiatry, 41,* 949–958.

Robinson, E. L. (1989). The relative effectiveness of cognitive restructuring and coping desensitization in the treatment of self-reported worry. *Journal of Anxiety Disorders, 4,* 197–207.

Rosen, H. (1989). Piagetian theory and cognitive therapy. In A. Freeman, K. M. Simon, L. E. Beutler, & H. Arkowitz (Eds.), *Comprehensive handbook of cognitive therapy* (pp. 189–212). New York: Plenum Publishing.

Rosen, J., & Fields, R. (1988). The long-term effects of extraordinary trauma: A look beyond PTSD. *Journal of Anxiety Disorders, 2,* 179–191.

Rothbaum, B. O., & Foa, E. B. (in press). Cognitive-behavioral treatment of post-traumatic stress disorder. In P. A. Saigh (Ed.), *Posttraumatic stress disorder: A behavioral approach to assessment and treatment.* Elmsford, NY: Pergamon Press.

Rothbaum, B. O., & Foa, E. B. (1988, September). *Treatments of post-traumatic stress disorder in rape victims.* Paper presented at the World Congress of Behaviour Therapy Conference, Edinburgh, Scotland.

Roy-Byrne, P., Mellman, T. A., & Uhde, T. W. (1988). Biological findings in panic disorder: Neuroendocrine and sleep-related abnormalities. *Journal of Anxiety Disorders, 2,* 17–29.

Runch, B. (1983). Research is changing views on obsessive-compulsive disorder. *Hospital and Community Psychiatry, 34,* 597–598.

Rupert, P. A., Dobbins, K., & Mathew, R. J. (1981). EMG biofeedback and relaxation instructions in the treatment of chronic anxiety. *American Journal of Clinical Biofeedback, 4,* 52–61.

Rychtarik, R. G., Silverman, W. K., Van Landingham, W. P., Prue, D. M. (1984). Treatment of an incest victim with implosive therapy: A case study. *Behavior Therapy, 15,* 410–420.

Rygh, J. L., & Barlow, D. H. (1986, November). *Treatment of social phobias with panic management techniques.* Paper presented at the annual meeting of the Association for Advancement of Behavior Therapy, Chicago, IL.

Salkovskis, P. M. (1985). Obsessional-compulsive problem: A cognitive-behavioural analysis. *Behaviour Research and Therapy, 25,* 571–583.

Salkovskis, P. M. (1989). Cognitive-behavioral factors and the persistence of intrusive thoughts in obsessive problems. *Behavior Research and Therapy, 27,* 677–682.

Salkovskis, P. M., & Clark, D. M. (1990). Affective responses to hyperventilation: A test of the cognitive model of panic. *Behaviour Research and Therapy, 28,* 51–61.

Salkovskis, P. M., & Dent, H. R. (1989). *Intrusive thoughts, impulses, and imagery: Cognitive and behavioral aspects.* Manuscript in preparation.

Salkovskis, P. M., & Harrison, J. (1984). Abnormal and normal obsessions: A replication. *Behaviour Research and Therapy, 22,* 549–552.

Salkovskis, P. M., Jones, D. R. O., & Clark, D. M. (1986). Respiratory control in the treatment of panic attacks: Replication and extension with concurrent measurement of behaviour and pCO2. *British Journal of Psychiatry, 148,* 526–532.

Salkovskis, P. M., & Kirk, J. (1989). Obsessional disorders. In K. Hawton, P. M. Salkovskis, J. Kirk, & D. M. Clark (Eds.), *Cognitive behaviour therapy for psychiatric problems: A practical guide* (pp. 129–168). Oxford: Oxford Medical Publications.

Salkovskis, P. M., & Warwick, H. M. C. (1985). Cognitive therapy of obsessive-compulsive disorder: Treating treatment failures. *Behavioural Psychotherapy, 13,* 243–255.

Salkovskis, P. M., & Warwick, H. M. C. (1988). Cognitive therapy of obsessive-compulsive disorder. In C. Perris, I. M. Blackburn, & H. Perris (Eds.), *The theory and practice of cognitive therapy* (pp. 376–395). Heidelberg: Springer-Verlag.

Salkovskis, P. M., & Westbrook, D. (1987). Obsessive-compulsive disorder: Clinical strategies for improving behavioural treatments. In H. R. Dent (Ed.), *Clinical psychology: Research and development* (pp. 200–213). London: Croon Helm.

Salkovskis, P. M., & Westbrook, D. (1989). Behaviour therapy and obsessional ruminations: Can failure be turned into success? *Behaviour Research and Therapy, 27,* 149–160.

Sanderson, W. C., & Barlow, D. H. (1986). *Domains of worry within the DSM-III-R generalized anxiety disorder category: Reliability and description.* Paper presented at the annual meeting of the Association for Advancement of Behavior Therapy, Boston, MA.

Sanderson, W. C., Rapee, R. M., & Barlow, D. H. (1989). The influence of an illusion of control on panic attacks induced via inhalation of 5.5% carbon dioxide-enriched air. *Archives of General Psychiatry, 46,* 157–162.

Sank, L. I., & Shaffer, C. S. (1984). *A therapist's manual for cognitive behavior therapy in groups.* New York: Plenum Publishing.

Schelver, S. R., & Gutsch, K. U. (1983). The effects of self-administered cognitive therapy on social-evaluative anxiety. *Journal of Clinical Psychology, 39,* 658–666.

Scheppele, K. L., & Bart, P. B. (1983). Through women's eyes: Defining danger in the wake of sexual assault. *Journal of Social Issues, 39,* 63–81.

Schlenker, B. R., & Leary, M. R. (1982). Social anxiety and self-presentation: A conceptualization and model. *Psychological Bulletin, 92,* 641–669.

Schneier, F. R., Martin, L. Y., Liebowitz, M. R., Gorman, J. M., & Fyer, A. J. (1989). Alcohol abuse in social phobia. *Journal of Anxiety Disorders, 3*, 15–24.

Schwartz, G. E., Davidson, R. J., & Goleman, D. J. (1978). Patterning of cognitive and somatic processes in the self-regulation of anxiety: Effects of meditation versus exercise. *Psychosomatic Medicine, 40*, 321–328.

Seligman, M. E. P. (1971). Phobias and preparedness. *Behavior Therapy, 2*, 307–320.

Shea, C. A., Uhde, T. W., Cimbolc, P., Vittone, B. J., & Arnkoff, D. B. (1988, May). *Social phobia: Behavioral versus drug therapies.* Paper presented at the Annual Meeting of the American Psychiatric Association, Montreal, Canada.

Sheehan, D. V., & Raj, A. B. (1988). Monoamine oxidase inhibitors. In C. L. Last & M. Hersen (Eds.), *Handbook of anxiety disorders* (pp. 478–503). Elmsford, NY: Pergamon Press.

Silver, R. L., Boon, C. L., & Stones, M. H. (1983). Searching for meaning in misfortune: Making sense of incest. *Journal of Social Issues, 39*, 81–102.

Smith, D. (1982). Trends in counseling and psychotherapy. *American Psychologist, 37*, 802–809.

Smith, R. E., & Sarason, I. G. (1975). Social anxiety and the evaluation of negative interpersonal feedback. *Journal of Consulting and Clinical Psychology, 43*, 429.

Smith, T. (1982). Irrational beliefs in the cause and treatment of emotional distress: A critical review of the rational-emotive model. *Clinical Psychology Review, 2*, 505–522.

Sokol, L., Beck, A. T., Greenberg, R. L., Wright, F. D., & Berchick, R. J. (1989). Cognitive therapy of panic disorder: A nonpharmacological alternative. *The Journal of Nervous and Mental Disease, 177*, 711–716.

Spielberger, C. D. (1983). *Manual for the State-Trait Anxiety Inventory (STAI Form Y).* Palo Alto, CA: Consulting Psychologists Press.

Spielberger, C. D., Gorsuch, R. E., & Lushene, R. E. (1970). *Manual for the State-Trait Anxiety Inventory (Self-evaluation questionnaire).* Palo Alto, CA: Consulting Psychologists Press.

Staub, E., Tursky, B., & Schwartz, G. E. (1971). Self-control and predictability: Their effects on reactions to aversive stimulation. *Journal of Personality and Social Psychology, 18*, 157–162.

Steketee, G. (1987). *Social support as a predictor of long-term outcome following behavioral treatment of obsessive-compulsive disorder.* Paper presented at the annual meeting of the Association for Advancement of Behavior Therapy, Boston, MA.

Steketee, G., & Foa, E. B. (1985). Obsessive-compulsive disorder. In D. Barlow (Ed.), *Clinical handbook of psychological disorders* (pp. 69–144). New York: Guilford Press.

Steketee, G., & Foa, E. B. (1987). Rape victims: Post-traumatic stress responses and their treatment: A review of the literature. *Journal of Anxiety Disorders, 1*, 69–86.

Steketee, G., Foa, E. B., & Grayson, J. B. (1982). Recent advances in the treatment of obsessive-compulsives. *Archives of General Psychiatry, 39*, 1365–1371.

Steketee, G., & White, K. W. (1990). *When once is not enough.* Oakland, CA: New Harbinger Press.

Stern, R. S., & Marks, I. (1973). Brief and prolonged flooding: A comparison of agoraphobic patients. *Archives of General Psychiatry, 28*, 270–276.

Stewart, J. R. (1983). *The effects of two therapeutic approaches on anxiety reduction and client satisfaction with consideration of client hemisphericity.* Unpublished doctoral dissertation, University of Toledo, Toledo, OH.

Stoyva, J. M. (1979). Guidelines in the training of general relaxation. In J. V. Basmajian (Ed.), *Biofeedback—principles and practice for clinicians.* Baltimore, MD: Williams & Wilkins.

Stravynski, A. (1983). Behavioral treatment of psychogenic vomiting in the context of social phobia. *Journal of Nervous and Mental Disease, 171*, 448–451.

Stravynski, A., Marks, I., & Yule, W. (1982). Social skills problems in neurotic outpatients: Social skills training with and without cognitive modification. *Archives of General Psychiatry, 39*, 1378–1385.

Street, L., Craske, M. G., & Barlow, D. H. (1989). Sensations, cognitions, and the perception of cues associated with expected and unexpected panic attacks. *Behaviour Research and Therapy, 27*, 189–198.

Sturgis, E. T., & Scott, R. (1984). Simple phobia. In S. M. Turner (Ed.), *Behavioral theories and treatment of anxiety* (pp. 91–141). New York: Plenum Publishing.

Suinn, R. (1976). Anxiety management training to control general anxiety. In J. Krumboltz & C. Thoresen (Eds.), *Counseling methods*, New York: Holt, Rinehart & Winston.

Suinn, R. M. (1984). Generalized anxiety disorder. In S. M. Turner (Ed.), *Behavioral theories and treatment of anxiety*. New York: Plenum Publishing.

Taylor, C. B., & Arnow, B. (1988). *The nature and treatment of anxiety disorders*. New York: Free Press.

Taylor, S., & Rachman, S. (1990). *The fear and avoidance of aversive affective states*. Paper presented at the annual meeting of the Association for Advancement of Behavior Therapy, San Francisco.

Taylor, S. E., Wood, J. V., & Lichtman, R. R. (1983). It could be worse: Selective evaluation as a response to victimization. *Journal of Social Issues, 39*, 19–40.

Teasdale, J. D. (1985). Psychological treatments for depression: How do they work? *Behaviour Research and Therapy, 23*, 157–165.

Telch, M. J. (1987). *The Panic Appraisal Inventory*. Unpublished scale. University of Texas.

Telch, M. J., Agras, W. S., Taylor, C. B., Roth, W. T., & Gallen, C. (1985). Combined pharmacological and behavioral treatment for agoraphobia. *Behaviour Research and Therapy, 23*, 325–335.

Telch, M. J., Brouillard, M., Telch, C. F., Agras, W. S., & Taylor, C. B. (1989). Role of cognitive appraisal in panic-related avoidance. *Behaviour Research and Therapy, 27*, 373–383.

Telch, M. J., Lucas, J. A., & Nelson, P. (1989). Nonclinical panic in college students: An investigation of prevalence and symptomatology. *Journal of Abnormal Psychology, 98*, 300–306.

Thyer, B. A. (1987). *Treating anxiety disorders*. Newbury Park, CA: Sage Publications.

Thyer, B. A., Parrish, R. T., Curtis, G. C., Cameron, O. G., & Nesse, R. M. (1985). Ages of onset of DSM-III anxiety disorders. *Comprehensive Psychiatry, 26*, 113–122.

Tomlin, P., Thyer, B. A., Curtis, G. C., Nesse, R. M., Cameron, O. G., & Wright, P. (1984). Standardization data of the Fear Survey Schedule based upon patients with a DSM-III anxiety disorder. *Journal of Behavior Therapy and Experimental Psychiatry, 15*, 123–126.

Trower, P., & Turland, D. (1984). Social phobia. In S. Turner (Ed.), *Behavioral theories and treatment of anxiety* (pp. 321–365). New York: Plenum Publishing.

Turner, R. M., Meles, D., & DiTomasso, R. (1983). Assessment of social anxiety: A controlled comparison among social phobics, obsessive-compulsives, agoraphobics, sexual disorder and simple phobics. *Behaviour Research and Therapy, 21*, 181–183.

Turner, R. M., Steketee, G. S., & Foa, E. B., (1979). Fear of criticism in washers, checkers, and phobics. *Behaviour Research and Therapy, 17*, 79–81.

Turner, S. M. (1979). *Systematic desensitization of fears and anxiety in rape victims*. Paper presented at the annual meeting of the Association for the Advancement of Behavior Therapy, San Francisco, CA.

Turner, S. M., & Beidel, D. C. (1988). *Treating obsessive compulsive disorder*. Elmsford, NY: Pergamon Press.

Turner, S. M., & Beidel, D. C. (1989). Social phobia: Clinical syndrome, diagnosis, and comorbidity. *Clinical Psychology Review, 9*, 3–18.

Turner, S. M., Beidel, D. C., Dancu, C. V., & Keys, D. J. (1986). Psychopathology of social phobia and comparison to avoidant personality disorder. *Journal of Abnormal Psychology, 95,* 389–394.

Turner, S. M., Beidel, D. C., Dancu, C. V., & Stanley, M. A. (1989). An empirically derived inventory to measure social fears and anxiety: The Social Phobia and Anxiety Inventory. *Psychological Assessment: A Journal of Consulting and Clinical Psychology, 1,* 35–40.

Turner, S. M., Beidel, D. C., Stanley, M. A., & Jacob, R. G. (1988). A comparison of fluoxetine, flooding, and response prevention in the treatment of obsessive-compulsive disorder. *Journal of Anxiety Disorders, 2,* 219–226.

Turner, S. M., McCann, B. S., Beidel, D. C., & Mezzich, J. B. (1986). DSM-III classification of the anxiety disorders: A psychometric study. *Journal of Abnormal Psychology, 95,* 168–172.

Turner, S. M., McCann, M., & Beidel, D. C. (1987). Validity of the social avoidance and distress and fear of negative evaluation scales. *Behaviour Research and Therapy, 25,* 113–115.

Uhde, T. W., Roy-Byrne, P. P., Vittone, B. J., Boulenger, J. P., & Post, R. M. (1985). Phenomenology and neurobiology of panic disorder. In A. H. Tuma & J. D. Maser (Eds.), *Anxiety and the anxiety disorders* (pp. 557–576). Hillsdale, NJ: Lawrence Erlbaum Associates.

Uhlenhuth, E. H., Balter, M. B., & Lipman, R. S. (1978). Minor tranquilizers: Clinical correlations of use in an urban population. *Archives of General Psychiatry, 35,* 650–665.

van der Holk, B., Greenberg, M., Boyd, H., & Krystal, J. (1985). Inescapable shock, neurotransmitters, and addiction to trauma: Toward a psychology of post-traumatic stress. *Biological Psychology, 20,* 314–325.

van der Molen, G. M., van den Hout, M. A., Vroemen, J., Lousberg, H., & Griez, E. (1986). Cognitive determinants of lactate-induced anxiety. *Behaviour Research and Therapy, 24,* 677–680.

Veronen, L. J., & Kilpatrick, D. G. (1980). Self-reported fears of rape victims: A preliminary investigation. *Behavior Modification, 4,* 383–396.

Veronen, L. J., & Kilpatrick, D. G. (1983). Stress management of rape victims. In D. Meichenbaum & M. E. Jaremko (Eds.), *Stress reduction and prevention* (pp. 341–374). New York: Plenum Publishing.

Von Korff, M., & Eaton, W. W. (1989). Epidemiological findings on panic. In R. Baker (Ed.) *Panic disorder: Theory, research, and therapy* (pp. 35–50). West Sussex, England: John Wiley & Sons, Ltd.

Von Korff, M., Eaton, W., & Keyl, P. (1985). The epidemiology of panic attacks and panic disorder: Results of three community surveys. *American Journal of Epidemiology, 122,* 970–981.

Walen, S., DiGiuseppe, R., & Wessler, R. (1980). *A practitioner's guide to rational-emotive therapy.* New York: Oxford University Press.

Walk, R. D. (1956). Self-ratings of fear in a fear-invoking situation. *Journal of Abnormal and Social Psychology, 52,* 171–178.

Walsh, T. A. (1982). *Rational-emotive therapy and progressive relaxation in the reduction of trait anxiety of college undergraduate students who enroll in anxiety reduction workshops.* Unpublished doctoral dissertation, University of the Pacific, Stockton, CA.

Warren, R., Good, G., & Velten, E. (1984). Measurement of social-evaluative anxiety in junior high school students. *Adolescence, 19,* 643–648.

Warren, R., McLellarn, R., & Ponzoha, C. (1988). Rational-emotive therapy vs. general cognitive-behavior therapy in the treatment of low self-esteem and related emotional disturbances. *Cognitive Therapy and Research, 12,* 21–38.

Warren, R., & Warren, T. (1985). *Tender talk: A practical guide to intimate conversations.* Portland, OR: The Portland Press.

Warren, R., & Winkler, C. (1990). *Emergency management of panic attacks: A pilot study and suggested protocol.* Manuscript submitted for publication.

Warren, R., & Zgourides, G. (1989). Evidence of validity for the Malouff and Schutte Belief Scale. *Journal of Rational-Emotive Therapy, 7,* 166–172.

Warren, R., Zgourides, G., & Jones, A. (1989). Cognitive bias and irrational belief as predictors of avoidance. *Behaviour Research and Therapy, 27,* 181–188.

Watson, J. P., & Friend, R. (1969). Measurement of social-evaluative anxiety. *Journal of Consulting and Clinical Psychology, 33,* 448–457.

Watson, J. P., Gaind, R., & Marks, I. M. (1972). Physiological habituation to continuous phobic stimulation. *Behaviour Research and Therapy, 20,* 269–278.

Wegner, D. M., Schneider, D. J., Carter, S. R., & White, T. L. (1987). Paradoxical effects of thought suppressing. *Journal of Personality and Social Psychology, 53,* 5–13.

Weissman, M., & Merikangas, K. (1986). The epidemiology of anxiety and panic disorders: An update. *Journal of Clinical Psychiatry, 47,* 11–17.

Weissman, M. M., Klerman, G. L., Markowitz, J. S., & Quellette, R. (1989). Suicidal ideation and suicide attempts in panic disorder and attacks. *The New England Journal of Medicine, 321,* 1209–1214.

Weissman, M. M., Myers, J. K., & Harding, P. S. (1978). Psychiatric disorders in a U.S. urban community. *American Journal of Psychiatry, 135,* 459–462.

Wessler, R. A., & Wessler, R. L. (1980). *The principles and practice of rational-emotive therapy.* San Francisco: Jossey-Bass.

Williams, S. L. (1987). On anxiety and phobia. *Journal of Anxiety Disorders, 1,* 161–180.

Williams, S. L., Doosemen, G., & Kleifield, E. (1984). Comparative effectiveness of guided mastery and exposure treatments for intractible phobias. *Journal of Consulting and Clinical Psychology, 52,* 505–518.

Williams, S. L., Turner, S. M., & Peer, D. F. (1985). Guided mastery and performance desensitization treatments for severe agoraphobia. *Journal of Consulting and Clinical Psychology, 53,* 237–247.

Willoughby, R. R. (1932). Some properties of the Thurstone Personality Schedule and a suggested revision. *Journal of Social Psychology, 3,* 401–424.

Wilson, G. T. (1990). Fear reduction methods and the treatment of anxiety disorders. In C. M. Franks, G. T. Wilson, P. C. Kendall, & J. P. Foreyt, *Review of behavior therapy.* (vol. 12, pp. 72–102). New York: Guilford Press.

Wilson, J. P. (1989). A person-environment approach to traumatic stress reactions. In J. P. Wilson (Ed.), *Trauma transformation and healing: An integrated approach to theory, research, and post-traumatic therapy* (pp. 3–21). New York: Brunner/Mazel.

Wittchen, H. U. (1986). Epidemiology of panic attacks and panic disorders. In I. Hand & H. U. Wittchen (Eds.), *Panic and phobias: Empirical evidence of theoretical models and long-term effects of behavioral treatments.* Berlin: Springer-Verlag.

Wolff, R. (1977). Systematic desensitization and negative practice to alter the aftereffects of a rape attempt. *Journal of Behavior Therapy and Experimental Psychiatry, 8,* 423–425.

Wolpe, J., & Lang, P. (1977). *Manual for the Fear Survey Schedule.* San Francisco: Educational and Industrial Testing Service.

Wolpe, J., & Lang, P. J. (1969). A fear survey schedule for use in behavior therapy. *Behaviour Research and Therapy, 2,* 27–30.

Woods, S. W., & Charney, D. S. (1988). Benzodiazepines: A review of benzodiazepine treatment of anxiety disorders: Pharmacology, efficacy, and implications for pathophysiology. In C. G. Last & M. Hersen (Eds.), *Handbook of anxiety disorders* (pp. 413–444). Elmsford, NY: Pergamon Press.

Woodward, R., & Jones, R. B. (1980). Cognitive restructuring treatment: A controlled trial with anxious patients. *Behaviour Research and Therapy, 18,* 401–407.

Wortman, C. B. (1983). Coping with victimization: Conclusions and implications for future research. *Journal of Social Issues, 39,* 195–221.

Yankura, J., & Dryden, W. (1990). *Doing RET: Albert Ellis in action.* New York: Springer Publishing Company.

Yaryura-Tobias, J. A. (1977). Obsessive-compulsive disorders: A serotonergic hypothesis. *Journal of Orthomolecular Psychiatry, 6,* 317–326.

Young, H. S. (1974). *A rational counseling primer.* New York: Institute for Rational-Emotive Therapy.

Zarate, R., Rapee, R. M., Craske, M. G., & Barlow, D. H. (1988). *The effectiveness of interoceptive exposure in the treatment of simple phobia.* Paper presented at the annual meeting of the Association for Advancement of Behavior Therapy, New York.

Zgourides, G. D. (1987). Paruresis: Overview and implications for treatment. *Psychological Reports, 60,* 1171–1176.

Zgourides, G. D. (1988). Bethanechol chloride as an adjunct to prolonged *in vivo* exposure therapy in the treatment of paruresis. *Perceptual and Motor Skills, 66,* 319–322.

Zgourides, G. D., & Warren, R. (1988). Further evidence of construct and discriminant validities for the Malouff and Schutte Belief Scale. *Psychological Reports, 63,* 801–802.

Zimbardo, P. G. (1977). *Shyness: What it is and what to do about it.* Reading, MA: Addison-Wesley.

Zohar, J., & Insel, T. R. 1987. Obsessive-compulsive disorder: Psychobiological approaches to diagnosis, treatment, and pathophysiology. *Biological Psychiatry, 22,* 667–687.

Zung, W. W. (1971). A rating instrument for anxiety disorders. *Psychosomatics, 12,* 371–379.

Author Index

Subject Index

About the Authors

Ricks Warren, Ph. D., is director of the Anxiety Disorders Clinic of the Pacific Institute for Rational-Emotive Therapy and a psychologist in private practice. He is an Associate Fellow and Certified Supervisor of the Institute for Rational-Emotive Therapy in New York and Adjunct Professor of Psychology at the School of Professional Psychology, Pacific University in Forest Grove, Oregon. Dr. Warren is also coauthor, with Terri Warren, of *Tender Talk: A Practical Guide to Intimate Conversations* and *The Updated Herpes Handbook*.

George D. Zgourides received his Psy.D. degree in clinical psychology in 1989 from Pacific University (Forest Grove, Oregon). Dr. Zgourides is an Assistant Professor of Psychology at the University of Portland, with academic and clinical interests in the areas of anxiety, sexual dysfunctions, cognitive therapy, and health psychology. He maintains a private practice at the Anxiety Disorders Clinic in Lake Oswego, Oregon and is a member of the adjunct psychology staff at Tualatin Valley Mental Health Center in Portland, Oregon.

Psychology Practitioner Guidebooks

Editors
Arnold P. Goldstein, Syracuse University
Leonard Krasner, Stanford University & SUNY at Stony Brook
Sol L. Garfield, Washington University in St. Louis

Elsie M. Pinkston & Nathan L. Linsk—CARE OF THE ELDERLY:
A Family Approach

Donald Meichenbaum—STRESS INOCULATION TRAINING

Sebastiano Santostefano—COGNITIVE CONTROL THERAPY WITH
CHILDREN AND ADOLESCENTS

Lillie Weiss, Melanie Katzman & Sharlene Wolchik—TREATING BULIMIA:
A Psychoeducational Approach

Edward B. Blanchard & Frank Andrasik—MANAGEMENT OF CHRONIC
HEADACHES: A Psychological Approach

Raymond G. Romanczyk—CLINICAL UTILIZATION OF
MICROCOMPUTER TECHNOLOGY

Philip H. Bornstein & Marcy T. Bornstein—MARITAL THERAPY:
A Behavioral-Communications Approach

Michael T. Nietzel & Ronald C. Dillehay—PSYCHOLOGICAL
CONSULTATION IN THE COURTROOM

Elizabeth B. Yost, Larry E. Beutler, M. Anne Corbishley & James R.
Allender—GROUP COGNITIVE THERAPY: A Treatment Approach for
Depressed Older Adults

Lillie Weiss—DREAM ANALYSIS IN PSYCHOTHERAPY

Edward A. Kirby & Liam K. Grimley—UNDERSTANDING AND
TREATING ATTENTION DEFICIT DISORDER

Jon Eisenson—LANGUAGE AND SPEECH DISORDERS IN CHILDREN

Eva L. Feindler & Randolph B. Ecton—ADOLESCENT ANGER
CONTROL: Cognitive-Behavioral Techniques

Michael C. Roberts—PEDIATRIC PSYCHOLOGY: Psychological
Interventions and Strategies for Pediatric Problems

Daniel S. Kirschenbaum, William G. Johnson & Peter M. Stalonas, Jr.—
TREATING CHILDHOOD AND ADOLESCENT OBESITY

W. Stewart Agras—EATING DISORDERS: Management of Obesity,
Bulimia and Anorexia Nervosa

Ian H. Gotlib & Catherine A. Colby—TREATMENT OF DEPRESSION:
An Interpersonal Systems Approach

Walter B. Pryzwansky & Robert N. Wendt—PSYCHOLOGY AS A
PROFESSION: Foundations of Practice

Cynthia D. Belar, William W. Deardorff & Karen E. Kelly—THE
PRACTICE OF CLINICAL HEALTH PSYCHOLOGY

Paul Karoly & Mark P. Jensen—MULTIMETHOD ASSESSMENT OF
CHRONIC PAIN

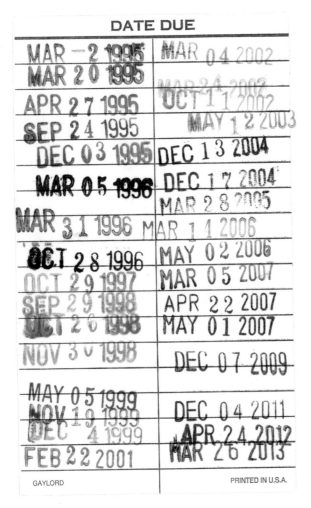

DATE DUE

MAR - 2 1995	MAR 04 2002
MAR 20 1995	MAR 24 2002
APR 27 1995	OCT 11 2002
SEP 24 1995	MAY 12 2003
DEC 03 1995	DEC 13 2004
MAR 05 1996	DEC 17 2004
MAR 31 1996	MAR 28 2005
OCT 28 1996	MAR 11 2006
OCT 29 1997	MAY 02 2006
SEP 29 1998	MAR 05 2007
OCT 26 1998	APR 22 2007
NOV 30 1998	MAY 01 2007
MAY 05 1999	DEC 07 2009
NOV 19 1999	DEC 04 2011
DEC 4 1999	APR 24 2012
FEB 22 2001	MAR 26 2013

GAYLORD   PRINTED IN U.S.A.